Understanding Research Methods

An Overview of the Essentials

Ninth Edition

Mildred L. Patten

Pyrczak Publishing

P.O. Box 250430 • Glendale, CA 91225

"Pyrczak Publishing" is an imprint of Fred Pyrczak, Publisher, A California Corporation.

Although the author and publisher have made every effort to ensure the accuracy and completeness of information contained in this book, we assume no responsibility for errors, inaccuracies, omissions, or any inconsistency herein. Any slights of people, places, or organizations are unintentional.

This edition was written in collaboration with Randall R. Bruce.

Project Director: Kyle Dump.
Editor: Danielle Dobies.

Editorial assistance provided by Cheryl Alcorn, Amber Avines, Jenifer Dill, Jack Petit, Karen Sommerfeld, Erica Simmons, Meredith Simonds, Pamela Wray-Biron, and Sharon Young.

Cover design by Robert Kibler and Larry Nichols.

Printed in the United States of America by Edwards Brothers Malloy, Inc.

CONTENTS

Continued →

Continued →

Tables

Index

INTRODUCTION TO THE NINTH EDITION

Understanding Research Methods provides an overview of basic research methods.

The distinctive features of this book are as follows:

- The division of the material into short sections instead of long chapters, which will help students to take small steps through this exciting—but highly technical—field of study. The long chapters in other research methods books prompt students to take big gulps, which often are not easily digested.

- When one topic builds directly on the previous topic, the second topic begins with a reminder of what students should have mastered already. This helps students to keep their eyes on the big picture and to make a smooth transition from one topic to the next.

- Technical jargon is defined in plain English and numerous examples make abstract research concepts concrete. In field tests, students agreed that this book is comprehensible.

- The material on statistics is presented at the conceptual level. It shows students how to interpret statistical reports but does not include computational details.

- The exercises at the end of the topics encourage students to pause and make sure they have mastered one topic before moving on to another. This is important because much of the material in this book is cumulative. Thorough mastery of an earlier topic is frequently a prerequisite for ease in mastering a later topic. The first part of each exercise tests comprehension of factual material. The second part asks students to interpret and apply the material they have mastered. This will help students to internalize the concepts and will stimulate classroom discussions. Finally, the third part provides questions that help students consider major issues in planning a research project.

Why should students have an overview of research methods?

- Leaders in all fields are increasingly relying on the results of research to make important decisions, such as how to help those who are dependent on welfare, which types of educational programs to fund, and how to adjust work environments to improve employees' output and satisfaction. If students hope to become decision makers in their fields, they must master research methods in order to be effective at sorting through the conflicting claims often found in the research literature.

- Many students will be expected to conduct simple but important research on the job. For instance, clinical psychologists are expected to track improvements made by their clients, teachers are expected to experiment with new methods in the classroom, and social workers are expected to collect data on their clients.

- All students will be making lifestyle decisions on the basis of research reported in the media. Should an individual take vitamin supplements? How should individuals dress for success on the job? Which make of automobile is superior if the buyer's primary concern is safety? Answers based on research are often offered in newspapers, magazines, and television newscasts. As a result of studying research methods, students will become knowledgeable, critical consumers of research.

- Students may need to read and report on published research in other classes. They will be more skilled at doing this if they have a solid understanding of basic methods of research.

New to the Ninth Edition

In this edition, the material on citing sources and preparing reference lists has been expanded. This material now covers important elements of sociological as well as psychological style. Finally, new examples from published research have been added to keep this best-seller up-to-date.

Acknowledgments

Dr. Anne Hafner and Dr. Robert Morman, both of California State University, Los Angeles, provided many helpful comments on the first draft of this book. New material for subsequent editions was reviewed by Dr. Robert Rosenthal of Harvard University and the University of California, Riverside; Dr. Deborah M. Oh of California State University, Los Angeles; and Dr. Richard Rasor of American

River College. Material for the current edition was reviewed by Drs. George W. Burruss, Nicholas A. Corsaro, and Matthew Giblin of Southern Illinois University, Carbondale. All these individuals made important contributions to the development of this book. Errors and omissions, of course, remain the author's responsibility.

Mildred L. Patten

PART A

INTRODUCTION TO RESEARCH METHODS

This part of the book defines what is meant by the term *empirical research* and provides an overview of the characteristics of the major approaches to this type of research. Broad issues that underlie all types of research—such as the nature of research hypotheses, how researchers define the variables they plan to study, ethical considerations in research, and the role of theory in research—are also covered.

NOTES

TOPIC 1 INTRODUCTION TO EMPIRICAL RESEARCH

The **empirical approach** to knowledge is based on observations.[1] Everyone uses the empirical approach in his or her daily life. For instance, if a teacher observes students becoming restless during a certain lesson, he or she might say they "know" the lesson is boring. As useful as everyday observations often are, they can be misleading and are often misinterpreted. For instance, the teacher may have misinterpreted the reason for the students' restlessness. The time and day, such as a warm Friday afternoon, might be the source of the students' restlessness and *not* the dullness of the lesson. Even if the lesson is indeed boring to this teacher's students, the teacher might conclude that the lesson is boring to students *in general*, when it might, in fact, be interesting to other students at other ability levels, with different backgrounds, and so on.

When researchers use the empirical approach, they strive to avoid misleading results and poor interpretations. The key to doing so is careful planning of **why** they want to make observations, **whom** they want to observe, and **how** and **when** to observe.

The question of *why to observe* establishes the need for the study. Perhaps a better method for helping students acquire a certain mathematics skill is needed. After considering their own experiences and reviewing related literature on the topic, researchers prepare a formal statement of their research purpose, such as "whether the use of hands-on manipulatives to teach Topic X will result in greater student achievement than a workbook approach." A researcher might also have a **hypothesis**, which is a statement indicating what results are expected. For instance, a researcher might hypothesize that students who use manipulatives will have higher scores than those who are exposed to a workbook approach. The question of *why* is explored throughout Parts A and F of this book.

When researchers plan *whom to observe*, they first decide whether to observe an entire population (such as all fifth-grade students in a school district) or just a sample of the population. If a sample is to be observed, which is often the case, researchers consider how to obtain a sample that is not biased against any types of individuals or subgroups. For instance, asking students to volunteer to take a mathematics lesson might result in a sample of students who are more interested in mathematics than are the students in the population as a whole. Such a sample would be biased against those who are less interested. Methods of drawing unbiased samples are discussed in Part D of this book.

When researchers plan *how to observe*, they select among available measures,[2] such as objective tests, interviews, and direct observation of behavior, with an eye to selecting the most valid measure(s). If none is judged to be reasonably valid for their purposes, they develop new measures. In addition, researchers need to decide *when* they will use the measures to obtain the most valid results. These issues are explored in detail in Part E of this book.

The observations researchers make may result in **data** in the form of numbers, which are analyzed statistically. Widely used statistical techniques are described in Part G of this book. Note that some scientific observations are *not* reduced to numbers but are expressed in words. For instance, interview data may be described in a narrative that points out themes and trends. Such research is referred to as *qualitative research*. The differences between qualitative and quantitative research are described in Topics 9 and 10. In addition, qualitative research methods are discussed in some detail in Part I of this book.

One of the most fundamental distinctions in scientific research is whether research is **experimental** or **nonexperimental**. In *experimental* research, treatments are given for the research purpose, such as treating some students with hands-on manipulatives and others with a workbook approach in order to determine which treatment *causes* greater math achievement.[3] Of course, researchers are not always interested in cause-and-effect questions. For instance, they might want to know whether teachers believe they need more training in the use of manipulatives for teaching mathematics. For this particular research purpose, a researcher should ask teachers about their needs without giving treatments, such as training them how to use manipula-

---

[1] Examples of other approaches are (1) *deduction*, such as when one deduces a proof in mathematics on the basis of certain assumptions and definitions, and (2) *reliance on authority*, such as relying on a dictator's pronouncements as a source of knowledge.

[2] *Measures* are sometimes called *instruments*.

[3] The design of experiments is discussed in Part F of this book.

tives. Thus, *nonexperimental* research is needed for this research purpose. The distinction between ex- perimental and nonexperimental research is ex- plored in the next two topics of this book.

EXERCISE ON TOPIC 1

1. On what is the empirical approach to knowledge based?

2. Is the empirical approach used in everyday living?

3. What does the question of *why* establish?

4. How is the term *hypothesis* defined in this topic?

5. According to the topic, are samples often observed?

6. What do researchers do when they plan *how* to observe?

7. What is an alternative term for *measures*?

8. The results from which type of research ("quantitative" *or* "qualitative") are *not* reduced to numbers?

9. Are treatments given for the research purpose in "experimental research" *or* in "nonexperimental research"?

10. If a researcher asked students for their opinions on switching from the semester system to the quarter system, would the researcher be conducting "experimental research" *or* "nonexperimental research"?

Questions for Discussion

11. Briefly describe a time when you were misled by an everyday observation (i.e., when you reached a con- clusion on the basis of an everyday observation that you later decided was an incorrect conclusion).

12. You have probably encountered conflicting research reported in the mass media. For example, one study might indicate that X increases blood pressure while another study indicates that X does not. Speculate on the reasons why various researchers might obtain different results when studying the same problem.

For Students Planning Research

13. Name a general problem area in which you might conduct research. At this point, your problem area may still be broad, such as "social phobia," *or* it may be narrow, such as "effectiveness of behavior modifica- tion in the treatment of social phobia among children." Note that you may want to name several problem areas for research and make a final selection at a later time.

14. Have you already made observations in your problem area(s)? If so, briefly describe them. (Keep in mind that observations may be direct, such as observing aggressive behavior on a playground, *or* indirect, such as asking adolescents for self-reports on their alcohol consumption.)

In **experiments, researchers give treatments and** observe if they cause changes in behavior. A classic simple experiment is one in which a researcher forms two groups at random and gives each group a different treatment. To form two groups at random, a researcher can put the names of the available participants on slips of paper, mix them thoroughly, and pull some names for each group.[1] Notice that random assignment gives each participant an equal chance of being in either group.

Below are three examples of experiments.

Example 1
Fifty students were divided into two groups at random. One group received math instruction via a correspondence course on the Internet. The other group was given instruction on the same math skills using a traditional textbook. The purpose was to see if instruction via the Internet was more effective than traditional textbook instruction.

In Example 1, the group receiving the new type of instruction via the Internet is referred to as the **experimental group**, while the group receiving the instruction with a textbook is called the **control group.** When the participants are divided at random (such as through the drawing of names from a hat to determine who will be in the experimental group and who will be in the control group), the experiment is called a **true experiment**. Not all experiments are true experiments,[2] as illustrated by Example 2.

Example 2
A psychiatrist identified 100 clinically depressed clients who volunteered to take a new drug under her direction. She also identified 100 nonvolunteers with the same diagnosis and similar demographics (i.e., background characteristics such as age and gender) to serve as controls. The study was conducted to investigate the effectiveness of the new drug in treating depression.

In Example 2, the experiment was conducted by comparing the volunteers who were given the new drug with a group of nonvolunteers who were *not* given the new drug. This study is an experiment even though random assignment was not used. Note

that if a researcher administers treatments or arranges for their administration, the study is called an experiment regardless of whether the groups of participants are formed at random.

Some experiments are conducted with only one group of participants, as illustrated in Example 3, in which the extra verbal praise is the treatment.

Example 3
The students in one classroom were observed for an hour each day for a week, and their inappropriate out-of-seat behaviors were counted. During the next week, the teacher provided extra verbal praise when students were in their seats at appropriate times. During the third week, the teacher stopped providing the extra verbal praise. The results showed less inappropriate out-of-seat behavior during the second week of the experiment than in the other two weeks.

In **nonexperimental studies, researchers do not** give treatments. Rather, they observe participants in order to describe them as they naturally exist, without experimental treatments. One of the most common types of nonexperimental studies is a **survey** or **poll** in which participants are interviewed, questioned, or otherwise observed so that their attitudes, beliefs, and behaviors as they exist without experimental intervention are determined.

Nonexperimental studies come in many forms, which are explored in more detail in Topic 4. At this point, however, readers should be able to distinguish between nonexperimental and experimental studies by determining whether treatments were administered for experimental purposes.

Note that consumers of research cannot distinguish between nonexperimental and experimental studies based on the type of measure used. Measures such as paper-and-pencil tests, interview schedules, and personality scales are used in both types of studies. The act of measurement is usually not considered to be a treatment. In fact, researchers try to measure in such a way that the act of measuring does not affect or change the participants. This is true in both experimental and nonexperimental studies.

By now, it should be clear that the purpose of an experiment is to explore cause-and-effect relationships (i.e., treatments are given to see how they affect the participants). The next topic describes how nonexperimental studies are also sometimes used for this purpose.

---

[1] Other methods for drawing random samples are discussed in Part D of this book.
[2] Types of experiments are explored more fully in Part F, where the advantages of true experiments are discussed.

Exercise on Topic 2

1. Are treatments given in nonexperimental studies?

2. In an experiment, Group A was given verbal praise for being on time for appointments while Group B was given no special treatment. Which group is the control group?

3. Is it necessary to have at least two groups of participants in order to conduct an experiment?

4. What is the purpose of a nonexperimental study?

5. Is a survey an experiment?

6. Does knowing that a multiple-choice test was used in a study help a consumer of research determine whether the study was experimental *or* nonexperimental?

7. What is the purpose of an experiment?

8. A political scientist polled voters to determine their opinions on a decision by the Supreme Court. Is this an "experimental study" *or* a "nonexperimental study"?

9. A teacher compared the effectiveness of three methods of teaching handwriting by using different methods with different students. Did the teacher conduct an "experimental study" *or* a "nonexperimental study"?

Questions for Discussion

10. Suppose you read that an outbreak of intestinal disorders occurred in a town and the source was traced to contaminated chicken served in a popular restaurant. Is it likely the study that identified the source was "experimental" *or* "nonexperimental"? Why?

11. Have you ever conducted an informal experiment by giving a treatment to a person or a group and then observing the effects? If so, briefly describe it. Would you have obtained better information by including a control group? Explain.

12. Suppose you wanted to know whether having parents read to preschool children has a positive effect on the children's subsequent reading achievement. Do you think it would be better to conduct an "experimental study" *or* a "nonexperimental study"? Why?

For Students Planning Research

13. At this point, do you anticipate using an "experimental" *or* a "nonexperimental" approach in your research? If it will be experimental, what treatments do you plan to administer?

14. If you plan to conduct experimental research, have you already conducted an informal experiment on your topic? If so, did you use a control group? Was it a true experiment? How will the experiment you are planning differ from the informal experiment you already conducted?

As indicated in Topic 2, an **experiment** is a study in which treatments are given in order to observe their effects. When researchers conduct experiments, they ask, "Does the treatment (i.e., the input or stimulus) given by the researcher *cause* changes in participants' behavior (i.e., changes in the output or response)?"

When researchers want to investigate cause-and-effect relationships, they usually prefer experimental over nonexperimental studies. However, for physical, ethical, legal, or financial reasons, sometimes it is not possible to conduct an experiment. For example, it would be unethical (because of potential harm to the participants) to treat some participants with smoke (such as requiring them to smoke a pack of cigarettes a day for 15 years) in order to observe the effects of smoking on health in comparison with a nonsmoking control group (which is forbidden to smoke for 15 years). Clearly, for this research problem, researchers cannot conduct an experiment. Notice that even if it were ethical to conduct such an experiment, it might not be practical because researchers probably would not want to wait 15 years to determine the answer to such an important question.

When it is impossible or impractical to conduct an experiment to answer a causal question, a researcher must settle for information derived from nonexperimental studies. For instance, a researcher could identify individuals who currently have lung cancer as well as a control group without lung cancer but with similar **demographics** (i.e., background characteristics such as socioeconomic status). Then, the researcher could examine differences between the two groups in terms of previous lifestyle characteristics that might affect health, such as diet, exercise, smoking, prescription drug use, illicit substance abuse, and so on.

A finding that smoking differentiates between the two groups who have similar demographics suggests that smoking is a possible cause of lung cancer. However, there are several dangers in this interpretation. First, smoking and cancer might have a common cause. For example, perhaps stress causes cancer and also causes individuals to smoke excessively. If this is the case, banning smoking will not prevent cancer, only reducing stress will. Another danger is that the researcher may have failed to identify control participants who were properly matched with those who have lung cancer. Perhaps

most of those with lung cancer reside in urban areas while most of those in the control group reside in rural areas. Because urban areas tend to have more smog than rural areas, smog might be the cause, and smoking might be coincidental. These types of problems would not arise in an experiment in which participants are divided at random to form two groups: one of which is made to smoke and the other forbidden to smoke. They would *not* exist because the random assignment would produce two groups that are equally likely to experience stress and equally likely to live in either rural or urban areas and, in fact, be about equal[1] in terms of all other potential causes of cancer.[2]

The example of smoking and lung cancer illustrates a specific type of nonexperimental study known as a **causal-comparative study** (sometimes called an **ex post facto study**).[3] The essential characteristics of this type of nonexperimental study are (1) researchers observe and describe some current condition (such as lung cancer) and (2) researchers look to the past to try to identify the possible cause(s) of the condition. Notice that researchers do *not* give treatments in causal-comparative studies. Instead, they only describe observations. Hence, they are conducting nonexperimental studies.

Although the causal-comparative method has more potential pitfalls than the experimental method, it is often the best researchers can do when attempting to explore causality. Note that when it is used properly, and the comparison groups are selected carefully, the causal-comparative method is a powerful scientific tool that provides data on many important issues in all the sciences.

---

[1] Because of the laws of probability, the larger the sample, the more likely that two groups formed at random will be equal in terms of their characteristics. Sample size is covered in Topics 29 and 30.

[2] The relationship between smoking and health has been examined in many hundreds of causal-comparative studies. On this basis, almost all experts agree that alternative interpretations are without merit. However, the results of some of the early studies on the health effects of smoking were disputed because the studies were not true experiments (i.e., they did not have random assignment to groups).

[3] Other types of nonexperimental studies are covered in the next topic.

EXERCISE ON TOPIC 3

1. According to the topic, do "experimental" *or* "causal-comparative" studies have more potential pitfalls when one is trying to identify cause-and-effect relationships?

2. Researchers look to the past for a cause in which type of study?

3. Is causal-comparative research a type of experiment?

4. Are treatments given by researchers in causal-comparative studies?

5. Random assignment to treatments is used in which type of study?

6. How is the term *demographics* defined in this topic?

7. A researcher compared the health of low-income adolescents who had received free lunches during their elementary school years with the health of a comparable group of low-income adolescents who had not received free lunches. The purpose was to determine the effects of free lunches on health. Did the researcher conduct an "experimental" *or* a "causal-comparative" study?

8. A researcher divided diabetes patients who were being released from the hospital into two groups. Upon their release, the researcher provided brief counseling for individuals with diabetes to one group while providing the other group with extended counseling. The purpose was to determine the effects of the two types of counseling on patients' compliance with physicians' directions during the first month after hospitalization. Did the researcher conduct an "experimental" *or* a "causal-comparative" study?

9. What is another name for a causal-comparative study?

Questions for Discussion

10. If you wanted to investigate the causes of child abuse, would you use the "experimental" *or* the "causal-comparative" method? Explain.

11. Suppose you read that a causal-comparative study indicates that those who take vitamins A and E tend to be less overweight than the general population. Are there any possible dangers in the interpretation that the vitamins *cause* individuals to maintain a healthy weight?

For Students Planning Research

12. If you will be conducting a nonexperimental study, will it be causal-comparative (i.e., looking to the past for the causes of some current condition)? If yes, briefly explain why you chose this method of research instead of the experimental method.

TOPIC 4   TYPES OF NONEXPERIMENTAL RESEARCH

As indicated in Topics 2 and 3, researchers do not give treatments to participants in nonexperimental studies. Rather, they observe (i.e., measure) in order to describe the participants without trying to change them.

Nonexperimental studies take many forms because they serve many purposes. The most common types of nonexperimental studies are briefly described here.

As indicated in the previous topic, **causal-comparative research** is research in which researchers look to the past for the cause(s) of a current condition. It is used primarily when researchers are interested in causality, but it is *not* possible to conduct an **experiment**.

Another type of nonexperimental research is the **survey** or *poll*. The purpose of surveys is to describe the attitudes, beliefs, and behaviors of a population. Researchers draw a sample of a population, study the sample, then make inferences to the population from the sample data. For instance, a researcher could survey a sample of individuals receiving food stamps to determine what types of food they purchase with the stamps. The results obtained from studying the sample could be generalized to the population (assuming that a good sample has been drawn).[1] Note that if a researcher decides not to sample but, instead, interviews everyone in the population (i.e., all individuals receiving food stamps), the study is called a **census**. A census is a count (or study) of all members of a population.

While surveys usually include hundreds or even thousands of participants, a **case study** usually involves only one. For instance, some important theories in clinical psychology were developed from intensive one-on-one case studies of individuals. In a case study, the emphasis is on obtaining thorough knowledge of an individual, sometimes over a long period of time. Researchers do not confine themselves to asking a limited number of questions on a one-shot basis as they would do in a survey.

When researchers repeatedly measure traits of the participants over a period of time in order to trace developmental trends, they are conducting **longitudinal research**. For instance, a researcher could measure the visual acuity of a sample of infants each week for a year to trace their development.

In **correlational research**, researchers are interested in the degree of relationship among two or more *quantitative variables*. For instance, scores on a college admissions test and GPAs are quantitative, and because individuals *vary* or differ on both of them, they are variables.[2] If a researcher conducts a study in which he or she is asking, "Did those with high admissions scores tend to earn high GPAs?" the researcher is asking a correlational question. To the extent that the answer to the question is true, the researcher can assert that the test works (i.e., it has validity for predicting GPAs).[3]

Experiments and all the types of research mentioned so far in this topic belong to the class of research called **quantitative research**. A distinctive feature of quantitative research is that researchers gather data in such a way that the data are easy to quantify, allowing for statistical analysis. For instance, to measure attitudes toward Asian American immigrants, a quantitative researcher might use a questionnaire and count how many times respondents answer "yes" to statements about Asian Americans, and then calculate the percentage who answered "yes" to each statement.

In contrast, in **qualitative research**, researchers gather data (such as responses to open-ended interview questions on attitudes toward Asian Americans) that must be analyzed through the use of informed judgment to identify major and minor themes expressed by participants. Most published qualitative research is collected through semi-structured interviews in which there is a core list of questions from which the interviewers may deviate as needed to obtain in-depth information.

Other differences between qualitative and quantitative research are explored in Topics 9 and 10. In addition, Part I of this book describes qualitative research methods in detail.

In **historical research**, information is examined in order to understand the past. Note that good historical research is not just a matter of developing a chronological list of so-called facts and dates.

---

[1] Characteristics of good samples for quantitative research are explored in detail in Part D of this book. Considerations in sampling for qualitative research are described in Topics 68 and 69 in Part I of this book.

[2] Types of variables are described in Topics 5 and 6.

[3] Validity is explored in Part E of this book. Correlational studies employ a statistic called a *correlation coefficient*, which is described in Topic 57.

Rather, it is an attempt to understand the dynamics of human history. As such, it is driven by theories and hypotheses. In other words, by reviewing historical evidence, researchers are able to develop theories that may explain historical events and patterns. These theories lead to hypotheses, which are evaluated in terms of additional historical data that are collected. Historical researchers may use qualitative methods (e.g., examining historical documents, using insight and judgment to identify themes) or quantitative methods (e.g., counting certain types of statements made in historical documents). Historical research is typically taught in history departments and is not considered further in this book.

EXERCISE ON TOPIC 4

1. Suppose a researcher administered an intelligence test to young children each year for five years in order to study changes in intelligence over time. The researcher was conducting what type of study?

2. Is the study in Question 1 experimental?

3. If a researcher conducts a poll to estimate public support for free childcare for mothers on welfare, the researcher is conducting what type of nonexperimental study?

4. A researcher determined the degree of relationship between vocabulary scores and reading comprehension scores. The researcher was conducting what type of nonexperimental study?

5. According to this topic, what is a distinctive feature of quantitative research?

6. Most published qualitative research is collected using what?

Questions for Discussion

7. Name a topic in your field of study that you might explore with a nonexperimental study. Which type of nonexperimental study would be most appropriate for your topic?

8. Think of a survey in which you were asked to serve as a participant. (You may have been sent a questionnaire in the mail, such as a consumer satisfaction survey, or you may have been contacted in person or by phone.) Did you cooperate and respond? Why? Why not?

9. Name two quantitative variables that might be studied through the use of correlational research.

10. Suppose someone prepared a list of educational events and their dates of occurrence in the past 100 years. Would the list be an example of good historical research? Explain.

For Students Planning Research

11. If you will be conducting a nonexperimental study, which type will it be? Explain the basis for your choice.

A **variable** is a trait or characteristic with two or more categories. Participants *vary* in terms of the categories to which they belong. Example 1 has two variables.

EXAMPLE 1
A sample of registered voters was surveyed. Each voter was asked first to name his or her gender (male or female), then to name the candidate for whom he or she planned to vote (Doe, Jones, or Smith). The purpose was to explore gender differences in voting preferences.

The two variables in Example 1 are (1) gender, with two categories; and (2) the preferred candidate, with three categories (i.e., three possible candidates).

Be careful not to confuse a variable with its categories. For instance, "male" is one of the two categories of the variable called "gender." "Male" is not a variable. Here is how to visualize it:

| One Variable ⇨ | *GENDER* | |
| Two Categories ⇨ | Male | Female |

All variables have **mutually exclusive categories**. That is, each respondent to the survey in Example 1 will belong to one—and *only one*—category. For instance, the categories for "preferred candidate" are mutually exclusive because a researcher would ask, "For which *one* candidate do you plan to vote?" When conducting such a survey, a researcher would not allow a participant to name two candidates (i.e., two categories) for the same political office.

Researchers define variables in such a way that the categories are **exhaustive**. To be exhaustive, a variable must have a category for each respondent's opinion. For instance, a researcher would want to add a fourth choice of "undecided" for respondents who have not yet chosen from among the three candidates in Example 1.

Notice that both variables in Example 1 are *naming* variables (more properly called *categorical* variables).[1] Each participant *names* his or her gender and *names* the preferred candidate. Other variables have quantitative categories that describe the amount of a characteristic. Consider Example 2.

---
[1] *Naming data* are obtained from the *nominal scale of measurement*. Scales of measurement are discussed in Topic 49.

EXAMPLE 2
The college admissions scores on the *Scholastic Aptitude Test* (*SAT*) were compared with students' freshman GPAs to determine how valid the *SAT* is for predicting GPAs.

Both the College Board's *SAT* scores (ranging from 200 to 800 per subtest) and GPAs (usually ranging from 0.00 to 4.00) are quantitative. In other words, each possible score is a category. A student who earns an *SAT* score of 550 belongs to the category called "550." Likewise, a student who has a GPA of 2.9 belongs to the category called "2.9."

Variables in nonexperimental studies are sometimes classified as either **independent or dependent**. For instance, when researchers conduct a causal-comparative study (see Topic 3 to review), the presumed cause (such as smoking) is called the *independent* variable, and the response or outcome (such as lung cancer) is called the *dependent* variable.

> The *independent variable* (stimulus or input) causes changes in the *dependent variable* (response or output).

Some researchers refer to any variable that comes first (whether or not it is presumed to be a cause) as *independent* and to the one that comes later as *dependent*. For instance, *SAT* scores (the predictor variable) are usually determined before students earn their college GPAs. Thus, some researchers would call the *SAT* the independent variable and the GPA the dependent variable. It is also common to call the independent variable the **predictor** and the outcome variable (such as GPA) the **criterion**. The term *criterion* means *standard*. Hence, GPA is the standard by which the *SAT* is often judged. Ideally, high scores on the *SAT* should be associated with high GPAs, while low *SAT* scores should be associated with low GPAs. To the extent that this is true, the *SAT* is judged to be valid. To the extent that it is not true, the *SAT* is judged to be invalid. Procedures for determining the validity of a test are described in Part E of this book.

EXERCISE ON TOPIC 5

1. Adults who were taking a course to learn English as a second language were asked to name their country of birth and their number of years of formal education. In this example, how many variables were being studied?

2. In Question 1, which variable is a categorical variable?

3. In Question 1, which variable is quantitative?

4. A sample of adults was asked their level of agreement with the statement, "The president of the United States is doing a good job of handling foreign relations." They were permitted to respond with either "strongly agree," "agree," "disagree," or "strongly disagree." How many variables were being studied?

5. What is meant by *mutually exclusive categories*?

6. A researcher looked for the causes of social unrest by examining economic variables such as poverty, income, and so on. Is social unrest an "independent" *or* a "dependent" variable?

7. If a researcher administers a basic math test to middle school children to see if the basic math test scores predict grades in high school algebra, what is the criterion variable?

8. Suppose a researcher asks participants to identify their age group using these categories: "under 21," "21–39," "40–55," and "56+." Are these exhaustive categories?

9. In Question 8, how many variables are being studied?

10. What is the minimum number of categories that each variable must have?

Questions for Discussion

11. Suppose you want to measure income on a self-report questionnaire on which each participant will check off his or her income category. Name the categories you would use. Are they exhaustive and mutually exclusive? Explain.

12. Name a quantitative variable of interest to you, and name its categories. Are the categories mutually exclusive and exhaustive? Explain.

For Students Planning Research

13. If you will be conducting a nonexperimental study, name the major variables you will be studying. For each, indicate whether the categories will be quantitative.

All experiments have at least one **independent variable** and one **dependent variable**. The purpose of experiments is to estimate the extent to which independent variables cause changes in dependent variables.

As indicated in the previous section, an independent variable is a stimulus or input variable. Note that in experiments, researchers *physically manipulate* independent variables. Examples of physical manipulation are (1) giving a new drug to some participants while giving a placebo to others, (2) providing some students with computers while denying computers to others, and (3) using group counseling with some clients while using individual counseling with others. Thus, to *physically manipulate* means to physically administer treatments.

Note that in *nonexperimental* studies, researchers do *not* physically manipulate independent variables. Instead, they observe independent variables as they occur (or have occurred) naturally. For instance, researchers observe the health of individuals who have smoked cigarettes in nonexperimental studies—researchers do not provide participants with cigarettes, nor do they expose participants to smoke. (See Topic 3 to review other differences between experimental and nonexperimental studies of causation.)

In a simple experiment, as in Example 1, there is only one independent variable and only one dependent variable.

EXAMPLE 1
On alternate weeks, a disruptive first-grade student is given extra praise for being in her seat when appropriate. The purpose of the study is to see if the extra praise will increase the amount of appropriate in-seat behavior.

In Example 1, the physical manipulation is giving or not giving extra praise, which is the independent variable (i.e., the stimulus or input variable). The dependent variable (i.e., the response or outcome variable) is the change in the student's in-seat behavior.

Often, experiments have more than one dependent variable. For instance, in Example 1, a researcher could observe not only if the treatment causes (1) more in-seat behavior, but also (2) improvement in the student's achievement and (3) improvement in the student's attitude toward school during the weeks in which the extra praise is given. If a researcher did this, the researcher would have three dependent variables.

Many experiments also have more than one independent variable. Often, these experiments are more interesting than those with only one independent variable because they provide insights into the causal effects of combinations of variables. Consider Example 2, which has two independent variables (i.e., childcare and transportation money).

EXAMPLE 2
Voluntary, free job training was offered to all mothers on welfare in a small city. Four groups of the mothers were formed at random to explore the effects of these two independent variables: (1) providing or not providing free childcare while in training and (2) providing or not providing transportation money to get to the job-training site. Each group was assigned at random to one of the four treatment conditions shown here:

GROUP 1 childcare *and* transportation money	GROUP 3 *no* childcare *and* transportation money
GROUP 2 childcare *and* *no* transportation money	GROUP 4 *no* childcare *and* *no* transportation money

It was predicted that those in Group 1 (the group that was given *both* childcare and transportation money) would have the highest attendance rates in the job-training program, those in Group 2 would have the next highest, those in Group 3 would have the next highest, and those in Group 4 would have the lowest.

Notice that in Example 2, a researcher can determine (1) how effective childcare is, (2) how effective transportation money is, and (3) the effectiveness of both childcare *and* transportation money *in combination*. Thus, a researcher would get more information by looking at two independent variables in one study than by looking at each independent variable in a separate experiment (in which case, a researcher could determine only points 1 and 2).

EXERCISE ON TOPIC 6

1. All experiments have at least how many dependent variables?

2. In an experiment, what is the name of a stimulus or input variable?

3. What does *physically manipulate* mean in an experimental context?

4. Are dependent variables physically manipulated?

5. Can an experiment have more than one independent variable?

6. Every other customer entering a shoe store was given one of two different coupons. One coupon offered a second pair of shoes for 50% off. The other coupon offered to reduce the total price by 25% if two pairs of shoes were purchased. The purpose was to determine which coupon was more effective in getting individuals to buy two pairs of shoes. In this experiment, what is the independent variable?

7. In Question 6, what is the dependent variable?

8. A teacher showed an educational film on daily nutritional needs to one group of students and gave a handout on the same material to another group. The purpose was to determine which method of instruction was more effective in increasing students' knowledge of daily nutritional needs. In this experiment, what is the dependent variable?

9. In Question 8, what is the independent variable?

Questions for Discussion

10. Name a variable that would be easy for a researcher to physically manipulate in an experiment. Then, name a variable that might be affected by the manipulation.

11. Name a variable that you would be unwilling to physically manipulate due to ethical or legal concerns.

For Students Planning Research

12. If you will be conducting an experiment, name the independent and dependent variables you will be studying.

TOPIC 7   RESEARCH HYPOTHESES, PURPOSES, AND QUESTIONS

A **research hypothesis** is a prediction of the outcome of a study. The prediction may be based on an educated guess or a formal theory. Example 1 is a hypothesis for a nonexperimental study.

EXAMPLE 1
It is hypothesized that first-grade girls have better reading comprehension than first-grade boys.

In Example 1, the researcher is predicting that he or she will find higher reading comprehension among girls than boys. To test the prediction, a nonexperimental study would be appropriate because nothing in the hypothesis suggests that treatments will be given.

A simple research hypothesis predicts a relationship between two variables. The two variables in Example 1 are (1) gender and (2) reading comprehension. The hypothesis states that reading comprehension is related to gender.

Example 2 is a hypothesis for an experimental study.

EXAMPLE 2
It is hypothesized that children who are shown a video with mild violence will be more aggressive on the playground than those who are shown a similar video without violence.

In Example 2, the independent variable is violence (mild vs. no violence), and the dependent variable is aggressiveness on the playground.

The hypotheses in Examples 1 and 2 are examples of **directional hypotheses**. In a directional hypothesis, researchers predict which group will be higher or have more of some attribute.

Sometimes researchers have a **nondirectional hypothesis**. Consider Example 3.

EXAMPLE 3
It is hypothesized that the child-rearing practices of Tribe A are different from those of Tribe B.

The author of Example 3 is saying that there will be a difference, but the author does not predict the direction of the difference. This is perfectly acceptable when there is no basis for making an educated guess as to the outcome of a study.

Instead of a nondirectional hypothesis, a researcher might state a **research purpose**. Example 4 shows a research purpose that corresponds to the nondirectional hypothesis in Example 3.

EXAMPLE 4
The research purpose is to explore the differences in child-rearing practices between Tribe A and Tribe B.

A **research question** may also be substituted for a nondirectional hypothesis. Example 5 shows a research question that corresponds to the nondirectional hypothesis in Example 3 and the research purpose in Example 4.

EXAMPLE 5
The research question is, "How do the child-rearing practices in Tribe A and Tribe B differ?"

When using a research question as the basis for research, researchers usually do *not* state it as a question that can be answered with a simple "yes" or "no," as is the case in Example 6.

EXAMPLE 6
The research question is, "Do the child-rearing practices in Tribe A and Tribe B differ?"

Example 6 merely asks, "Do they differ?" This is not a very interesting research question because it implies that the results of the research will be only a simple "yes" or "no." Example 5 is superior because it asks, "*How* do they differ?"—a question that implies that the results will be complex and, thus, more interesting and informative.

The choice between a nondirectional hypothesis, a research purpose, and a research question is purely a matter of personal taste—all are acceptable in the scientific community. Of course, when researchers are willing and able to predict the outcome of a study, they state a directional hypothesis—not a research purpose or question. In other words, a research purpose or a research question is a suitable substitute for a nondirectional hypothesis. It is inappropriate to use these as substitutes for a directional hypothesis.

Those who have read research reports in journals may have encountered references to another type of hypothesis: the **null hypothesis**. This is a *statistical hypothesis*, which needs to be considered when analyzing results obtained from samples in quantitative research studies. The null hypothesis need not be considered at this point. However, it will be explored in detail in Part G of this book.

EXERCISE ON TOPIC 7

1. Which type of statement (hypothesis, purpose, or question) predicts the outcome of a study?

2. "It is hypothesized that college students who have firm career goals achieve higher GPAs than those who do not have firm career goals." Is this a "directional" *or* a "nondirectional" hypothesis?

3. "It is hypothesized that children of immigrants and children of native-born citizens differ in their attitudes toward school." Is this a "directional" *or* a "nondirectional" hypothesis?

4. "The goal of this study is to examine college students' attitudes toward religion." Is this statement a "hypothesis" *or* a "purpose"?

5. "Are children of alcoholics different from children of nonalcoholics in their social adjustment?" Is this research question stated appropriately? Why? Why not?

6. When researchers are willing to predict the outcome of a study, should they state a "directional" *or* a "nondirectional" hypothesis?

7. What are the two alternatives to stating a nondirectional hypothesis?

8. Consider nondirectional hypotheses, research purposes, and research questions. Are "all three acceptable in the scientific community" *or* is "one type preferred over the others"?

Questions for Discussion

9. Restate this hypothesis as a research purpose: "It is hypothesized that there is a difference in job satisfaction between those who receive regular feedback on their job performance and those who receive irregular feedback."

10. Is the hypothesis in Question 9 "directional" *or* "nondirectional"? Explain.

11. Could an experiment be conducted to test the hypothesis in Question 9? Explain.

12. Restate the following hypothesis as a research question: "It is hypothesized that those who exercise regularly and those who do not exercise regularly differ in other behaviors that affect health."

For Students Planning Research

13. State a research hypothesis, purpose, or question for the research you are planning. (Note: You may have more than one of each.)

14. If you stated a hypothesis in response to Question 13, is it "directional" *or* "nondirectional"?

TOPIC 8 OPERATIONAL DEFINITIONS OF VARIABLES

Dictionaries provide **conceptual definitions** of variables. For instance, a researcher in speech communication might be interested in students' ability to *recite*, which has a dictionary definition along these lines: "to repeat or speak aloud from or as from memory, especially in a formal way." This definition is perfectly adequate if a researcher merely wants to communicate the general topic of his or her research to other individuals.

Suppose, however, that the researcher wants to conduct an experiment on the effectiveness of two memory aids on the ability to recite. As the researcher plans the research, it will become clear that a conceptual definition is not adequate because it does not indicate the precise concrete or physical steps the researcher will take in order to identify the variable. Redefining a variable in terms of physical steps is called *operationalizing* a variable. When a researcher operationalizes a variable, he or she is creating an **operational definition**. Example 1 shows the first attempt at creating an operational definition of students' ability to recite.

EXAMPLE 1
For the research project, the ability to recite is defined as the number of words mispronounced, missing, or misplaced when students repeat aloud from memory Christian Abzab's poem *The Road Taken* in front of a panel of three teachers.

Notice that the definition in Example 1 is not fully operational because there might still be questions about the *physical arrangements*, such as "Will the students stand while reciting?" "In what type of room will the recitation take place (a classroom or auditorium)?" "Will the teachers be male or female?" and "Will the teachers already know the students?"

It is important to note that no attempt at operationalizing a variable will result in a completely operational definition because there are an infinite number of physical characteristics that might be addressed in any definition (e.g., the humidity in the room, the level of lighting, the type of flooring, the color of the walls). Thus, instead of striving for completely operational definitions, researchers try to produce definitions that are adequate to permit a **replication** in all important respects by another researcher. A replication is an attempt to confirm the results of a study by conducting it again in the same way. Of course, there is much subjectivity in apply-

ing this criterion of adequacy (i.e., sufficiently operational to permit replication), and all researchers may not agree on when it has been met.[1]

Notice that a highly operational definition is not necessarily meaningful or relevant. For example, clients' self-esteem could be operationalized with the definition in Example 2.

EXAMPLE 2
Positive self-esteem is defined as answering "yes" to the written question, "Do you feel good about yourself?"

The definition in Example 2 is reasonably operational because it indicates what specific question to ask in writing and what response to anticipate. However, the definition is quite narrow. For instance, it does not tap self-esteem in the various dimensions of clients' lives, such as self-esteem in the workplace, in social settings, and so on. Thus, Example 2 illustrates that a definition can be operational without being adequate in other respects, such as being fully multidimensional.

Treatments given in experiments also should be operationalized. For instance, "verbal praise" given in an experiment could be operationalized in terms of the types of words used when giving praise, the frequency of the praise, the conditions under which the praise will be given, and so on.

Notice that if a researcher fails to provide operational definitions of all key variables in a research report, the report is vague at best and the results are often of limited usefulness. For instance, if research shows that a certain program is helpful in reducing spousal abuse but the researcher fails to provide a highly operational definition, consumers of research will not know how to conduct the program in applied settings.

---

[1] Confidence in results of a study is increased when the results have been independently replicated by other researchers. This is the case because a given researcher may have blind spots, unconscious biases, and so on. Also, a given researcher may have been unlucky and have results that were influenced by large random errors. Independent replications by others reduce the odds that these factors are the cause of a particular finding.

EXERCISE ON TOPIC 8

1. Which type of definition indicates physical steps?

2. In practice, are operational definitions ever fully operationalized?

3. Which of the following definitions of *gregarious* is more operational?
   A. Talking on the phone with friends for at least two hours each week.
   B. Being open and friendly when in social gatherings with others.

4. Which of the following definitions of being *computer literate* is more operational?
   A. Having taken at least two formal courses of instruction in an accredited school on the use of computers.
   B. Having knowledge of the origins and uses of computers in modern society and their implications.

5. Which of the following definitions of administering *nonverbal praise* (in an experiment) is more operational?
   A. Using various positive gestures involving various body parts without speaking.
   B. Nodding the head slightly in an up-down direction while smiling lightly with the lips closed.

6. To replicate the research of others, do researchers need "operational" *or* "conceptual" definitions?

7. Is it possible for a definition to be highly operational, yet inadequate in other respects?

Questions for Discussion

8. Suppose you read a research report claiming that low-socioeconomic-status (SES) children have lower self-concepts than high-SES children do. In the report, the only definition of self-concept is "feeling good about oneself." How much credence would you give the results in light of the definition? What additional information, if any, would you want about the definition if you were planning to replicate the study?

9. In a research report, job satisfaction is defined as "the number of times each participant said 'yes' to a set of questions such as 'Do you look forward to going to work most mornings?'" Is this definition completely operational? If not, what is missing from the definition?

10. Is the definition in Question 9 too narrow in terms of how you normally think about job satisfaction? Why? Why not?

11. Write a highly operational definition of "success in college."

12. Write a highly operational definition of "motivation to succeed on the job."

For Students Planning Research

13. Name the major variables you will be studying. Define each variable, trying to be as operational as possible. (Note: After you have read published research on your topic, you may want to come back here and redefine some of your definitions in light of how other researchers have defined them.)

The results of **quantitative research** are presented as quantities or numbers (i.e., statistics). In **qualitative research**, the results are presented as discussions of trends and/or themes based on words, not statistics. In addition to the difference in how results are presented, there are a number of characteristics that distinguish the two types of research. To understand some of the major ones, consider this research problem: A metropolitan police force is demoralized, with signs such as high rates of absenteeism, failure to follow procedures, and so on. Furthermore, the press has raised questions about the effectiveness of the force and its leadership. In response, the police commission is planning to employ a researcher to identify possible causes and solutions.

If a researcher with a quantitative orientation is retained, he or she will probably begin with a review of the research literature on demoralized police departments. From the review, the researcher will attempt to develop hypotheses to be tested by research. This is a deductive approach to planning the research. That is, the researcher is deducing from the literature possible explanations (i.e., hypotheses) to be tested. In contrast, a qualitative researcher will tend to use an inductive approach to planning the research. For example, he or she might begin to gather data on the specific police force in question by making preliminary observations and conducting informal interviews. The resulting preliminary findings might be used as a basis for planning what additional types of information to collect and how to collect them. Thus, rather than approaching the research task with preconceived notions based on published theory and research, a qualitative researcher will emphasize induction from the preliminary data that he or she collected.

Note that qualitative researchers (like quantitative researchers) typically examine previously published literature and include reviews of it in their research reports. However, quantitative researchers use literature as the basis for planning research, while qualitative researchers tend to deemphasize it.

When deciding what types of measures (sometimes called *instruments*) to use, quantitative researchers prefer those that produce data that can be easily reduced to numbers, such as structured questionnaires or interview schedules with objective formats, such as multiple-choice questions. In contrast, qualitative researchers prefer measures that yield words that are not easily reduced to numbers. These can be obtained through the use of measures such as unstructured interviews or direct, unstructured observations.

Quantitative researchers tend to select large samples to use as participants.[1] Quantitative researchers are able to work with large samples because objective measures such as anonymous, objective questionnaires usually are easy to administer to large numbers of participants in a short amount of time. In contrast, qualitative researchers tend to use smaller samples because of the amount of time required to use their measures, such as extended, in-depth, one-on-one unstructured interviews and extensive observations over time.

When deciding which individuals to use as research participants, quantitative researchers prefer to select a random sample in which all participants have an equal chance of being selected. This can be done, for instance, through the drawing of names from a hat. (The uses of random samples and their relationship to statistics are discussed in later topics.) Qualitative researchers, on the other hand, are more likely to select a purposive sample of individuals whom the researchers believe are key informants in terms of social dynamics, leadership positions, job responsibilities, and so on. In other words, qualitative researchers prefer to use informed judgment in selecting participants, while quantitative researchers prefer to leave the selection of participants to chance (i.e., random selection).

While working with the participants, qualitative researchers would be open to the possibility of making adjustments in the measures, such as rewording questions or adding questions based on earlier responses by participants. On the other hand, quantitative researchers seldom make such adjustments during the course of a research project. Instead, quantitative researchers plan their research in detail and follow the plan closely throughout the study because midstream deviations might be viewed as introducing subjectivity to the study. It is important to note that while quantitative researchers emphasize objectivity, qualitative researchers believe all

---

[1] Note that the term *participants* implies that the individuals being studied have voluntarily agreed to participate in a given research project. When individuals are being observed without their consent, they are more likely to be called *subjects*.

observational processes are inherently subjective and open to interpretation. Because of this, qualitative researchers sometimes mention relevant details of their personal backgrounds (such as having a mother who was a police officer) in order to inform readers of their research about possible sources of bias in their collection and interpretation of the data.

For data analysis, quantitative researchers tend to summarize all responses with statistics and seldom report on the responses of individual participants. Qualitative researchers, on the other hand, tend to cite individuals' responses (e.g., by quoting individual participants) in the Results section of a research report.

Finally, quantitative researchers tend to generalize the results to one or more population(s), while qualitative researchers tend to limit their conclusions to only the individuals who were directly studied.

Should the police commission select a researcher with a "quantitative" or a "qualitative" orientation? Criteria for making such a decision are described in the next topic.

EXERCISE ON TOPIC 9

1. Do "qualitative" *or* "quantitative" researchers tend to rely more on published research literature in planning research?

2. Which method of research relies on the inductive approach?

3. Which method of research is more likely to lead to a statistical report of results?

4. In which method of research would a researcher be more likely to make adjustments to the interview questions during the course of a research project?

5. Which method of research tends to have smaller samples?

6. Do "qualitative" *or* "quantitative" researchers prefer random sampling?

7. There are more likely to be quotations from participants in the Results sections of reports in which type of research?

8. In which type of research do researchers have more interest in generalizing the results to populations?

Questions for Discussion

9. In general, are you more likely to believe research results that are presented as themes and trends expressed in words *or* results described with statistics? Explain. (If you have not read academic research extensively, consider secondary reports of research such as those found in newspapers, magazines, and textbooks.)

10. Do you believe that both qualitative and quantitative research have valuable roles in advancing knowledge in your field of study? Why? Why not?

For Students Planning Research

11. At this point, are you leaning toward conducting "qualitative" *or* "quantitative" research? Explain the basis for your choice. (Note that you will be learning more about qualitative research in the next topic.)

The last topic finished with the question, "Should the police commission select a researcher with a 'quantitative' *or* a 'qualitative' orientation?" Some of the criteria that are usually used when making such a decision are as follows:

A. Some research questions inherently lend themselves more to the quantitative than to the qualitative approach. For instance, "What is the impact of terrorism on the U.S. economy?" is a question that lends itself to quantitative research because economic variables readily lend themselves to quantitative analysis. On the other hand, "What is the emotional impact of terrorism on at-risk healthcare workers?" is a question that lends itself more to the qualitative approach because this question focuses on emotional impact, which is more difficult to quantify. Note, however, that the second question could be examined with either qualitative or quantitative research.

B. When little is known about a topic, qualitative research should usually be initially favored. New topics are constantly emerging in all fields, such as new diseases (like SARS), new criminal concerns (such as domestic terrorism), and new educational techniques (such as using the Internet for instructional purposes in classrooms). On new topics, there often is little, if any, previously published research. In its absence, quantitative researchers may find it difficult to employ the deductive approach (i.e., to deduct hypotheses from previously published research). Also, quantitative researchers might find it difficult to write structured questions about a little-known topic. (How can a researcher know exactly what to ask when he or she knows little about a topic?) In contrast, qualitative researchers could start with broad questions and refine them during the course of the interviews as various themes and issues start to emerge. Based on the qualitative results, theories might be developed from which hypotheses can be deduced and subsequently tested with quantitative research.

C. When the participants belong to a culture that is closed or secretive, qualitative research should usually be favored. A skilled qualitative researcher who is willing to spend considerable time breaking through the barriers that keep researchers out is more likely to be successful than a quantitative researcher who tends to spend much less time interacting with participants.

D. When potential participants are not available for extensive interactions or observation, the quantitative approach should be considered. For instance, it might be difficult to schedule extensive interviews with chief executives of major corporations. However, the chief executives might be willing to respond to a brief objective-type questionnaire, which would provide data that can be analyzed with statistics.

E. When time and funds are very limited, quantitative research might be favored. Although this is an arguable criterion for choosing between the two types of research, it is suggested because quantitative research can be used to provide quick, inexpensive snapshots of narrow aspects of research problems. Qualitative methods do not lend themselves to the more economical, snapshot approach.

F. When audiences require hard numbers (which legislators or funding agencies sometimes do, for example), quantitative research should be favored or, at least, incorporated into a qualitative research project. When someone says, "Just the numbers, please," themes and trends illustrated with quotations are unlikely to impress him or her. For such an audience, one should start by presenting statistics when possible. This might open the door to consideration of more qualitative aspects of the findings. Notice that implicit in this criterion is the notion that both qualitative and quantitative approaches might be used in a given research project, with each approach contributing a different type of information.

Up to this point, quantitative and qualitative research have been presented as though they are opposites. However, researchers conduct research that is a blend of the two approaches. For instance, a quantitative researcher who uses semi-structured interviews to collect data, reduces the data to statistics, but also reports quotations from participants to support the statistics, is conducting research that has some of the characteristics of both approaches.

Clearly, the hypothetical police commission needs to make a complex decision. How would you answer the question in the first paragraph of this topic? What is the basis for your answer? For more information on the characteristics of qualitative research, consult Part I of this book.

Exercise on Topic 10

1. Which of the following lends itself more to quantitative research?
   A. How do the social relations of adolescents who use illicit drugs differ from those who do not use them?
   B. How do school attendance and grades differ between adolescents who use illicit drugs and those who do not use them?

2. Which of the following lends itself more to qualitative research?
   A. What are the differences between the social interactions of students at commuter colleges and students who live on campus?
   B. To what extent does family income predict whether a student will choose to attend a commuter college or a college where most students live on campus?

3. Suppose a researcher wants to conduct research on members of a secretive fraternity. According to the information in this topic, which type of researcher is more likely to be successful in conducting the research?

4. If little is known about a new topic, which type of research is recommended for initial use?

5. For which type of research must participants usually be available for extensive interactions with researchers?

6. Which type of research is more suitable for getting a quick snapshot of a problem?

Questions for Discussion

7. How would you answer the two questions in the last paragraph of this topic?

8. Suppose a team of researchers wants to identify the characteristics of professors whom students perceive as being excellent. Would you advise them to conduct "qualitative" *or* "quantitative" research? Why?

9. Name a problem in your field of study that would probably lend itself more to the quantitative than the qualitative approach.

For Students Planning Research

10. In light of the information in this topic, have you changed your mind about your answer to Question 10 in the Exercise on Topic 9? Explain.

Consider a school that receives a foundation grant for a new program that emphasizes parental involvement and shared decision making. In this program, decisions are made by an administrator with the advice and consent of both teachers and parents. The ultimate purpose is to help students improve on a variety of academic and social skills. In this case, as in most others, the granting agency requires a report on the implementation and effectiveness of the programs for which they provide funding. To prepare such a report, researchers conduct a **program evaluation** by engaging in *evaluation research.*

At first glance, it might appear that a researcher should conduct *experimental research*. As indicated in Topic 2, in experimental research, researchers give treatment(s) (in this case, a program) in order to observe their effects. Indeed, while elements of evaluation research resemble experimental work, there are some major differences.

First, program evaluation is almost always *applied research* (i.e., research in which researchers wish to apply the findings directly to such practical decisions as whether to continue funding the program and whether to modify it). Experimental research, on the other hand, is often *basic research* in which researchers are attempting to understand underlying theories that explain behavior without necessarily looking for direct, immediate applications.

Second, new programs are, or should be, based on a *needs assessment*. A needs assessment is nonexperimental research in which researchers attempt to determine the practical needs of those who will be served by the program. For a school-based program, a researcher might ask questions such as, "What types of skills do the students need to acquire?" and "What types of program interventions to promote these skills will be most readily accepted by students, parents, and teachers?" Pure experimental research is seldom preceded by a formal needs assessment, which is associated with program evaluation because a major focus of evaluation is to estimate the extent to which a program has met the needs revealed in a needs assessment.

Third, the programs, which are analogous to treatments in an experiment, are usually subject to change during the course of the evaluation. For instance, perhaps a program is designed to give teachers a major role in decision making, with only a minor role for parents. If, in midstream, it is found that the parents are seeking more involvement, adjustments may be made in the program procedures to give parents a greater voice in decision making. Although it is almost unheard of for an experimental researcher to make changes in the nature of a treatment during the course of an experiment, skilled program evaluators are open to such modifications. In fact, program evaluators collect information during the course of a program that assists in the process of modifying the program while it is being implemented. Collecting this information is called **formative evaluation.**

Formative evaluation has two prongs. First, information is collected on the *process* of implementing a program. For instance, when looking at the process, a researcher might ask, "Were the parents notified of the program in a timely manner?" and "Were the proposed meetings of parents and teachers conducted?" These questions clearly ask about the process, not the ultimate goals of student improvement. The second prong of formative evaluation involves collecting information on the *progress toward the ultimate goals*. For example, periodic achievement tests might be administered to determine if students are showing signs of improvement. If not, evaluators and program administrators might rethink the program they are implementing and make appropriate changes. By looking at *progress,* those responsible for the program can often prevent disappointment in the final results of a program evaluation.

When evaluators collect information about participants' attainment of the ultimate goals at the end of the program (e.g., at the end of a school year), the activity is called **summative evaluation.** A summative evaluation report contains information about the final or long-term benefits of the program for its ultimate clients (such as students). Summative evaluation often involves a comparison with a control group. For instance, students in a program might be compared with similar students in other schools who are not in the program. Note that while experimental researchers typically strive to use random assignment (like pulling names out of a hat) to form experimental and control groups, program evaluators usually have to find an external group (such as students at another school) to serve as the control group.

The final program evaluation research report should provide an overview of the needs assessment that led to the development of the program, the results of the formative evaluation (i.e., data on program implementation and client progress), and data on the summative evaluation (i.e., the extent to which clients reached the ultimate program goals). The report should also contain recommendations regarding extending the program in the future and recommendations for improving the program's implementation.

EXERCISE ON TOPIC 11

1. Is "program evaluation" *or* "experimental research" almost always *applied research*?

2. Is a needs assessment associated with "experimental research" *or* with "program evaluation"?

3. Is it acceptable to modify the treatments (programs) during the course of a program evaluation?

4. Suppose that in a program evaluation, an evaluator asks, "How many children were reading at grade level by the end of the program?" Is this question relevant to "formative" *or* to "summative" evaluation?

5. Suppose that in a program evaluation, an evaluator asks, "Are the clients in the job-placement program writing better résumés?" Is this question relevant to "formative" *or* to "summative" evaluation?

6. Suppose that in a program evaluation, an evaluator asks, "Were key program personnel hired on time?" Is this question relevant to "formative" *or* to "summative" evaluation?

7. When a researcher looks at the process of implementing a program, is the researcher conducting "formative" *or* "summative" evaluation?

8. Is examining program participants' *progress* toward attaining the ultimate goals of the program part of "formative" *or* "summative" evaluation?

9. Is the attainment by participants of the final goals of a program a topic for "formative" *or* for "summative" evaluation?

Questions for Discussion

10. Suppose you were on the board of a foundation that was giving a grant to a social welfare agency's program. Would you prefer to have the program evaluated by an employee of the program (such as the program director) *or* by an external, independent evaluator? Why?

11. Government agencies and organizations sometimes fund certain programs despite prior negative summative evaluations. Speculate on some of the possible reasons for this. Are any of the reasons justifiable?

For Students Planning Research

12. Will you be evaluating a program in your research? If yes, name the program and indicate whether you will be conducting both "formative" *and* "summative" research.

TOPIC 12 ETHICAL CONSIDERATIONS IN RESEARCH

When planning research, it is imperative to consider potential harm to participants. Certain treatments that researchers may want to administer in experimental studies may present hazards. For instance, a research psychologist might expose an experimental group to an anxiety-provoking stimulus in a study designed to advance a theory on the sources and effects of anxiety. Clearly, some participants might suffer mental anguish as a result of being exposed to the treatment.

Participants also might be harmed in nonexperimental studies. For instance, the process of exploring sensitive topics (e.g., relationships with abusive parents) might cause participants to focus on them again, leading to renewed anxiety, sleeplessness, and so on.

Because of such potential problems, the research community has developed a body of ethical values regarding the use of humans as participants. The primary value is that participants must be *protected from both physical and psychological harm*. Unfortunately, it is not always possible to anticipate all the potential for harm, especially when using new treatments or measuring tools. Because of this, most universities and large school districts have research committees (often called the Institutional Review Boards or IRBs) that review research plans for potential harm to participants.

Another important value is that participants *have a right to privacy.* For instance, most individuals would probably agree that it would be a violation of parents' rights to privacy if researchers questioned children about discord between their parents without parental consent, even if the results might be very useful to educators, sociologists, psychologists, and other professionals.

A related value is that participants have a right to have data collected about them kept *confidential.* Even if participants freely and knowingly provide information to researchers, the researchers have an obligation not to disclose the information to others *unless* the identities of the participants are disguised or hidden, which is often accomplished through the use of statistics such as group averages.

Also, almost all researchers agree that participants have a right to *knowledge of the purpose* of the research before they participate. Having this knowledge, they are in a better position to determine whether they want to participate. Unfortunately, complete honesty with participants about the purpose of a study sometimes makes it difficult or impossible to conduct research on important topics. For instance, suppose researchers want to study the influence of lobbyists on a group of state legislators. The researchers might persuade some legislators to allow the researchers to shadow them (i.e., follow them around unobtrusively) if the purpose is only vaguely described as "to understand the state's political process." However, how many legislators (especially those who allow themselves to be unduly influenced by lobbyists) would agree to being shadowed if researchers revealed the true purpose of their research? Is it ethical to present only a vague general purpose that does not reveal specific goals? Do government employees have a right to privacy on the job? These types of questions illustrate the difficulties in balancing the need to protect participants with the need to collect information of benefit to society.[1]

A key to promoting ethical values is *informed consent*. To obtain informed consent, researchers inform the participants of (1) the general purpose of the research, (2) what will be done to them during the research, (3) what the potential benefit(s) to them and others might be, (4) what the potential for harm to them might be, and (5) the fact that they may withdraw at any time without penalty, even midstream. This information should be provided in writing, and the participants (or their guardians) should sign an informed consent form to indicate that they understand it and freely agree to participate.

Another key to promoting ethical values is to *debrief* participants after their participation in a study. Debriefing consists of reviewing the purpose(s) of the study and the procedure(s) used, and offering to share the results with the participants when the results become available. The process of debriefing should also include reassurances that the data will remain confidential. In addition, participants should be allowed to ask for information about any aspect of the study in which they participated. During debriefing, researchers should try to identify participants who may need more help in overcoming unanticipated harm to them than a

---

[1] For more information on this topic, refer to *Ethical Principles in the Conduct of Research With Human Subjects*, published by the American Psychological Association. Visit www.apa.org for more information.

standard debriefing session provides. At the debriefing session, information should be provided on how participants can contact the researchers in the future, either for more information or to request assistance with any harmful effects that might reveal themselves at a later date.

EXERCISE ON TOPIC 12

1. Should researchers take steps to prevent psychological harm as well as physical harm to participants?

2. Should participants be told that they are free to withdraw from a study at any time without penalty?

3. Under the principle of informed consent, is it acceptable to hide the general purpose of a study from the participants?

4. Should informed consent be in writing?

5. Is debriefing done "before" or "after" a study is conducted?

6. What does debriefing cover?

7. Should information about participants be kept confidential even if the participants freely provided it to researchers?

Questions for Discussion

8. How would you answer these two questions posed in the topic?
   A. Is it ethical to present only a vague general purpose that does not reveal specific goals?
   B. Do government employees have a right to privacy on the job?

9. Suppose a researcher wants to keep a class of third-grade students in from recess to administer an attitude-toward-school scale. The purpose is to help teachers to understand their students' attitudes and how they might affect students' achievement in school. Is there potential for harm in this case? Would it be wise to seek informed consent from the parents? Why? Why not?

10. A researcher interviewed adolescents on their possible use of marijuana (with their informed consent). During the course of the interviews, some participants named other individuals who use marijuana but who have not provided informed consent to the researcher. Does this raise ethical concerns? What, if anything, can the researcher do to protect the other individuals?

11. Suppose one of your instructors asks you to be a participant in a research project but does not tell you the purpose of the research. Would you ask for information on the purpose before deciding whether to participate? Would you feel pressured to participate because the researcher is your instructor?

For Students Planning Research

12. Do you anticipate that the study you are planning has the potential to harm the participants? Will you be obtaining informed consent? Will you have your consent form reviewed by your professor? By a university committee? By others? Explain.

A theory is a unified explanation for discrete observations that might otherwise be viewed as unrelated or contradictory. One of the most widely studied theories in learning is reinforcement theory. It defines positive reinforcement as anything that increases the frequency of a response from an animal or individual. For instance, it is common to give praise to reward a dog for sitting. To the extent that the praise increases the sitting behavior, it constitutes positive reinforcement.

At first, reinforcement theory sounds obvious, and in a way, it is self-defining. So why has it been so carefully studied? Because it explains many apparently contradictory observations. For instance, suppose at first an individual praises a dog regularly for sitting and after a while becomes lax and offers praise intermittently. Common sense might suggest that the sitting behavior will decrease with the decrease in praise. However, the individual might actually observe an increase in sitting because reinforcement theory indicates that intermittent reinforcement[1] is, under many circumstances, more effective than consistent reinforcement. Thus, reinforcement theory is a unified set of principles that helps explain why certain behaviors increase in their frequency. Without it, behaviors that do not seem to be consistent or related to each other would be observed.

One of the major functions of research is to test hypotheses derived from an existing theory. To do this, a researcher deduces hypotheses that are consistent with the theory. For instance, an axiom of self-regulated learning theory states that the goals students adopt determine their level of cognitive engagement. From this, a researcher might deduce that when students know they will be tested again on the same material, those who have lower goals (e.g., a goal of getting 70% right) should ask for less feedback about wrongly answered test items than those who have higher goals.[2] A study that confirms this hypothesis lends support to the underlying theory. Assuming the study is methodologically strong, failure to confirm a hypothesis calls the theory (or parts of it) into question, causing theorists to consider reformulating it to account for the discrepancy.

Another major function of research is to provide the observations and conclusions on which researchers can induce theory. That is, researchers try to develop theories that explain events they have observed. Researchers who practice qualitative research often refer to this as **grounded theory** (i.e., theory that is grounded on observations).[3] Grounded theory is often thought of as evolutionary. That is, it is usually developed during the process of making observations, and it is regularly revised (i.e., it evolves) as new observations warrant.

That scientists wish to develop theories on all major aspects of human experience should not be surprising. Unified explanations of phenomena are clearly more useful than a collection of unrelated "facts" collected via nontheoretical research.

Students who are looking for a research topic for a thesis or term project would be well advised to consider a theory of interest. Testing some aspect of the theory makes a potential contribution to the understanding of all aspects of behavior related to the theory. In addition, students will find it easier to defend their selection of a research topic and write the introduction to the research report if it can be shown that the study has implications for validating and refining an important theory.

When thinking about theory as a basis for research, keep in mind that no theory of human behavior is universal (i.e., there are almost always exceptions to the rule). This is why researchers usually examine *trends across groups* in order to test or develop theories. However, do not overlook the possibility of designing a study specifically to examine those individuals who do not perform as predicted by a theory. Understanding how the dynamics of their behavior differ from those of individuals who act in the way predicted by theory may help in refining a theory to take account of exceptions.

---

[1] Technical terms for various schedules of reinforcement are not discussed here.

[2] For more information on this theory and to see an example of research based on the theory, see van der Werf, G., Kuyper, H., & Minnaert, A. (2013). Emotions, self-regulated learning, and achievement in mathematics: A growth curve analysis. *Journal of Educational Psychology*, *105*, 150–161.

[3] For more information on the use of the grounded theory approach to research, see Part I of this book. Also see: Zarif, T. (2012). Grounded theory research: An overview. *Interdisciplinary Journal of Contemporary Research In Business*, 969–979.

EXERCISE ON TOPIC 13

1. How is a *theory* defined in this topic?

2. Do researchers use "induction" *or* "deduction" to derive a hypothesis from a theory?

3. What are the two major functions of research mentioned in this topic?

4. If a hypothesis derived from a theory is not confirmed, what implications does this have for the theory?

5. Is grounded theory based on "induction" *or* on "deduction"?

6. Is the use of grounded theory more likely to be associated with "qualitative" *or* with "quantitative" research?

Question for Discussion

7. Examine the discussion of a theory in a textbook in your field. Does the author of the textbook cite research that supports it? Does he or she suggest unresolved issues relating to the theory that might be explored in future research? Explain.

For Students Planning Research

8. Is the purpose of your research to test a hypothesis deduced from a theory? (This is typically done by quantitative researchers. See Topics 9 and 10 for a brief explanation of the differences between qualitative and quantitative research.) Explain.

9. Is the purpose of your research to make observations on which a theory may be built? (This is typically done by qualitative researchers. See Topics 9 and 10 for a brief explanation of the differences between qualitative and quantitative research.) Explain.

10. Will you be conducting research without reference to theory? (Note that it is possible to plan and conduct research on practical matters without explicit reference to theory. For instance, suppose your local schools went on double shifts because of overcrowding, and you want to investigate the effects of the double shifts on students' attitudes and achievements. While there may be several theories that relate to this situation, you might conduct your research *as a practical, nontheoretical matter* in order to better inform decision makers and taxpayers on this matter.) If you will not be referencing theory, will the results of your research still have important practical implications? Explain.

PART B

REVIEWING LITERATURE

Reviewing the research conducted by others is often the first step in planning a new research project. In this part of the book, the reasons for reviewing literature and how it helps researchers to identify a suitable idea for additional research are discussed. Because it is assumed that you already know how to locate books and articles in mass-circulation periodicals and newspapers, the emphasis here is on how computerized databases can make a search of academic journals more efficient and precise. Finally, some basic principles for writing literature reviews, including how to cite references, are described.

NOTES

TOPIC 14 REASONS FOR REVIEWING LITERATURE

A researcher begins by identifying a broad problem area. This could be a practical problem such as "the education of bilingual children" or it could be a more theoretical one such as "How valid is attribution theory in informal learning situations?"

Next, a researcher examines the literature about the problem area. Examining both the theoretical and research literature may help in identifying a testable hypothesis or a specific research purpose or research question.[1] In fact, authors of published research often make specific suggestions for future research in the last section of their research reports.[2]

After examining the literature, a researcher may decide to replicate a study that has already been published.[3] In a strict replication, researchers try to mimic the original study in all important respects because the purpose of a strict replication is to see if the same types of results as those of the original study will be obtained. Of course, a strict replication should be undertaken only for studies with potentially important implications. Note that if the results of a study cannot be replicated by other researchers, the results of the original study may be viewed as invalid.

Another possibility is to locate an important study and conduct a modified replication (i.e., a replication with some major modification[s], such as examining a new population or using an improved measurement technique).

Because there are many topics on which the results of published research are conflicting, a third possibility is to plan a study designed to resolve a conflict. Published reviews of research often point out such conflicts and offer possible explanations for them.

After examining the existing research in a problem area, a researcher may arrive at a creative idea that is *not* a direct extension of existing research. While there are important cases of this in the history of science, they are rare. Thus, it is extremely unlikely that a novice researcher will have such an insight at the beginning of his or her professional career. Put another way, new research almost always has its origins in existing research.

In addition to helping to identify purposes for future research, reviewing published research provides three additional benefits. First, a researcher may identify *measuring tools* (also called *instruments*) that were used successfully by other researchers. He or she may also identify seriously flawed measures, which can be avoided in future research.

Second, a researcher may be able to identify and avoid dead ends (i.e., ideas for research may have already been thoroughly investigated and shown to be unsuccessful, such as treatments that failed to produce the desired effects in experiments).

Third, researchers can get ideas on how to organize and write research reports by paying careful attention to the style and organization used by previous researchers.

When writing research reports, researchers are expected to cite relevant research. When writing a research report for publication in a journal, it is typical to integrate the literature into the introduction. (In theses and dissertations, the **literature review** is often presented in a separate chapter immediately following the chapter that contains the introduction.) Note that a well-crafted review of research shows readers the context within which the researcher was working. It can also help to justify a study if the literature is used to establish the importance of a research topic and to show how the research being reported on flows from previously published research.

For students conducting research, writing reviews of research allows the students to demonstrate to instructors, thesis committee members, and others that they were able to locate research relevant to their research purposes and write critical reviews that synthesize what is known about a topic.

In the next topic, methods for searching for literature electronically are explored. Then, specific techniques for writing literature reviews are explored in the remaining topics in this part of the book.

---

[1] See Topic 7 to review hypotheses as well as purposes and questions, which are alternatives to hypotheses, as the heart of research. A testable hypothesis is one that can be tested through direct observation.

[2] The last section is usually labeled "Discussion." See Part J of this book for more information on the typical structure of research reports.

[3] Check with your professor to see if this is acceptable in light of the objectives for the course.

EXERCISE ON TOPIC 14

1. When planning research, which should come first?
   A. Identify a broad problem area.
   B. Develop a testable hypothesis or research problem.

2. Suppose a researcher conducted a replication of a study but used a sample from a population different from the one used in the first study. What type of replication did the researcher conduct?

3. Should a researcher be surprised to find conflicting results in the research literature on a given topic?

4. According to this topic, students would be wise to try to find a creative, new research idea (not derived from the literature) to explore in their first research project. Is this statement "true" *or* "false"?

5. In journal articles, the literature review is usually integrated into which part of the article?

6. How can a researcher use a review of literature to help justify a study they have undertaken?

Question for Discussion

7. Has the information in this topic convinced you that reviewing published literature is an important part of the research-planning process? Explain.

For Students Planning Research

8. Have you begun reading the literature on your problem area? If yes, are you planning a strict replication of a previous study? A modified replication? A study that might resolve a conflict in the literature? Explain.

9. Was your research purpose or hypothesis explicitly suggested in the literature you have read? Explain.

The use of electronic databases (i.e., databases accessible via computer) to locate articles in academic journals is explored in this topic. Note that journal articles are a major source of original reports of empirical research, as well as the primary source of information on established and emerging theories.

Four of the major databases in the social and behavioral sciences are (1) *Sociological Abstracts*, covering journal articles published in more than 1,800 journals; (2) *PsycINFO*, which now contains more than 3 million records; (3) *PsycARTICLES*, with full-text journal articles dating as far back as 1894; and (4) *ERIC*, which contains abstracts of articles in education found in more than 1,165 journals dating from 1966 to the present.[1]

Unlike most other databases, access to *ERIC is free* of charge to any user, and it can be accessed from any computer connected to the Internet without restrictions such as passwords. (Other electronic databases are usually free of charge to students through their college libraries, which pay license fees that permit students and professors to use them without additional charge.)

ERIC defines *education* very broadly and has references to topics of interest to students in all the behavioral and social sciences. For instance, go to www.ERIC.ed.gov and enter *drinking* as a search term. As the time of this writing, ERIC identified 5,965 sources of information. Among other things, the column on the left shows "Descriptors," which might be helpful to use as search terms. One of the Descriptors is *alcohol abuse*. Because this is a more specific term than *drinking*, clicking on *alcohol abuse* yields only 1,526 results. Clearly, the term *alcohol abuse* is a more specific descriptor than just the word *drinking*. If the researcher had *alcohol abuse* in mind when using the term *drinking*, the search has been refined. To further refine an ERIC search, click on "Advanced Search Tips."

At the time of this writing, the ERIC website is undergoing a major reconstruction, which may lead to some differences from what you are reading about here.

Consider another major database *PsycARTICLES*, which contains abstracts and the full text articles. Let us suppose a researcher wants to search for journal articles on the topic "alcohol abuse."

1. Go to www.APA.org and enter your User ID and Password. Your college library probably has a site license for this Internet site. Check with a librarian to determine how to access this site without a personal password.
2. Click on the "Publications" tab at the top of the page.
3. Click on the "Databases" link.
4. Click on the *PsycARTICLES* link.
5. Click on "Search *PsycARTICLES* Now." At this point, a list of journal titles will appear. To search *all* journals at the same time for the topic of interest, follow the next step.
6. Click on the "SEARCH" tab at the top of the page, which will produce a dialog box that can be used to refine a search.
7. Click on the box to the left of "Select ALL." This will uncheck all the possible sources.
8. Click on the box to the left of *PsycARTICLES*.
9. Search for articles on *alcohol abuse* by typing the term in the first open space and clicking on "Search." At the time of this writing, 2,603 articles were identified.

To restrict the search to only those articles most likely to deal with alcohol abuse in-depth, go back and change "Any Field" to "Abstract." The abstract is a summary of research. An article that deals mainly with alcohol abuse is very likely to use the term in its abstract (i.e., summary).

Another way to refine the search is to use AND. For example, leave *alcohol abuse* in the first box and change "Abstract" back to "Any Field." Then, type *children* to the right of AND in the next box. This search yields 186 journal articles that mention both alcohol abuse *and* children.

Changing AND to NOT leads to 436 articles that mention alcohol abuse but do not mention children.

Changing AND to OR leads to 16,407 articles that mention either alcohol abuse or children. The use of OR in this situation is clearly not productive.

---

[1] The emphasis in this topic is on journal articles. Note that *Sociological Abstracts* also abstracts dissertations, *PsycINFO* also abstracts books, and *ERIC* also abstracts unpublished documents, such as convention papers, which are available on microfiche.

EXERCISE ON TOPIC 15

1. Which database is free of charge to any user?

2. What is a major source of original reports?

3. When using ERIC to conduct a search which field will yield more references, the Abstract Field *or* Any Field?

4. Which of the following will yield a larger number of references?
    A. A search using "alcohol abuse *AND* treatment."
    B. A search using "alcohol abuse *OR* treatment."

5. Which of the following will yield a larger number of references?
    A. A search using "alcohol abuse *OR* treatment."
    B. A search using "alcohol abuse *NOT* treatment."

6. Which of the following will yield a smaller number of references?
    A. A search for the keyword "discipline" as well as a separate search for the keyword "rewards."
    B. A search for "discipline *AND* rewards."

Question for Discussion

7. If you have searched for journal articles electronically in the past, briefly describe your experience(s). Was it easy to do? What suggestions do you have for others who will be doing it for the first time?

For Students Planning Research

8. Name some keywords you might use in an electronic search of the literature. Have you searched a database using the keywords? Did the search yield a lot of references? Explain.

TOPIC 16 ORGANIZING A LITERATURE REVIEW

A straightforward approach for beginning a literature review is to identify the broad problem area and indicate why it is important. Example 1 shows the first two sentences of a literature review. The first sentence clearly identifies the topic (substance abuse among Latino youth), and the second sentence asserts that it is an important problem.

EXAMPLE 1
Substance use and abuse are among the most well-documented behavioral risks for Latino youth. There is evidence that lifetime drug-use rates for Latinos are increasing, and that use and related outcomes pose a significant public health problem for Latino communities (Martinez, Eddy, & DeGarmo, 2003; Vega & Gil, 1999).[1]

The importance of a topic may also be established through the citing of statistics that indicate how many individuals are affected by a particular problem (e.g., the number of victims of armed assault last year) or the size of the population of interest (e.g., the number of children enrolled in special classes for the gifted). Some major sources for statistics are described in Appendix B.

Another straightforward way to begin a literature review is to start with a conceptual definition[2] of a key variable. Example 2 illustrates the beginning of a review that starts with a definition of fear of cancer recurring (FCR) in its first paragraph.

EXAMPLE 2
FCR is defined as "the fear or worry that the cancer will return or progress in the same organ or in another part of the body" (Simard & Savard, 2009; Vickberg, 2003). The current literature suggests that moderate to high levels of FCR affect 33% to 56% of cancer patients (Llewellyn, Weinman, McGurk, & Humphris, 2008; Vickberg, 2003). FCR is associated with impairment in functioning, psychological distress, stress-response symptoms, and lower quality of life (Dow, Ferrell, Leigh, Ly, & Gulasekaram, 1996; Mellon, Northouse, & Weiss, 2006....)[3]

---

[1] Martinez, C. R. Jr. (2006). Effects of differential family acculturation on Latino adolescent substance use. *Family Relations, 55,* 306–317.

[2] See Topic 8 for a discussion of the differences between conceptual and operational definitions. Conceptual definitions may also be integrated throughout a literature review. Operational definitions are usually provided in the Methods section of research reports.

[3] Lebel, S., Beattie, S., Arès, I., Bielajew, C. (2013). Young and worried: Age and fear of recurrence in breast

Note that it is acceptable to cite a published conceptual definition, as was done in Example 2.

If a literature review starts with definitions, the definitions should be followed by statements (and statistics, if any) indicating the importance of the problem area. See Appendix C for examples of how various researchers started their reviews.

After establishing the importance of the research topic and providing definitions of key terms, the next step is to write a *topic-by-topic* description of relevant research. Provide major and minor sub-headings to guide readers through a long literature review. For instance, some of the **major headings** and *minor subheadings* used by Vaitl et al. (2005) in their review of research on altered states of consciousness are shown in Example 3.

EXAMPLE 3
Spontaneously Occurring Altered States of Consciousness (ASC)
  States of Drowsiness
  Daydreaming
  Sleep and Dreaming
  Near-Death Experiences
Physically and Physiologically Induced ASC
  Extreme Environmental Conditions
  Starvation and Diet
  Respiratory Maneuvers[4]

Avoid writing a series of abstracts (i.e., writing a summary of one article, then a summary of another article, and so on). Instead, group references together when they have something in common. For instance, in Example 2, there are two citations for the definition of FCR. The first reference cited for the definition has two authors (Simard & Savard), while the second reference cited for the definition has one author (Vickberg). The second sentence in Example 2, which cites some statistics, also has two references cited. The first one has four authors (Llewellyn, Weinman, McGurk, & Humphris), while the second one has only one author (Vickberg). Note that Vickberg is cited at two different points in the paragraph. This is possible because the paragraph summarizes content; it is not a summary of a particular author's work.

---

cancer survivors. *Health Psychology, 32,* 695–705. doi: 10.1037/a0030186

[4] Vaitl, D. et al. (2005). Psychobiology of altered states of consciousness. *Psychological Bulletin, 131,* 98–127.

EXERCISE ON TOPIC 16

1. This topic suggests two ways that a writer might begin a literature review. What is the first way that is mentioned?

2. This topic suggests two ways that a writer might begin a literature review. What is the second way that is mentioned?

3. This topic suggests that statistics can be cited to establish what?

4. What should be provided in order to guide readers through a long literature review?

5. Instead of writing a series of abstracts, what should the writer do?

6. Examine the paragraph in Example 1 in this topic. Note that two sources are referred to in the paragraph. Is this appropriate?

Question for Discussion

7. Consider the six literature review excerpts in Appendix C. Each excerpt shows the beginning paragraph(s) of a literature review in a research article. In your opinion, do they all convince you of the importance of the respective problem areas? Explain.

For Students Planning Research

8. Name some of the headings and subheadings you anticipate using to organize your literature review. (Note that these may change after you have carefully examined all the literature on your topic.)

A literature review should be a *critical* assessment of the literature on a topic. Novice writers often make two common mistakes that lead to *noncritical* reviews. First, they often take the results of each study to be "facts" that have been proven. As indicated below, all studies should be presumed flawed and, therefore, to offer only degrees of evidence, not "truths" to be accepted noncritically. Second, novice writers often discuss all studies as though they were equal in quality when some studies are methodologically superior to others.

To prepare to write a critical review, the writer should assess the quality of each research article that will be cited. The first important area that requires critical assessment is sampling. More often than not, researchers work with samples that are less than ideal (such as volunteers instead of random samples of the populations of interest). Weaknesses in sampling limit the generalizability of the results. For instance, the results of a study on learning theory using a sample of psychology students who volunteered to serve as participants would have limited generalizability to nonvolunteers.

The second important area that requires critical assessment is measurement (sometimes referred to as *instrumentation*). It is safe to presume that all measures are flawed to some extent. Furthermore, it is safe to presume that various methods of measuring a given variable might lead to somewhat different results. For instance, one researcher on nutrition might measure by asking overweight adolescents to keep diaries of what they eat throughout a day. Fearing that participants might not be completely truthful in diaries, another researcher on nutrition might observe the food choices of overweight adolescents in the school cafeteria. The second method has the limitation of being conducted in a highly structured environment, where the food choices might be limited. Neither method is right or wrong. Instead, both methods have limitations, which should be considered when critically assessing the results of the studies.

The third important area to consider when critically assessing studies that will be cited in a literature review applies only to experiments (i.e., studies in which treatments are administered to participants so that one can estimate the effects of the treatments on the participants' subsequent behaviors). Experiments are often flawed by having inappropriate control conditions (such as comparing a treatment group consisting of volunteers with a control group from the general population). Also, laboratory experiments (e.g., receiving rewards for making appropriate food choices in a laboratory setting) may have limited generalizability to receiving rewards in a natural environment (i.e., the rewards may have effects in the natural environment different from those in the laboratory setting).

Issues in sampling are discussed in detail in Part D of this book, while issues in measurement are covered in Part E, and considerations in the evaluation of experiments are covered in Part F. Careful attention to these parts of the book will help in making informed assessments of the results of published studies.

Fortunately, researchers often discuss the limitations of their studies, usually in the last section of their research reports. Examining researchers' self-assessments of the limitations of their research can help writers of literature reviews when citing the studies. Example 1 shows a portion of such a discussion of limitations.

EXAMPLE 1
However, this study does have limitations, including the small sample size and the nonrandomized controlled design. Consequently, observed changes in study end points may be explained by the natural course of postoperative recovery. Also, no biochemical verification was used to confirm self-report of smoking status. (p. 185)[1]

Because flaws are widespread in research, it is important to assess the seriousness of the flaws and use appropriate terms when describing the results. For instance, Example 2 shows some terms that might be used to describe the results of research with serious weaknesses.

EXAMPLE 2
Doe's (2013) study provides some evidence that….

Recent research by Doe (2013) raises the possibility that….

Preliminary evidence suggests that…(Doe, 2013)….

---

[1] Hoffman, A. J., Brintnall, R. A., Brown, J. K., von Eye, V., Jones, L. W., Alderink, G., & VanOtteren, G. M. (2013). Too sick not to exercise: Using a 6-week, home-based exercise intervention for cancer-related fatigue self-management for postsurgical non-small cell lung cancer patients. *Cancer Nursing, 36*, 175–188.

Of course, some studies provide strong evidence, such as a national survey using a large, representative sample. Also, sometimes there is a series of studies on the same topic, all of which have similar results, making the overall findings of the series highly reliable. Terms that might be used to refer to strong evidence are shown in Example 3.

EXAMPLE 3

Overall, this set of studies clearly indicates that....

 In summary, the five studies described provide nearly conclusive evidence that....

Doe's (2013) national survey demonstrates that....

It is not necessary to use terms such as those in Examples 2 and 3 to qualify every comment about each study cited in a literature review. However, keep in mind that when a writer presents a finding or statement from the literature without qualification, readers are likely to assume that the writer believes that the underlying methodology and logic are reasonably sound.

EXERCISE ON TOPIC 17

1. According to the topic, novice writers often make two common mistakes. What is the first one that is mentioned in this topic?

2. According to the topic, novice writers often make two common mistakes. What is the second one that is mentioned in this topic?

3. "More often than not, researchers work with samples that are less than ideal." According to this topic, is this statement "true" *or* "false"?

4. "It is safe to assume that flawed measures are rare in research." According to this topic, is this statement "true" *or* "false"?

5. Do researchers often discuss the limitations of their own studies?

6. When a writer presents a finding or statement from the literature without qualification, readers are likely to assume what?

Question for Discussion

7. Suppose this statement appeared in a literature review: "The results of Doe's (2011) study clearly prove that A is higher than B." In light of the information in this topic, is such a statement justified? Explain.

For Students Planning Research

8. In the past, have you ever written an *uncritical* literature review for a term project? Has this topic convinced you that such reviews can be misleading? Explain.

TOPIC 18   CREATING A SYNTHESIS

As indicated in the previous topic, a literature review should be based on a critical assessment of the literature on a topic. However, it should consist of more than just critical summaries of individual studies. Instead, a literature review should be a **synthesis**—providing a whole picture of what is known and what is not known as well as an attempt to show how diverse pieces of information fit together and make sense.

A key to creating a synthesis is to write a review that moves from subtopic to subtopic (not from one study to another), while citing whatever studies are relevant for each topic. See Example 3 in Topic 16 for an example of a topic outline for writing a literature review.

To further the creation of a synthesis, the writer of a review should explicitly point out major trends and commonalities in the results of previous research. Example 1 illustrates how this might be done.

EXAMPLE 1
A well-established body of research speaks to the multiple and varied indices of maladjustment associated with peer victimization, including emotional distress, suicidal ideation, externalizing behaviors, social isolation, school avoidance, and academic failure (Boivin, Petitclerc, Feng, & Barker, 2010; Bonanno & Hymel, 2010; Buhs, Ladd, & Herald, 2006; Hawker & Boulton, 2000; Heilbron & Prinstein, 2010; Troop-Gordon & Ladd, 2005).[1]

In addition, when there are major discrepancies in results, they should be pointed out, and possible explanations for the discrepancies should be noted. Example 2 points out an important difference in the samples used in the studies.

EXAMPLE 2
While the studies described previously support the prediction that X is greater than Y in samples of college students, a recent study of young adolescents found no difference in X and Y. It may be that X and Y operate differently within different age groups.

A whole picture of the literature on a research topic should also explicitly point out gaps in the literature, which is illustrated in Example 3. Note

that the purpose of research is often to fill a gap found in the literature.

EXAMPLE 3
Although a plethora of past research has studied bullying and peer victimization in face-to-face situations (e.g., Champion, 2009; Dijkstra, Lindeberg, & Veenstra, 2007; Gini, Albiero, Benelli, & Altoe, 2007), fewer studies have delved into the cyberbullying context....[2]

To facilitate providing readers with an overview, writers of reviews should avoid giving extensive, detailed descriptions of the research methodology used in each study. In other words, it is usually not necessary to provide details on how studies were conducted. The main exceptions are when the writer of the review wants to document a particular weakness in a study being cited (e.g., use of a small, unrepresentative sample) or when the details of the methodology might help to explain why two studies on the same topic arrived at substantially different results.

In addition, one or more paragraphs (or even whole sections) might be devoted to describing a particular author's written work when the work is central to one or more points being made in the literature review.

Because direct quotations break the flow of a presentation, they should be used very sparingly. Quotations normally should be used only for (1) presenting especially well-crafted definitions of key terms, (2) presenting concepts that are explained especially well with a particular set of words, and (3) clarifying differences of opinion in the literature when seeing that the differences in wording (such as the wording of theories) might help readers to understand the issues involved.

The flow of presentation can be facilitated through the use of appropriate transitional terms and phrases (e.g., *however*, *as a consequence*, and *indeed*) both within and at the beginning of paragraphs.

Finally, a brief summary of the literature review placed at the end of a review can help readers to grasp the whole of the literature review.

---

[1] Visconti, K. J., Sechler, C. M., & Kochenderfer-Ladd, B. (2013). Coping with peer victimization: The role of children's attributions. *School Psychology Quarterly*, *28*(2), 122–140. doi: 10.1037/spq0000014

[2] Freis, S. D., & Gurung, R. A. R. (2012). A Facebook analysis of helping behavior in online bullying. *Psychology of Popular Media Culture*, *2*(1), 11–19. doi: 10.1037/a0030239

Exercise on Topic 18

1. An effective literature review should consist solely of a set of critical summaries of individual studies. Is this statement "true" or "false"?

2. A key to creating a synthesis is to write a review that moves from subtopic to subtopic. Is this statement "true" or "false"?

3. Is it desirable to point out major trends and commonalities in the results of previous research?

4. Is it desirable to point out gaps in the literature?

5. Should the methodology employed in each of the studies cited in a review be described in detail?

6. When would it be appropriate to devote one or more paragraphs to describing a particular author's written work?

7. Why should direct quotations be used sparingly?

8. What can be placed at the end of a review to help readers grasp the whole of the literature review?

Questions for Discussion

9. When you wrote term papers in the past, did you include many direct quotations from the authors you cited? Are you surprised by the suggestion made in this topic regarding quotations? Explain.

10. Before you read this topic, would you have been likely to write a series of summaries of previous research in the belief that the series would produce an effective literature review? Explain.

For Students Planning Research

11. Have you started writing a literature review on your topic? If yes, what types of changes will you make in it based on what you learned in this topic?

Part C

In-Text Citations and Reference Lists

In a typical research proposal or report, a large number of sources usually are cited. While a source may be cited in any part of a proposal or report, most sources are cited in literature reviews (see Part B). This part (Part C) briefly describes some basics of two widely used methods for citing sources and preparing corresponding reference lists. One method is recommended by the American Psychological Association (APA) in the *Publication Manual of the American Psychological Association*. The other method is recommended by the American Sociological Association (ASA) in the *ASA Style Guide*, which is based primarily on *The Chicago Manual of Style*. A wide variety of disciplines in the behavioral and social sciences use either APA or ASA style for citing sources and for preparing reference lists.

NOTES

Organizations as diverse as the American Medical Association (AMA), International Business Machines Corporation (IBM), the Associated Press (AP), and the American Sociological Association (ASA) have published style guides to assist their authors and editors.

An important function of style guides is to provide answers to problematic questions. For instance, consider this question: Should academic degrees be capitalized? The *AMA Manual of Style* provides this answer: "Capitalize academic degrees when abbreviated but not when written out" (AMA 2007:378).[1] Thus, when writing for the AMA, an author should write the following two sentences, as shown here:

Jane Doe earned her master's degree at Stanford University.

Jane Doe, MA, will be the keynote speaker at this year's senior seminar.

The two sentences immediately above answer another problematic question: Should periods be used in abbreviations for academic degrees? As you can see, the answer is "no" if you are writing for the AMA. However, the answer is "yes" if you are writing for the Associated Press using *The Associated Press Stylebook* (2004:5). Neither style guide is right or wrong, but rather each of the two style guides has a different style on this issue.

A second important function of style guides is to specify the contents and organization of manuscripts. For example, the American Sociological Association's *ASA Style Guide* describes the contents of title pages for articles submitted for publication. If you guessed that the title page should contain the names of the authors and their institutions, you would be correct. However, relying just on your intuition you might fail to include the required word count, the running head, and a footnote acknowledging credits and grant numbers.

Third, style guides address issues faced by authors when using specialized technical vocabulary and jargon. For example, *The IBM Style Guide* covers the use of computer-related terms. Among numerous other pieces of advice, the guide admonishes writers to avoid using computer-related abbreviations and acronyms as verbs, as illustrated here:

Incorrect: "You can FTP the files to the server."

Correct: "You can use the FTP commands to send the files to the server."

Finally, style guides often review the basics of English grammar (e.g., subject-agreement), punctuation (e.g., using commas to separate independent clauses), and expression of ideas (e.g., avoiding unnecessarily wordy phrases).

The American Sociological Association's *ASA Style Guide*

The *ASA Style Guide* is published by the American Sociological Association, which is the major association for professional and academic sociologists in the United States.

Like most other style guides, the *ASA Style Guide*'s purpose is to assist authors and editors in preparing polished, properly punctuated, grammatically correct manuscripts that are consistent in style with each other. Consistency in style is especially important in scientific writing because inconsistency can cause confusion and errors.

The *Guide* is used by the association's editors of its books and journals. Members of the association are expected to use the *Guide* in their professional writing. In addition, students are often required to use it in preparation of term papers, projects, theses, and dissertations.

Despite its small size (4" x 7", 114 pages) the *ASA Style Guide* covers the same general territory as larger guides. However, as a result of its small size, the *Guide* has a limited number of examples and provides highly selective and concise guidance on many topics.[2]

The *Publication Manual of the American Psychological Association* (*APA Manual*)

The *APA Manual* covers the same general topics as the *ASA Guide*, but in greater detail. There are important similarities between the two styles. Similarities and differences between the two styles are described in the next four topics.

---

[1] (AMA 2007:378) is a "reference citation" written in the style described by the *ASA Style Guide*. In the citation, the year 2007 is the year of publication, and the number 378 is the page number on which the quotation appears. An issue covered by academic style guides concerns the preparation of citations and reference lists.

[2] The *ASA Guide* is based on the *Chicago Manual of Style*, which is comprehensive and detailed.

Exercise on Topic 19

1. Does the American Medical Association publish its own style guide?

2. Do all major style guides agree on the issue regarding capitalization of academic degrees?

3. Do style guides specify the contents and organization of manuscripts?

4. What is the full name of the organization that publishes the *ASA Style Guide*?

5. Does the ASA require a word count for articles submitted for publication?

6. After reading this topic, should you be surprised to find that a style guide provides a review of basic English grammar?

7. Consistency in style is especially important in what type of writing?

8. Is the *ASA Style Guide* a large book?

9. What is the full name of the organization that publishes the *APA Manual?*

10. Are there similarities between APA and ASA styles?

Question for Discussion

11. Are you surprised to learn that many diverse organizations publish their own style guides? Explain.

For Students Planning Research

12. Have you selected a style guide to use while you write your research proposal and research report? If so, what is the name of the style guide? Why did you select that style guide? How familiar are you with the style guide?

TOPIC 20   IN-TEXT CITATIONS: ASA STYLE

The American Sociological Association's *ASA Style Guide* specifies a version of the "author–date" method for in-text citations. This method can be parenthetical or non-parenthetical, as described below. For each in-text citation, there should be a full bibliographic reference in the reference list at the end of the manuscript. The preparation of reference lists in ASA style is described in the next topic.

Example 1 illustrates a **parenthetical in-text citation**, in which the last name of the author being cited and the year of publication are placed in parentheses at the end of a sentence in the text.

EXAMPLE 1
New data suggest that the influence of the mass media on social norms and customs is growing very rapidly (Doe 2013).

Example 2 illustrates ASA style for an in-text citation of a source with two authors.

EXAMPLE 2
The influence of peer group pressure on bullying behavior by girls needs more large-scale investigations (Edwards and Jones 2013).

If a source with **one or two authors** is cited more than once in a given manuscript, it should be cited in the same way each time. However, when there are **three authors** of a given source, the first time the authors are cited, all names are used. Then, in subsequent citations, only the first author's last name followed by "et al." is used, as illustrated in Example 3.

EXAMPLE 3
First time the source with three authors is cited:
More research is needed on the origins of gender-role socialization (Washington, Yu, and Galvan 2013).

The second and subsequent times the source is cited:
Large-scale research on gender-role socialization is relatively rare (Washington et al. 2013).

When a source being cited has **four or more** authors, use "et al." the first and all subsequent times the source is cited.

Often, two or more sources are in substantial agreement. For instance, there might be three sources with data indicating that the XYZ program is strongly supported by most parents. These three sources may be cited within a single set of parentheses, as illustrated in Example 4. Note that semicolons are used to separate sources and that the sources are listed in alphabetical order.

EXAMPLE 4
In three recent surveys, a majority of parents expressed strong support for the XYZ program (Black 2012; Brown et al. 2011; White and Bright 2013).

When the source is a group such as a professional organization, government agency, corporation, or similar entity, cite its authorship using the full name of the group, as shown in Example 5.

EXAMPLE 5
The origins of the BEST program have been traced "as far back as the 1920s" (Association for Hypothetical Studies 2012:7–8).

When an author quotes directly from a source, the author should include the page number(s) in the in-text citation. Illustrated in Example 5 above, the page numbers (7–8) appear immediately after the colon without a space and without an abbreviation for the word *page*. This is also done when an author wants to call attention to a particular part of a source.

The *ASA Style Guide* also permits **non-parenthetical in-text citations**. In this type of citation, the authors' last names become part of a sentence, while the year of publication remains parenthetical. Typically, the authors' last names become the subject of a sentence in non-parenthetical citations, as illustrated in Example 6, which contains the same information as Example 3.

EXAMPLE 6
First time the source is cited: Washington, Yu, and Galvan (2013) claim that more research is needed on the origins of gender-role socialization.

The second and subsequent times the source is cited: Washington et al. (2013) point out that large-scale research on gender-role socialization is relatively rare.

You can see non-parenthetical citations emphasize the authorship by making the author's names more prominent than parenthetical citations do. Neither is right or wrong. The decision on which one to use depends on whether the writer wants to emphasize the authorship or the content.

The next topic will describe the basics for preparing a reference list in ASA style.

Exercise on Topic 20

1. Is the following sentence an example of a parenthetical in-text citation? If "no," explain.

   Doe (2012) points out that reducing bullying in the schools has become a concern of several major foundations that fund school research.

2. Is the following sentence an example of a parenthetical in-text citation? If "no," explain.

   The most recent study of the topic yielded data that are consistent with the predictions made by the theory (Smith 2013).

3. Is the following sentence an example of a parenthetical in-text citation that has been correctly formatted in ASA style for a source with two authors? If "no," explain.

   The questionnaire used in this study has been criticized for using difficult vocabulary complex sentences (Jones et al. 2014).

4. Is the following an example of a parenthetical in-text citation in ASA style for the *first* citation for a source with four authors? If "no," explain.

   The researchers recommend that larger and more representative samples be used in future studies of this topic (Adams et al. 2014).

5. Are there any errors in the following parenthetical in-text citation in ASA style for a source with one author that is being quoted? If "yes," explain.

   The senator called his opponent a "small-time thief" (Clinton 2013, pp. 9–10).

6. Which type of in text-citation emphasizes authorship?

   A. Parenthetical   B. Non-parenthetical

Question for Discussion

7. Examine the excerpts from literature reviews in Appendix C near the end of this book. Do the authors use both parenthetical and non-parenthetical in-text citations? Do they tend to prefer one type of citation over the other? Explain.

For Students Planning Research

8. Do you anticipate using primarily parenthetical or non-parenthetical citations? Explain.

As you know from the previous topic, the American Sociological Association's *ASA Style Guide* specifies a version of the "author–date" method for in-text citations. For each in-text citation, there should be a full bibliographic reference in the **reference list** at the end of the manuscript.

Example 1 is a reference list that illustrates how to format selected types of references in ASA style. In it, the references are listed in alphabetical order, and each reference is formatted with a **hanging indent**.[1] A paragraph with a hanging indent has its second line and all subsequent lines indented from the left margin.

EXAMPLE 1

References

Adams, Eric. S. 2014. "Review of the Origins of Social Sports Theories." *Journal of Hypothetical Social Studies in Sports*, 34(2):119–21.

Suresh, Geetha and Richard Tewksbury. 2013. "Locations of Motor Vehicle Theft and Recovery." *American Journal of Criminal Justice*, 38(2):200–215. doi 10.1007/s12103-012-9161-7.

U.S. Travel Association. 2013. "Senate Judiciary Approves Immigration Bill with Important Travel Facilitation Provisions." Washington DC: U.S. Travel Association. Retrieved June 11, 2013 (http://www.ustravel.org/news/press-releases/senate-judiciary-approves-immigration-bill-important-travel-facilitation-provisi).

Viceroy, Steven J. and José Salinas. 2013. *The Little Book of Big Words*. 2nd ed. Any City, NC: False Hopes Press.

West, Fred A, Steve Tobble, and Catherine C. Chin. 2012. "Life as Observed from Below." Pp. 12–20 in *Motivations of Successful Professors*, edited by J. Doe, M.M. Bush, and V.N. Carter. New York: Pretend Publishers.

The first two sources in Example 1 above are for journal articles. The first one (Adams) illustrates a reference for a journal article with only one author. The seven elements in the reference to Adams' journal article are:

1. Author's name inverted.

2. Year of publication.

3. Title of journal article in "quotation marks."

4. Title of journal in *italics*.

5. Volume number, which is 34. (Typically, Volume 1 refers to the first year of publication; Volume 2 refers to the second year of publication; and so on.)

6. Issue number in parentheses immediately followed by a colon. (Typically, there are four to 12 issues per year.) In this case, the issue number is 2, which indicates it is the second issue of the year.

7. Page numbers, 119–21, which are elided (contain an abbreviation). The "21" stands for 121.[2]

The second reference in Example 1 (Suresh and Tewksbury) illustrates a reference for a journal article with two authors. Only the name of the first author (Suresh) is inverted. Also the word *and* is used between the authors' names.[3] In addition, the second reference in Example 1 illustrates a reference for a journal article published on *and* retrieved from the web. It has a DOI number. This number stands for "Digital Object Identifier." It is a unique case number assigned to that journal article.[4] Go to www.doi.org, type in a valid DOI, and the source of the article will be identified.

Typing the DOI for Suresh and Tewksbury in the search box at www.doi.org takes a reader to a website maintained by the publisher of the journal with directions for purchasing the article or for accessing it if your institution maintains a subscription for electronic access to the publisher's journals.

The third reference (U.S. Travel Association) illustrates a reference to a document written by an organization and published on the web. It includes the date of retrieval from the web.

The next reference (Viceroy and Salinas) in Example 1 is for the second edition of a book, and the last reference, which has three authors, is for a book.

See the *ASA Style Guide* for additional information on other types of reference materials.

---

[1] To create a hanging indent in most versions of Word, click anyplace in the reference you want to change. Then click on *Format* at the top of the screen. A drop-down window will appear. Click on *Paragraph*, click on the down arrowhead to the right of *Special*, and then click on *Hanging*.

[2] For information on elided numbers, see Appendix I.

[3] APA uses the symbol & instead of the word *and*.

[4] The uppercase letters *DOI* are used when discussing digital object identifiers. However, in an ASA reference list, the lowercase is used.

EXERCISE ON TOPIC 21

1. What organization is the sponsor of the *ASA Style Guide*?

2. Describe a paragraph with a hanging indent.

3. In a reference for a source that has two authors, what word or symbol should be placed between the two author's names?

4. Below is the beginning of a reference for a journal article. In terms of ASA style, what is wrong with it?

    Doe, John C. and Smith, Maria. 2012. "A modified survey of the…."

5. Below is a reference for a journal article. In terms of ASA style, what is wrong with it?

    Best, Andrea A. 2012. "The Origins of Modern Hypnotic Techniques." *Journal of the Unusual.*
    (3) 285–302.

6. Below is a reference for a journal article. In terms of ASA style, what is wrong with it?

    Kelp, Fra A. 2013 "The Origins of Modern Hypnotic Techniques." *Journal of the Association for the Study of the Unusual."* (1)54.

7. Below is a reference for a book. In terms of ASA style, what is wrong with it?

    Jackson, Steven J. and Maria Solis. 2012. "The Little Grammar Book." 3rd ed. Centerville, GA: Pleasant Press.

8. What does "DOI" stand for?

Question for Discussion

9. The examples in this topic illustrate certain types of journal articles and books. What other types of sources (other than journal articles and books) might you need to reference in your academic work?

For Students Planning Research

10. Will you be using the *ASA Style Guide*? How familiar are you with it?

Topic 22 In-Text Citations: APA Style

The *Publication Manual of the American Psychological Association* specifies a version of the "author–date" method for in-text citations. This method can be parenthetical or non-parenthetical, as described below. For each in-text citation, there should be a full bibliographic reference in the reference list at the end of the manuscript. The preparation of reference lists in APA style is described in the next topic.

Example 1 illustrates a **parenthetical in-text citation**, in which the last name of the author being cited and the year of publication are placed in parentheses at the end of a sentence in the text.

EXAMPLE 1
New data suggest that the influence of the mass media on social norms and customs is growing very rapidly (Doe, 2013).[1]

Example 2 illustrates APA style for an in-text citation of a source with two authors.

EXAMPLE 2
The influence of peer group pressure on bullying behavior by girls needs more large-scale investigations (Edwards & Jones, 2013).[2]

If a source with **one or two authors** is cited more than once in a given manuscript, it should be cited in the same way each time. However, when there are **three to five authors** of a given source, the first time the authors are cited, all names are used. Then, in subsequent citations, only the first author's last name followed by "et al." is used, as illustrated in Example 3.

EXAMPLE 3
First time the source with three authors is cited: More research is needed on the origins of gender-role socialization (Washington, Yu, & Galvan, 2013).

The second and subsequent times the source is cited: Large-scale research on gender-role socialization is relatively rare (Washington et al., 2013).

When a source being cited has **six or more** authors, use "et al." the first and all subsequent times the source is cited.

Often, two or more sources are in substantial agreement. For instance, there might be three sources with data indicating that the XYZ program is strongly supported by most parents. These three sources may be cited within a single set of parentheses, as illustrated in Example 4. Note that semicolons are used to separate sources and that the sources are listed in alphabetical order.

EXAMPLE 4
In three recent surveys, a majority of parents expressed strong support for the XYZ program (Blackstone, 2012; Brown et al., 2011; White & Bright, 2013).

When the source is a group, such as a professional organization, government agency, corporation, or similar entity, cite its authorship using the full name of the group, as shown in Example 5.

EXAMPLE 5
The origins of the theory have been traced "as far back as the 1950s" (International Association of Unlicensed Practitioners, 2012, p. 285).

When an author quotes directly from a source, the author should include the page number(s) in the in-text citation, as illustrated in Example 5 above. This is also done when an author wants to call attention to a particular part of a source.

APA style also permits **non-parenthetical in-text citations**. In this type of citation, the authors' last names become part of a sentence, while the year of publication remains parenthetical. Typically, the authors' last names become the subject of a sentence in non-parenthetical citations, as illustrated in Example 6, which contains the same information as Example 3.

EXAMPLE 6
First time the source is cited: Washington, Yu, and Galvan (2013) claim that more research is needed on the origins of gender-role socialization.[3]

The second and subsequent times the source is cited: Washington et al. (2013) point out that large-scale research on gender-role socialization is relatively rare.

Non-parenthetical citations emphasize the authorship by making the author's names more prominent than parenthetical citations do. Neither is right

---

[1] As illustrated in Topic 20, the parenthetical in-text citation for a single author of a reference in ASA style does not contain a comma.

[2] Note that APA style uses an ampersand (&), while ASA uses the word *and* in this type of citation.

[3] Note that while APA uses an ampersand in parenthetical citations, it uses the word *and* in non-parenthetical citations.

or wrong. The decision on which one to use depends on whether the writer wants to emphasize the authorship or the content.

The next topic will describe the basics for preparing a reference list in APA style.

EXERCISE ON TOPIC 22

1. Is the following sentence an example of a parenthetical in-text citation? If "no," explain.

   Reducing bullying in the schools has become a concern of several major foundations that fund school research (Doe, 2012).

2. Is the following sentence an example of a parenthetical in-text citation? If "no," explain.

   Smith (2013) points out that data from the most recent study of the topic are consistent with the predictions made by the theory.

3. Is the following in-text citation correctly formatted in APA style for a source with two authors? If "no," explain.

   The questionnaire used in this study has been criticized for using difficult vocabulary and complex sentences (Jones and Smith 2014).

4. Is the following in-text citation correctly formatted in APA style for the *first* citation of a source with six authors? If "no," explain.

   The researchers recommend that larger and more representative samples be used in future studies of this topic (Adams et al., 2014).

5. Is the following in-text citation correctly formatted in APA style for the *second* citation of a source with six authors? If "no," explain.

   They also recommend not relying exclusively on self-report measures (Adams et al., 2014).

6. Are there any errors in the following parenthetical in-text citation in APA style for a source with one author that is being quoted? If "yes," explain.

   The mayor called her opponent a "back-room operator" (Smith 2013:9).

7. Which type of in-text citation emphasizes content rather than the authorship of a source?

   A. Parenthetical   B. Non-parenthetical

Question for Discussion

8. Examine the excerpts from literature reviews in Appendix C near the end of this book. Do the authors use both parenthetical and non-parenthetical in-text citations? Do they tend to prefer one type of citation over the other? Explain.

For Students Planning Research

9. Do you anticipate using primarily parenthetical or non-parenthetical citations? Explain.

The *Publication Manual of the American Psychological Association* specifies a version of the "author–date" method for in-text citations. For each in-text citation, there should be a full bibliographic reference in the **reference list** at the end of the manuscript.

Example 1 is a reference list that illustrates how to format selected types of references in APA style. In it, the references are listed in alphabetical order, and each reference is formatted with a **hanging indent**.[1] A paragraph with a hanging indent has its second line and all subsequent lines indented from the left margin.

EXAMPLE 1

References

Adams, E. S. (2014). Review of the origins of social sports theories. *Journal of Hypothetical Social Studies in Sports, 34*, 119–121.

Suresh, G., & Tewksbury, R. (2013). Locations of motor vehicle theft and recovery. *American Journal of Criminal Justice, 38*, 200–215. doi 10.1007/s12103-012-9161-7.

U.S. Travel Association. 2013. *Senate Judiciary Approves Immigration Bill with Important Travel Facilitation Provisions*. Washington DC: U.S. Travel Association. Retrieved from http://www.ustravel.org/news/pressreleases/sena te-judiciary-approves-immigration-billimportant -travel-facilitation-provisi).

Viceroy, S. J., & Salinas, J. 2013. *The little book of big words*. (2nd ed.). Any City, NC: False Hopes Press.

West, F. A., Tobble, S., & Chin, C. C. (2012). Life as observed from below. In J. Doe, M.M. Bush, and V.N. Carter (Eds.), New York: Pretend Publishers.

The first two references in Example 1 above are for journal articles. The first one (Adams) illustrates a reference for a journal article with only one author. The seven elements contained in the reference to Adams' journal article are:

1. Author's name inverted. Only initials are used for first and middle names.

2. Year of publication enclosed in parentheses.

3. Title of journal article (no quotation marks).

4. Title of journal *in italics*.

5. Volume number, which is *34*, in italics.[2]

6. Issue numbers are almost always omitted in APA style.[3]

7. Page numbers, 119–121.[4]

The second reference in Example 1 (Suresh & Tewksbury) illustrates a reference for a journal article with two authors. Both authors' names are inverted. Note that instead of the word *and*, an ampersand (*&*) is used between the authors' names.

In addition, the second reference in Example 1 illustrates a reference for a journal article published in hard copy and available on the Internet. It has a DOI number. This number stands for "Digital Object Identifier." It is a unique case number assigned to that journal article.[5] Go to www.doi.org, type in a valid DOI, and the source of the article will be identified.

Typing the DOI for Suresh and Tewksbury in the search box at www.doi.org takes a reader to a website maintained by the publisher of the journal with directions for purchasing the article or for accessing it if your institution maintains a subscription for electronic access to the publisher's journals.

The third reference (U.S. Travel Association) illustrates a reference to a document written by an organization and published on the web. It includes the date of retrieval from the Internet.

The next reference (Viceroy and Salinas) in Example 1 is for the second edition of a book, and the last reference is for a book.

See APA's *Publication Manual* for additional information on formatting many other types of reference materials such as theses and dissertations as well as newspaper and magazine articles.

---

[1] To create a hanging indent in most versions of Word, click anyplace in the reference you want to change. Then click on *Format* at the top of the screen. A drop-down window will appear. Click on *Paragraph*, click on the down arrowhead to the right of *Special*, and then click on *Hanging*.

[2] Typically, Volume 1 refers to the first year of publication, Volume 2 refers to the second year of publication, and so on.

[3] In the rare case in which page numbers are not consecutively numbered throughout a volume, the issue number should be included. See the *Publication Manual* for details.

[4] Unlike ASA style, APA style does not use elided (abbreviated) numbers.

[5] The uppercase letters *DOI* are used when discussing digital object identifiers. However, in an APA reference list, the lowercase is used.

EXERCISE ON TOPIC 23

1. What is the full title of the style guide discussed in this topic?

2. Describe a paragraph with a hanging indent.

3. In a reference for a source that has two authors, what word or symbol should be placed between the two author's names?

4. Below is the beginning of a reference for a journal article. In terms of APA style, what is wrong with it?

> Doe, John C. F., & Smith, M. M. 2012. "A national survey of the…."

5. Below is a reference for a journal article. In terms of APA style, what is wrong with it?

> Best, A. A. (2013). "The origins of modern hypnotic techniques." *Journal of the Unusual.* *42*, 285–302.

6. Below is a reference for a journal article. In terms of APA style, what is wrong with it?

> Kelp, F. A. (2013). The origins of modern hypnotic techniques. *Journal of the Association for the Study of the Unusual, 54–66.*

7. Below is a reference for a book. In terms of APA style, what is wrong with it?

> Jackson, S. J. & M. Solis. 2014. "The Little Grammar Book." 3rd ed. Centerville, GA: Pleasant Press.

8. What does "DOI" stand for?

Question for Discussion

9. The examples in this topic illustrate certain types of journal articles and books. What other types of sources (other than journal articles and books) might you need to reference in your academic work?

For Students Planning Research

10. Will you be using the *APA Publication Manual*? How familiar are you with it?

PART D

SAMPLING

When it is impractical to study an entire population, researchers draw a sample, study it, and infer that what is true of the sample is probably also true of the population. Because an inference to a population is only as good as the method used to draw the sample, the advantages and disadvantages of various methods of sampling are explored in detail in this part of the book. The issue of sample size is also considered.

NOTES

Topic 24 Biased and Unbiased Sampling

Researchers frequently draw a **sample** from a **population**, which is the group in which researchers are ultimately interested. A population may be large, such as all social workers in the United States, or small, such as all social workers employed by a specific hospital. If a researcher studies every member of a population, the researcher is conducting a **census**. For large populations, however, it is more efficient to study a sample instead of conducting a census. After drawing a sample, researchers study it and then make inferences to the population. That is, researchers infer that the characteristics of the sample probably are the characteristics of the population.[1]

Obviously, the quality of a sample affects the quality of the inferences made from a sample to the population. Thus, a poor sample is likely to lead to incorrect inferences. The two questions researchers ask when evaluating a sample are "Is the size adequate?" (a question that is discussed in Topics 29 and 30) and "Is the sample biased?"

A researcher can select an **unbiased** sample by giving every member of a population an equal chance of being included in the sample. One way to do this is to put the names of all individuals in the population on slips of paper, mix them up, and draw as many as needed for the sample. The result is called a **simple random sample**.[2]

Note that researchers cannot give every member of a population an equal chance of being included unless the researchers are able to identify all members of the population of interest. Failure to identify all members of a population is a major source of bias in sampling. For instance, if the population of interest consists of all homeless individuals in a city but researchers can identify only those who seek public assistance, researchers can sample only from those members of the population. This creates a bias against the less-visible homeless, who may be less resourceful, more destitute (or less destitute), and so on. To the extent that a sample is biased against less-visible homeless individuals, the inferences about all homeless individuals will be incor-

rect to an unknown extent (i.e., it is not possible to estimate how much error a bias of this type has caused because researchers do not have information on less-visible homeless individuals).

Researchers also obtain biased samples when they use **samples of convenience** (also known as *accidental samples*). For instance, if a psychology professor wants to study a principle of learning theory as it applies to all college sophomores but only uses those students who happen to be enrolled in his or her introductory psychology class, the sample is biased against all other college sophomores. This introduces many possibilities for error. For instance, the professor may have a reputation for giving high grades and thus may attract students with learning styles that are different from those of the general population of college sophomores. Also, of course, different colleges attract different types of students, and this professor has sampled only from students enrolled at the college where he or she teaches.

A third major source of bias is **volunteerism**. Volunteerism takes two forms. First, sometimes researchers simply issue a call for volunteers. This is often done in medical research in which researchers advertise for potential participants, such as those with chronic heart conditions, in order to test new methods of treatment. What is wrong with this? The possibilities are almost endless. For instance, some individuals may volunteer because they are becoming desperate as their condition worsens, whereas those who are doing better may be less inclined to expose themselves to experimental treatment, *or* those who volunteer may be more persistent and resourceful (and thus in better health) than the general population of those with heart conditions. These two opposing possibilities illustrate why researchers strive to eliminate bias—because they often cannot even speculate accurately on the direction in which a given bias might affect the results of a study.

Second, volunteerism might bias a sample even if a researcher begins by identifying a random sample from an entire population. For instance, a researcher might draw a random sample of all freshmen at a college and contact them to take part in a study of attitudes toward the use of instructional technology in higher education. For a variety of reasons, many of those in the random sample the researcher has selected may refuse to participate. Those who do participate, in effect, are volunteers

---

[1] The process of *inferring* from a sample to a population is also called *generalizing*. Inferential statistics, which are described in Part G of this book, assist in determining the reliability of inferences made from samples to populations.

[2] Another method for drawing a simple random sample is described in the next topic.

and may be fundamentally different from nonvolunteers—for instance, by being more interested in technology and more concerned about being successful in their educational pursuits.

Exercise on Topic 24

1. In this topic, how is *population* defined?

2. If a researcher studies every member of a population, what type of study is he or she conducting?

3. How can a researcher draw an unbiased sample?

4. Suppose a researcher drew a random sample from a population of college students but some of those selected refused to take part in the study. Are the students who participated in the study a "biased" *or* an "unbiased" sample of the population?

5. If a researcher mails questionnaires to all clients of a social worker and 50% of them are completed and returned, is the sample "biased" *or* "unbiased"?

6. Suppose a psychologist has his or her clients participate in an experiment simply because they are readily accessible (not drawn at random from the population of interest). What type of sample is being used?

7. Briefly describe one way a researcher can draw a simple random sample.

Questions for Discussion

8. Individuals who receive questionnaires in the mail often fail to return them, creating a bias because those who do return them are volunteers. Speculate on some things that a researcher can do to get more individuals to respond. (Consider mailed questionnaires you have received in the past and your reasons for responding or not responding.)

9. Are you convinced by the text that researchers should go to great lengths to avoid bias in their samples? Why? Why not?

10. Suppose you drew a random sample of all licensed clinical psychologists in your community to interview by phone. On the days you made the phone calls, some of the psychologists were not available to be interviewed, so you drew replacements for them at random from the population of licensed clinical psychologists. Speculate on whether the sample is "biased" *or* "unbiased" in light of the fact that replacements were drawn at random.

For Students Planning Research

11. Do you anticipate that you will be drawing a sample for your study, *or* will you be conducting a census?

12. If you will be sampling, do you anticipate that you will be using a biased sample? If yes, what do you anticipate will be the source of the bias? Is there anything you can do to reduce the bias? Explain.

TOPIC 25 SIMPLE RANDOM AND SYSTEMATIC SAMPLING

As indicated in the previous topic, **a simple random sample** is one in which every member of a population is given an equal chance of being included in a sample.

Putting names on slips of paper and drawing them from a hat is one way to obtain a random sample. Another way is to use a table of random numbers, a portion of which is reproduced in Table 1 near the end of this book. It consists of numbers that are unrelated to each other or to anything else. To use such a table, a researcher must give each member of a population a *number name*, and each name must contain the same number of digits. For instance, if there are 70 members of a population, the researcher should name one of the individuals 00 (it does not matter who the first individual is because the researcher is only renaming individuals with number names at this point—not selecting individuals). The researcher should name a second individual 01, name a third individual 02, and so on.[1]

After giving each individual a unique number name, the researcher can flip to any page in a book of random numbers (there is one page of such a book in Table 1 near the end of this book) and, without looking, point to a number—this is the number of the first individual selected. Assume that the first number pointed to is the first digit in the first row (Row #1) in Table 1, which is the number 2. The digit to the right of it is 1; together, they constitute the number 21. Thus, individual number 21 has been selected. Now, move two digits to the right. The next two digits are 0 and 4 (ignore the space between them, which is there only to help guide your eye). Thus, individual number 04 has been selected. The next two digits are 9 and 8. Because there are only 70 individuals in the population, no one is named 98. Thus, this number does not select anyone, so the researcher should continue to the right in the first row in the table. The next two digits are 0 and 8, which selects individual number 08. The researcher should continue in this manner until he or she has the number of participants needed for the sample.[2]

It is important to note that random samples are subject to error. For instance, quite by chance a random sample might contain a disproportionately large number of males, high achievers, and so on. Error created by random sampling is simply called **sampling error** by statisticians. Fortunately, if researchers use samples of adequate size (discussed in Topics 29 and 30), sampling errors are minimized. In addition, researchers can evaluate the effects of sampling errors by using inferential statistics, which are discussed in detail in Part G of this book.

Notice that bias also creates errors when sampling (see Topic 24). However, errors due to bias are nonchance errors, which are not reduced by increasing sample size. For instance, if a researcher samples for a political survey and the researcher's method is biased against Republicans (e.g., by including too many urban voters, who tend to be Democrats), increasing the sample size using the same biased sampling method yields a larger sample of voters who tend not to be Republicans. The larger sample is no less biased than the smaller one (it is just as biased as the smaller one). Thus, increasing sample size does not necessarily decrease bias.

Another method of sampling that many researchers regard as being essentially equivalent to simple random sampling is **systematic sampling**. In this type of sampling, every *n*th individual is selected. The number *n* can be any number, such as 2, in which case a researcher would select every second individual.[3] However, there is a potential problem with this method. Suppose someone has arranged the population in such a way that every second individual is somehow different from the others. Perhaps the population has been arranged in this order: man next to woman, next to man, next to woman, and so on. If a researcher draws every other individual, he or she will obtain a sample of all males or all females. Because a researcher cannot be sure that no one has ordered a list of the population in a way that might affect the sample, an alphabetical list (as opposed to any other kind, such as a classroom seating chart) is preferred when using systematic sampling. Note that a researcher should go completely through the alphabetical list (up to the letter Z) because different national origin

---

[1] Notice that because the population size (70) contains two digits, every member of the population is given a two-digit number name.

[2] Computer programs may also be used to select random samples. For instance, consult www.random.org.

[3] Divide the population size by the desired sample size to determine the value of *n*.

groups tend to concentrate at different points in the alphabet. Following this procedure yields a good sample, <u>but note that it is a *systematic sample*, and it should *not* be referred to as a random sample</u>.

EXERCISE ON TOPIC 25

1. Is there a sequence or pattern to the numbers in a table of random numbers?

2. This topic explains how to use a table of random numbers to draw what type of sample?

3. What is the term for errors created by random sampling?

4. How can researchers minimize sampling errors?

5. Can researchers minimize the effects of a bias in sampling by increasing the sample size?

6. Suppose a researcher wants to sample from a population of 99 clients, and the random starting point in Table 1 is the first digit in the last row (Row #26). What are the numbers of the first two clients selected?

7. Suppose a researcher wants to sample from a population of 500 clients and the random starting point in Table 1 is the first digit in the fifth row (Row #5). What are the numbers of the first two clients selected?

8. If a researcher draws every other individual from a list of the population, he or she is using what type of sampling?

9. What is the potential problem with systematic sampling?

10. How can a researcher get around the problem you named in the answer to Question 9?

Questions for Discussion

11. Suppose a friend was planning to use simple random sampling in a research project from which he or she wants to generalize to all students on a campus. Would you recommend drawing names from a hat *or* using a table of random numbers? Why?

12. Suppose a friend predicts that candidate Smith will win a local election, and the prediction is based on the opinions expressed by his or her friends and neighbors. What would you say to help your friend understand that this method of sampling is unsound?

For Students Planning Research

13. Will you use sampling to obtain participants for your research? If yes, do you plan to use random sampling, systematic sampling, *or* some other method of sampling? Explain.

14. Do you think that the method of sampling you plan to use might create a bias? Explain.

TOPIC 26   STRATIFIED RANDOM SAMPLING

As indicated in the previous two topics, simple random sampling gives each member of a population an equal chance of being included in a sample. The resulting sample is, by definition, *unbiased*, yet it may still contain *sampling errors*, which are errors created by chance (i.e., created by the random sampling process). The technical term for discussing the magnitude of sampling errors is *precision*. Results are more precise when researchers reduce sampling errors. The two major ways to reduce sampling errors are to increase sample size, which is discussed in Topics 29 and 30, and to use stratification in conjunction with random sampling, which is called **stratified random sampling**.

To obtain a stratified random sample, first divide a population into strata. For instance, researchers can easily divide a population into men and women because gender is easily identifiable. If a researcher draws separately at random from each stratum (i.e., separately from men and from women), he or she will obtain a stratified random sample.

Note that researchers usually draw the same percentage of participants, not the same *number* of participants, from each stratum.[1] Thus, if there are 600 women and 400 men in a population and a researcher wants a sample size of 100, he or she will draw 10% of the women (i.e., 600 × .10 = 60) and 10% of the men (i.e., 400 × .10 = 40). Thus, the resulting sample, consisting of 60 women and 40 men, is representative in terms of gender (i.e., it accurately represents the gender composition of the population). Note that while this stratified random sample will be accurate in terms of its gender composition, the sample from each gender might not be representative of its respective group. For instance, the sample of 60 women drawn at random might be unrepresentative of the 600 women in the population due to errors created by random sampling (i.e., unrepresentative by the luck of the random draw). Nevertheless, for studies in which there might be differences associated with gender, it is better to ensure that men and women are represented in the correct proportions by using stratified random sampling than to take a chance on misrepresentation of gender that might be obtained by using simple random sampling.

At first, some students think that men and women should have equal representation in the sample. To illustrate why this is wrong, suppose a researcher is trying to predict the outcome of a local proposition requiring equal pricing of services, such as dry cleaning, for men and women. Because women are traditionally charged more than men, women might be more likely to vote in favor of the proposition. Because there are more women voters in the population (600 women vs. 400 men), there should be more women voters in the sample (60 vs. 40).

Notice that if men and women do not differ in their opinions on a particular issue, stratification on the basis of gender will not increase the precision of the result. In other words, if men and women are the same in their opinions (perhaps 80% approve and 20% disapprove), it does not matter if a sample consists of all men, all women, or something in between because in any of these combinations, about 80% will say they approve. In other words, the stratification variable of gender is irrelevant if those in the various strata are the same in terms of what is being studied. Thus, stratification will improve precision only if the stratification is based on a variable that is relevant to the issue being studied.

Researchers can further increase precision (remember, this means reducing sampling errors) by using multiple strata in selecting a given sample. A researcher might, for instance, stratify on the basis of both gender and age by drawing separate random samples from each of the four subgroups shown here:

Women Ages 18–39	Men Ages 18–39
Women Ages 40+	Men Ages 40+

Of course, researchers are not confined to using just two variables for stratification: Having a larger number is better as long as the variables are relevant and *independent* of each other. To see what is meant by independence, suppose a researcher stratifies on both age and number of years employed. Because older individuals have had more years in which to be employed, the two variables tend to be highly correlated. Thus, stratifying on age has probably already accounted to a great extent for

---

[1] If equal numbers are drawn, the responses from each stratum can be statistically weighted to make the statistical result reflect the population proportions.

years of employment (i.e., they are not independent of each other).

Keep in mind the primary purpose of stratification, which is to ensure that different subgroups are represented in the correct proportions. <u>The goal in stratification is *not* to make comparisons across subgroups but to obtain a single sample that is representative in terms of the stratification variables.</u>

EXERCISE ON TOPIC 26

1. What is the technical term for discussing the magnitude of sampling errors?

2. Is it possible for a random sample to contain sampling errors?

3. What is the first step in stratified random sampling?

4. Does a researcher usually draw the "same number" *or* the "same percentage" from each stratum?

5. If the population of freshmen and the population of sophomores on a college campus are the same in their opinion on a particular issue on which a researcher will be conducting a survey, will it be to the researcher's advantage to stratify by drawing samples separately from each group?

6. What does stratification do to precision?

7. Is it possible to stratify on more than one variable?

8. Is the primary purpose of stratifying to be able to compare subgroups (such as comparing freshmen and sophomores in Question 5)?

Questions for Discussion

9. Think of an issue on which you might want to conduct a survey using the students at your college or university as the population. Name the issue and two variables you think would be relevant for stratification purposes when drawing a stratified random sample.

10. Students were given a test on a research article they read for class. (The article reported on the use of stratified random sampling.) One test question asked, "What type of sampling was used in the research?" Students who answered using only the term "random sampling" lost a point for the question. The instructor's comment was that the answer was ambiguous. Do you think the instructor was right in taking off the point? Why? Why not?

For Students Planning Research

11. If you planned to use simple random sampling (see Topic 25), do you now think your study would be improved if you used stratified random sampling instead? If yes, on what basis do you plan to stratify?

Simple random sampling, systematic sampling, and stratified random sampling are described in the previous two topics. In this topic, three additional methods are considered.

In **cluster sampling**, researchers draw groups (or clusters) of participants instead of drawing individuals. For instance, suppose a researcher wants to survey a sample of members of United Methodist churches throughout the United States. If the researcher obtains a membership list with addresses, he or she might draw a simple or stratified random sample of individuals and mail questionnaires to them. However, mailed questionnaires are notorious for their low response rates. The researcher might get a better response rate if he or she draws a sample of clusters—in this case, a sample of congregations—and contacts the ministers of the congregations to request that they personally distribute the questionnaires to their church members, collect the completed questionnaires, and mail them back to the researcher. If the ministers are convinced that the survey is appropriate and important, they might use their influence to help obtain responses from the members of their congregations (i.e., the clusters). Of course, for cluster sampling to be unbiased, a researcher must draw the clusters *at random*. This could be done by assigning a number to each congregation and using a table of random numbers to select a sample of the congregations. (See Topic 25 for a description of how to use a table of random numbers.)

A major drawback to cluster sampling results from the fact that each cluster tends to be more homogeneous in a variety of ways than the population as a whole. Suppose, for instance, that church members in the South tend to be more conservative than members in the North. Then, members of any one cluster in the South are unlikely to reflect accurately the attitudes of all members nationally. If a researcher draws only five clusters (i.e., congregations) at random, he or she might obtain a large number of participants, especially if one or two congregations have very large memberships. However, by drawing only five clusters, the researcher could easily obtain a sample in which most of the churches are in the South *or* most are in the North, potentially creating much sampling error. To avoid this problem, the researcher should draw a large

number of clusters.[1] To help increase precision, the researcher could also stratify on geography and draw a random sample of clusters from each stratum, which would assure, for instance, that the North and South are represented in the correct proportions.

Another method is **purposive sampling**. When researchers use this method, they purposively select individuals who they believe will be good sources of information. For instance, a researcher might observe over a long period that several members of the academic senate at a university consistently vote on the winning side on controversial issues. The researcher might decide that rather than interviewing a random sample drawn from the whole membership of the senate, he or she will interview only the consistent winners to predict the outcome of a new issue before the senate. While this method is interesting and may be useful at times, it is dangerous—in this case because professors may change their orientations or a new issue may raise different kinds of concerns from those raised by earlier issues. Qualitative researchers frequently use purposive sampling. For more information on sampling in qualitative research, see Topics 68 and 69 in Part I of this book.

Snowball sampling can be useful when attempting to locate participants who are difficult to find. For instance, suppose a researcher wants to study heroin addicts who have never had institutional contacts (e.g., who have never sought treatment or been arrested). How will the researcher find them? With the snowball technique, a researcher initially needs to find *only one*. If the researcher can convince this one individual that the research is important and that the data will remain confidential, this one participant might put the researcher in contact with several other potential participants. Each of these may help the researcher to contact several more. This technique is based on trust. If the initial participants trust the researcher, they may also identify other potential participants and convince them to trust the researcher. Of course, snowball samples

---

[1] Sample size for quantitative research is discussed in Topic 29. Note that statisticians consider each cluster to be a single participant. Thus, if five clusters are drawn, the sample size is 5. A comparison of sample sizes in both qualitative and quantitative research is discussed in Topic 69.

should be presumed to be biased because individuals are not drawn at random. However, without the use of snowball sampling, there would be many special populations that researchers would be unable to study, such as successful criminals (i.e., criminals who have never been caught), homeless individuals with no institutional contacts, and others who are difficult to identify and locate. Both quantitative and qualitative researchers use snowball sampling.

EXERCISE ON TOPIC 27

1. To conduct a survey on a campus, a researcher drew a random sample of 25 class sections and contacted the instructors, who then administered the questionnaires in class. This researcher used what type of sampling?

2. Which type of sampling is based on trust between participants and a researcher?

3. What is a major drawback to cluster sampling?

4. Which type of sampling is especially useful when attempting to locate participants who are difficult to find?

5. Briefly define purposive sampling.

6. What must researchers do in cluster sampling to obtain an unbiased sample of clusters?

7. Suppose a researcher has identified an individual who has engaged in an illegal activity to be a participant in a research project, and then the researcher identifies others who have engaged in the same activity through the first individual's contacts. The researcher is using what type of sampling?

Questions for Discussion

8. To study a sample of all nurses employed by hospitals in a state, a researcher drew two hospitals (clusters) at random, both of which happened, by chance, to be large public hospitals, each with hundreds of nurses, yielding a large sample. Are you impressed with the sample size? Why? Why not?

9. Name a population (other than those mentioned in the topic) for which snowball sampling might be better than other types of sampling. Explain the reason(s) for your answer.

For Students Planning Research

10. In light of Topics 24, 25, 26, and this topic, what type of sample do you plan to draw? If you will be using a less-than-satisfactory sample, explain why it will be necessary to draw such a sample.

Demographics are the background character-istics of the participants in research, such as gen-der, age, and income. Consider a research project conducted with participants at a local substance abuse counseling center. By collecting demo-graphic information on the participants (age, gen-der, marital status, types of substances used, length of use, and so on), the researcher can pro-vide readers of the research with a picture of the types of individuals who constituted the sample for the study. This information allows readers to make informed judgments regarding the extent to which the results may apply to their own settings. For instance, if the clients to whom a reader wants to generalize are similar in their demographics to the demographics of the participants in the study, the results are more likely to be generalizable.

Of course, certain demographic characteristics are more relevant for some studies than others. For instance, for a study on the use of a new method for teaching mathematics, grade level, age, and GPA are more relevant than political af-filiation, religious affiliation, and weight.

Sometimes, the demographics of a particular population are known, and these data can be use-ful for analyzing and interpreting the results of a study. For instance, suppose that the population consists of all students enrolled at a college, and the college has data indicating that 20% of the students in the population are Asian American. If a researcher draws a sample of the population and obtains a sample in which only 10% of the re-spondents are Asian American, he or she could make a statistical adjustment in the results, giving the Asian Americans in the sample more weight. For the example presented here, a researcher could count the responses of each Asian American in the sample *twice* when analyzing the results. This would boost the percentage of Asian Ameri-cans from 10% to 20% in the sample, yielding a sample with a correct percentage of Asian Ameri-cans in it.[1]

Even if a researcher does not make a statistical adjustment based on the difference between the demographics of a population and a sample, he or

she can warn readers that the sample differs from the population in terms of its demographics (e.g., Asian Americans are underrepresented in the sample).

When relying on voluntary participation in re-search, it is important to collect demographics that permit a comparison of volunteers with nonvolun-teers whenever possible. Consider research on an after-school reading program in which the pro-gram is offered to all students, but only 30% vol-unteer to participate. From school records, it may be possible to provide information on demo-graphic differences between the volunteers and nonvolunteers, such as previous grades in reading, gender differences, differences in age, and so on. Such information could be of value to readers who are interested in the application of the program in their local settings.

Mailed surveys are notorious for low response rates (low rates of volunteering), which create a bias in sampling. The fact that most mail is marked with zip codes provides a unique opportu-nity for researchers to collect demographic infor-mation for comparing volunteers with nonvolun-teers. Specifically, a researcher could keep track of the zip codes to which questionnaires were mailed as well as the zip codes from which com-pleted questionnaires were received. If the zip codes from which the questionnaires were re-ceived tended to be for higher-socioeconomic-status (SES) neighborhoods than the other zip codes to which they were mailed, the bias in favor of higher-income respondents could be noted in the research report (or statistical adjustments could be made).[2]

In experiments, a special type of sampling bias results from what researchers call **mortality**. As indicated in Topic 2, experiments are studies in which researchers administer treatments in order to examine their effects on participants. Consider an experiment in which a new prescription drug is administered to an experimental group while the control group receives no special treatment. If some of the participants drop out of the experi-

---

[1] For technical reasons that are beyond the scope of this book, such an adjustment is more sound for adjusting the results for an unbiased sample than for adjusting the results for a biased sample.

[2] For instance, suppose 50% were mailed to a high-SES zip code and 20% were returned from this zip code, while 50% were mailed to a low-SES zip code and 10% were returned from this zip code. The bias in fa-vor of the high-SES zip code could be noted.

ment at midcourse, *mortality* is said to have occurred. Because mortality does not occur at random, the result is presumed to bias the sample. For instance, those in the experimental group who experience less relief from the drug may get discouraged and drop out of the experiment before it is completed. This would bias the results of the experiment in favor of those for whom the drug is effective.

Because of mortality, it is important for experimenters to mention in their research reports whether there was mortality and, if so, the number and percentage who dropped out from each group. In addition, information on the demographics of those who dropped out and those who completed the experiments should be reported. For instance, did those who dropped out have more severe symptoms to begin with? Did the dropouts tend to be older? Answers to these types of questions can help readers to assess the severity of the effects of mortality on the outcome of experiments.

EXERCISE ON TOPIC 28

1. By collecting demographic information on the participants, a researcher can provide readers of the research with what?

2. Consider the demographic of marital status. Is this demographic likely to be equally relevant in all studies?

3. A researcher can do what two things if he or she compares the demographics of a sample with its population and finds that a subgroup is underrepresented?

4. According to this topic, is it important to compare the demographics of volunteers with the demographics of nonvolunteers?

5. What provides a unique opportunity for researchers who conduct mailed surveys to collect demographic information?

6. If some of the participants drop out of an experiment at midcourse, what is said to have occurred?

Question for Discussion

7. Consider a survey on campus services for freshmen. Name three demographic variables that might be especially relevant.

For Students Planning Research

8. Do you anticipate collecting demographics? If yes, do you anticipate using the demographic information in any of the ways mentioned in this topic? Explain.

In the previous topics in this part of the book, various methods of drawing samples were described,[1] with an emphasis on the importance of considering bias when evaluating the adequacy of a sample. **Sample size is an important but secondary consideration.** To understand why sample size is secondary to bias, consider this example: Suppose a student is conducting a survey on whether the main cafeteria on campus should remain open during evening hours. Being a commuter with only day classes, the student goes to the cafeteria at lunchtime and asks every 10th student who enters to participate in the survey. Of the 100 participants in the survey, 80% have no opinion and 20% want evening hours. After considering the results, the student decides that he or she should have used a larger sample, so the student obtains another 100 participants in the same way (asking every 10th student entering the cafeteria at lunchtime). This time, the student gets 85% with no opinion and 15% who want evening hours. Being very cautious, the student samples again, and this time obtains a 75%–25% split. Combining results from the three surveys, the student obtains the total results shown in the bottom row of this table:

	No Opinion	Want Evening Hours
Sample 1	80%	20%
Sample 2	85%	15%
Sample 3	75%	25%
Total	**80%**	**20%**

Notice that for all practical purposes, the three results are the same. That is, only a small minority want evening hours. With a total sample size of 300, the student might feel rather comfortable that he or she has pinned down an answer close to the truth. However, there is a serious problem in the method of sampling, which results from the fact that each time the student sampled, he or she sampled only from those entering the cafeteria at lunchtime. Thus, the sample is biased against those who are not on campus during lunch hours. Specifically, it is biased against evening students, who are the members of the population most likely to want eve-

ning cafeteria hours. If the student continues to increase the sample size by sampling only at lunchtime, obtaining the responses of many more hundreds of students, the increase in sample size will be of no benefit to correcting the bias. Instead, the student would get much more accurate results by using an unbiased sample—even if the student studies only a small, unbiased sample. As a rule, then, small, unbiased samples tend to yield more accurate results than biased samples, even if the sizes of the biased samples are large and the sizes of the unbiased samples are small.

Increasing sample size is of benefit in research because it increases **precision**. When researchers say that they have highly precise results, they are saying that the results will vary by only a small amount from sample to sample, which is what will happen if each sample is large. Notice that in the cafeteria example, the results of the three samples were reasonably close, so a researcher could correctly say that there is a reasonable degree of precision. However, because of the bias in the method of sampling, it would be more accurate to say that the results are *precisely wrong* to the extent that the bias has consistently thrown the results off in the same direction each time a sample was drawn. Thus, researchers should strive first to obtain an unbiased sample and then to seek a reasonably large number of participants.

If increasing the size of a sample increases precision, which is desirable, especially when using unbiased (random) sampling, then the larger the sample, the better—right? Yes, this is true, but researchers need to consider the principle of *diminishing returns* for each unit of increase in sample size. To understand this principle, consider the following two cases, in which the sample size was increased by 50 participants.

	Original Sample Size	Increase	New Sample Size
Researcher A	50	+50	100
Researcher B	3,000	+50	3,050

Considering the data in the box immediately above, it is clear that Researcher A gets a much bigger payoff for increasing her sample size by 50 because she has doubled her sample size, which gives her a big boost in precision. Researcher B, on the

---

[1] The topics on sampling in this part of the book emphasize sampling in quantitative research. For sampling in qualitative research, see Topics 68 and 69.

other hand, gets a very small increase in precision because the addition of 50 to his original sample of 3,000 can have little influence on the results. The responses of the 50 additional participants will be overwhelmed by the responses of the first 3,000. Thus, at some point, the returns (in terms of an increase in precision) diminish to the point that further increases in sample size (such as adding 50 participants) are of very little benefit. Because of this principle, even the most important and prestigious national surveys are often conducted with only about 1,500 respondents.

EXERCISE ON TOPIC 29

1. Is sample size the primary consideration when judging the adequacy of a sample?

2. Does increasing sample size reduce bias?

3. Does increasing sample size increase precision?

4. Researcher A increased his sample size from 200 to 250, and Researcher B increased her sample size from 1,000 to 1,050. Which researcher will get a bigger payoff in increased precision by adding 50 participants?

5. If a researcher uses a very large sample, is it still possible for the results to be wrong?

6. Does each additional participant a researcher adds to a sample make an equal contribution to increasing precision?

7. According to the topic, prestigious national surveys are often conducted with about how many respondents?

Questions for Discussion

8. A magazine editor conducted a poll by printing a questionnaire in an issue of the magazine for readers to fill out and mail back. Several thousand readers returned completed questionnaires. Suppose a friend reads the results of this poll and is convinced that it reflects the views of all adults in the United States. What would you say to convince him that he might be wrong?

9. Consider the statement, "The larger the sample, the better." Explain why this statement might be misleading to a novice researcher.

For Students Planning Research

10. What is the anticipated sample size for your study? On what basis did you make your decision on sample size? (Note that you will be learning more about sample size in the next topic.)

One of the first questions students ask when planning their theses or classroom research projects is, "How many participants do I need?" Students often ask this question even before a discussion of the purposes of the research and the procedures that will be used. Without considering these matters, however, it is impossible to make informed decisions on sample size.

The following are the major factors that influence researchers' decisions on how large samples should be.[1]

First, researchers frequently conduct **pilot studies**, which are studies designed to obtain preliminary information on how new treatments and measures work. For instance, when studying a new drug, a researcher might conduct a pilot study on the route of administration and the maximum tolerable dose. Also, a researcher might try out a new measure, such as a new questionnaire, to determine if there are ambiguous questions, questions that participants refuse to answer, and so on. Pilot studies are usually conducted with small sample sizes, such as 10 to 100. On the basis of the results, treatments and measures can be modified for use in more definitive future studies with larger samples.

Second, some research procedures are so expensive and time-consuming that researchers must limit the sizes of their samples. For instance, when conducting qualitative research, researchers might plan to spend considerable time interacting with each participant, and thus the researchers might have to be content with small samples.

Third, researchers might want to document the incidence of something rare, such as the incidence of heart attacks among men aged 18 to 30. If a researcher drew a small sample, such as 25 participants, and waited a year, he or she probably would not observe any heart attacks in such a small sample, but it would be a mistake to conclude that there are no heart attacks in this age group. For this type of research, if a researcher cannot afford to use very large samples, he or she should let another researcher with adequate resources conduct it because small samples are not useful for observing the incidence of rare events.

Fourth, researchers need to consider the **variability** in the population of interest. If there is very little variability (i.e., the population is homogeneous), researchers can obtain accurate results from a small sample. For instance, the population of small bags of Fritos® Corn Chips is homogeneous with respect to their weight because the manufacturer strives to be consistent in this respect. Studying a random sample of only 50 would give a researcher about the same information as studying a random sample of 1,000. In contrast, if a population is very heterogeneous, a researcher needs a large sample. Suppose, for instance, a researcher wants to study the rate of reading literacy among adults in a large metropolitan area. There undoubtedly is great variability, ranging from the totally illiterate to the exceptionally literate. If the researcher draws a small sample of 50 individuals from such a diverse population, the researcher might obtain a result with major errors, such as not having a single illiterate individual in the sample. Using a larger sample, however, the researcher would be more likely to capture the diversity of the entire population.

Fifth, if researchers are looking for small differences, they need to use large samples. For instance, suppose the population of women voters is just slightly more in favor of a ballot proposition than is the population of men voters. In small random samples of these voters, the random sampling errors could easily overwhelm the small difference and might even produce a result in which it appears that the men are slightly more in favor of the proposition than are women. Using large samples in this case is necessary if a researcher wants to identify the correct direction and size of such a small difference.

So what is large and what is small? The answer is relative to what is being studied and the traditional sample sizes used in various types of research. A national public opinion poll with a few hundred respondents, for instance, would be considered to have a small sample size because survey researchers have learned over the years that it takes about 1,500 respondents to get highly precise results at the national level. On the other hand, an experiment in which clients are given a new form of psychotherapy for several years might be considered to have a very large sample if the sample size were a few hundred because it is traditional in this type of research to use small numbers of partici-

---

[1] The topics on sampling in this part of the book emphasize sampling in quantitative research. For sampling in qualitative research, see Topics 68 and 69.

pants. Thus, it is important to read many instances of the type of research being planned in order to learn about the various research traditions—including traditional sample sizes—researchers use.

When a small population is of interest, Table 2 near the end of this book is helpful for estimating a sample size for survey research. Using the sample size (n) recommended in the table that corresponds to the population size (N) will usually hold the error down to about 5%. That is, the true percentage in the whole population should fall within 5% of the percentage obtained from the sample. For instance, the table indicates that for a population of 200, a researcher needs a sample size of 132 (more than half of the population), but for a population of 400, a researcher needs a sample size of only 196 (less than half of the population). This illustrates a practical application of the principle of diminishing returns discussed in the previous topic.

EXERCISE ON TOPIC 30

1. What are pilot studies?

2. Do researchers usually use "small" *or* "large" samples in pilot studies?

3. If a researcher suspects that a trait is rare in a population, should he or she use a "small" *or* a "large" sample to identify the incidence of the trait?

4. In what type of research might a researcher spend considerable amounts of time interacting with participants, and what effect might this have on sample size?

5. Suppose a researcher suspects that there is only a very small difference in the math abilities of boys and girls at the sixth-grade level. Should the researcher use a "small" *or* a "large" sample to measure this difference?

6. Suppose the population consists of church members in the Southern Baptist Convention. If a researcher believes the members of this population are very homogeneous in their belief in an afterlife, would it be acceptable to use a small sample to identify the percentage who hold such a belief?

7. According to Table 2 on page 215, if there is a population of 1,900 students in a school, what is the recommended sample size?

8. According to Table 2, if there are 130 nurses in a hospital, what is the recommended sample size?

9. What is the symbol for population size in Table 2?

Question for Discussion

10. Some research articles based on small samples in academic journals are characterized by their authors as pilot studies. Do you think the publication of pilot studies is justifiable? Why? Why not?

For Students Planning Research

11. In light of the information in this topic and in the previous topic, what is your anticipated sample size? Explain the basis for your decision. (Note that your decision may depend, in part, on practical matters such as the availability of participants and your financial resources.)

PART E

MEASUREMENT

In this part, the essentials of measurement, with an emphasis on how to assess the validity of tests and measures, are examined. Reliability, which is closely linked to validity, is also explored in detail. In addition, how norm groups help in the interpretation of scores and how to interpret scores that are not based on norm groups are considered. Finally, the distinguishing features of measures of optimum performance and measures of typical performance are explored.

This part of the book emphasizes measurement in quantitative research. For information on measurement in qualitative research, see Part I of this book.

NOTES

The generic term for any type of measurement device (e.g., test, questionnaire, interview schedule, or personality scale) is **measure**. In formal research reports, **measure** or **measures** is the term that serves as the heading for the section of the report where the measurement devices are described. An important issue that is often addressed in this section of a research report is the **validity** of the measures.

Note that some researchers use the term **instrument** as a synonym for the word *measure*, and the term **instrumentation** as the heading for the section of a research report in which the measures are described. This is especially true in older research literature.

Researchers say that a measure is **valid** to the extent that it measures what it is designed to measure and accurately performs the function(s) it is purported to perform. For instance, consider an achievement test that emphasizes knowledge of facts on the westward movement in the United States. It will be only *modestly valid* when administered to students whose instruction emphasized more than just the memorization of facts (such as critical appraisal of historical evidence on that period in history). Likewise, a typing test used by an employer is likely to be only *partially valid* if it is administered to applicants who are applying for a job that includes filing in addition to typing.

It is important to note that validity is *relative* to the purpose of testing. If the purpose is to measure the achievement of students exposed to instruction in critical thinking, a test that measures only factual knowledge will be largely lacking in validity. For the purpose of measuring the achievement of students exposed to instruction in which the acquisition of factual knowledge is emphasized, the same test will be much more valid. Thus, before researchers can assess the validity of a particular measure, the purpose for measuring must be clearly identified.

Also, note that validity is a *matter of degree*. Therefore, it is appropriate to discuss *how valid* a test is—not *whether* it is valid. Given the imperfect state of measurement practice, it is safe to say that no test is perfectly valid.

Consider some reasons why perfect validity is elusive. First, almost all tests tap only a *sample* of the behavior underlying the constructs being measured. Consider the construct of aptitude for college

(i.e., having the abilities to succeed in college). College aptitude tests emphasize verbal and mathematical skills and leave untapped other skills that relate to success in college, such as the ability to use a personal computer to do homework, knowledge of how to use an academic library, command of effective study skills, and having the maturity to persist in a difficult course. Even within the domains that are tapped by a college aptitude test, only a small sample of verbal and mathematical problems can be presented within a test of reasonable length. In the same way, when researchers sample participants from a population (see Part D of this book), some samples of material and skills covered by tests are better than others, and all samples are subject to error.

Another reason that perfect validity is elusive is that some traits researchers want to measure are inherently difficult to measure. Consider the trait of cheerfulness. Almost everyone has known individuals whose cheerfulness is contagious. However, even though it is known when it is seen, how can researchers measure this trait in a systematic way in order to study it? Researchers could, for instance, ask a series of questions on how participants interact with other individuals in various types of contexts, how they view adversity, and so forth. On the other hand, researchers might observe participants and rate them on the cheerfulness they exhibit in their interactions with others (e.g., Do they smile? Is the tone of their voice upbeat? and so on). While these procedures probably tap certain aspects of cheerfulness, they fail to capture the *full essence* of the trait. This illustrates the old principle that often the whole is greater than the sum of its parts. To compound the problem, researchers often examine only some of the parts when they measure a given trait (e.g., researchers look at only certain behaviors that indicate cheerfulness and do this in only certain specific settings).

The problem of elusiveness, at first glance, seems to plague those with a quantitative orientation more than those with a qualitative orientation because quantitative researchers seek to reduce elusive constructs, such as cheerfulness, to numerical scores. Qualitative researchers, on the other hand, tend to measure in ways (such as unstructured interviews) that yield words to describe the extent to which traits are present. Yet unless qualitative researchers refer to specific behaviors and events in their reports, they will fail to describe results in enough detail so that readers can picture the meanings that have been attached to a construct such as cheerfulness. While qualitative researchers' descriptions (including quoting participants' words) are less artificial than the numerical scores obtained by quantitative researchers, qualitative researchers can find it difficult to describe the essence of a trait, such as the feelings a genuinely cheerful individual creates when interacting with others.

The next three topics explore the major methods researchers use to assess the extent to which measures are valid.

EXERCISE ON TOPIC 31

1. What is the generic term for any type of measurement device?

2. A measure is said to be valid to the extent that it does what?

3. Suppose a researcher purchases a commercial reading test that is highly valid for students who receive reading instruction that emphasizes phonics. Is it possible that the test is of limited validity for students who are taught with a method that does not emphasize phonics?

4. According to this topic, is it safe to say that no test is perfectly valid?

5. Tapping only a sample of the behaviors underlying the constructs a researcher wants to measure has what effect on validity?

6. If a trait is elusive, is it "easy" *or* "difficult" to measure with a high degree of validity?

Questions for Discussion

7. Have you ever taken an achievement test in school that was seriously flawed in its validity? If so, describe the test and state why you believe it was seriously flawed. In your discussion, mention the purpose for testing.

8. Name a trait you think is *elusive* and thus may be difficult to measure with great validity. Be prepared to defend your answer.

For Students Planning Research

9. What types of measures (e.g., tests, questionnaires, interview schedules, or personality scales) do you plan to use in your research?

10. Will the measures you named in response to Question 9 measure only a *sample* of the behavior underlying the construct? Have you considered how to draw the sample? Explain.

11. Measuring the ability to add one-digit numbers is *not* very elusive. Are the traits you plan to measure inherently more *elusive* than measuring this mathematics skill? Explain.

TOPIC 32 JUDGMENTAL VALIDITY

To determine the **content validity** of a measure, researchers make judgments on the appropriateness of its contents. For achievement tests, this type of validity is essential.

Suppose a researcher wants to build an achievement test on the material in this book through Topic 31. What steps could the researcher take to maximize the content validity of the test? First, he or she would need to consider the amount of testing time and the types of test items to be used. For instance, the researcher could present many more multiple-choice items than essay items in a given amount of testing time. Assume the researcher decided to write 35 multiple-choice items, to be administered in a 50-minute period. The researcher could write one item on each of the 31 topics, assuring that a broad sample of the material was covered. Then, the researcher could allocate the remaining 8 items to those topics he or she deemed most important. Then, the researcher would need to decide which types of skills to measure. He or she could test primarily for facts and definitions (e.g., "Which of the following is the definition of validity?") or for higher-level skills (e.g., "Which one of the following statements from a test manual indicates something about the content validity of a test?").

Although the above example has been simplified, it illustrates three principles for writing achievement tests with high content validity. First, a broad sample of content is usually better than a narrow one. Second, important material should be emphasized. Third, questions should be written to measure the appropriate skills, such as knowledge of facts and definitions, application of definitions to new situations, drawing inferences, making critical appraisals, and so on. Of course, the skills should be those covered in instruction. Keeping these principles in mind, researchers can make *judgments* of the content validity of achievement tests.

Although content validity is most closely associated with achievement testing, it is sometimes applied when evaluating other types of measures. For instance, if a researcher wants to measure the broad construct called *self-concept* with a series of questions, he or she could consider sampling from each of the narrower constructs that constitute it, such as physical self-concept, academic self-concept, social self-concept, and so on, assuring that a broad sample has been covered. If the researcher believes one type of self-concept is more important than others

for his or her research purpose (e.g., academic self-concept for a study in a school setting), he or she might emphasize one type over the others by asking more questions about it. Finally, the researcher will need to write the questions in such a way that they elicit common, shared meanings from the examinees. To do this, the researcher should consider the participants' educational levels and the meanings they are likely to attach to particular words in the questions. Will the participants find some words too difficult to understand? Are some terms ambiguous in their meaning? Careful consideration of these points regarding the contents of measures helps to improve their validity.

Researchers also make judgments when they consider **face validity**. In this approach to validity, judgments are made on whether a measure appears to be valid *on the face of it*. In other words, on superficial inspection, does the measure appear to measure what it purports to measure? For instance, one might use a spatial relations test for selecting individuals for pilot training school. A test that uses drawings of geometric shapes moving in space would have less face validity than one that uses drawings of miniature airplanes moving in space. That is, the second one has more face validity in terms of its appearance, even though both tests might be equally valid for measuring the underlying ability to visualize objects moving in space. Thus, face validity is primarily a public relations concern. Note that researchers usually prefer to use tests that *look like* they are related to their purpose because this promotes public acceptance of testing and motivates examinees to do their best.

It is possible for a test to have high face validity for a certain purpose while having low content validity. An extreme example makes the point clear: A test consisting of a drawing of one airplane followed by a plus sign and two more airplanes might have some face validity for pilot selection (because of the drawings of airplanes) but would have essentially no content validity because the skill being tested (adding one-digit numbers) is not appropriate for selecting adults who are likely to be successful in pilot training.

Occasionally, researchers deliberately use measures with *low face validity*. For instance, in a survey on the drug Viagra (which is a potentially sensitive topic), the pollsters asked about a variety of drugs even though they were concerned only with attitudes toward Viagra. The face validity of the survey questions was deliberately diluted with questions about other drugs in the hope of reducing the potential sensitivity of the questions on the drug of interest. In general, low face validity is desirable when researchers want to disguise the true purpose of the research from the respondents. This can, of course, raise ethical issues (see Topic 12).

EXERCISE ON TOPIC 32

1. For which type of measure is content validity essential?

2. Should researchers consider the types of skills required by achievement test items when judging content validity?

3. To improve content validity, it is usually desirable to cover only a narrow sample of content from the broad content area to be covered by an achievement test. Is this statement "true" *or* "false"?

4. Is content validity relevant only to achievement tests?

5. Which type of validity is based on superficial inspection?

6. Which two types of validity rely on judgments?

7. Is it possible for a test to have high face validity but low content validity?

8. When might a researcher deliberately use a measure with low face validity?

Questions for Discussion

9. Suppose an instructor fails to tell students the types of items (e.g., multiple-choice or essay) that will be on a midterm examination. Could this affect the validity of the results? Explain.

10. Have you ever taken an achievement test in which the content emphasized was different from the content you concentrated on while studying for the test? If so, describe the discrepancy, and speculate on what caused it (e.g., Was there a miscommunication between you and the instructor?).

For Students Planning Research

11. Will you be evaluating the content validity of any measures you will be using in your research? Explain.

12. Do you anticipate that your measure(s) will have high face validity? Explain.

In the empirical[1] approach to validity, researchers make planned comparisons to see if a measure yields scores that relate to a **criterion**. To understand this approach to validity, consider Example 1.

EXAMPLE 1

Nine applicants for the position of clerk-typist were administered an employment test, yielding scores from 15 to 35. Because there was a labor shortage, all nine were hired even though some had low test scores. After six months on the job, the employees were rated on their job performance by their supervisors on a scale from 10 (excellent performance) to 1 (poor performance). Here are their scores and ratings:

Employee	Test Score	Supervisors' Ratings	
Jose	35	9	Top third on test.
Jane	32	10	
Bob	29	8	
Fernando	27	8	Middle third on test.
Sue	25	7	
Debbie	22	8	
Milly	21	6	Bottom third on test.
Ling	18	4	
John	15	5	

Comparing the test scores with the supervisors' ratings provides information about the validity of the new employee test. The set of ratings is called the *criterion*, which is the standard by which the test is being judged. Because the purpose of an employment test is to *predict* success on the job, the most appropriate test of its validity is **predictive validity**, which poses this question: To what extent does the test predict the outcome it is supposed to predict?

So how valid is the employee test in Example 1? A researcher can begin to answer the question by examining the table. First, notice that those in the bottom third on the test are also in the bottom third in terms of ratings, suggesting that the test is highly valid for identifying those who will get low ratings on the job. Next, notice that the results for the top and middle thirds are more mixed. For instance, Bob, who is in the top third on the test with a score of 29, has a rating of 8, which is the same as the ratings of Fernando and Debbie, who are in the

middle third. Thus, while the test has some validity at these high levels, it is less than perfectly valid.

A researcher can obtain more information on the test's predictive validity by looking at the rank order of individuals on the test in comparison to their rank order on the ratings. In Example 1, the individuals are already ordered from high to low in terms of test scores. Notice that their order on ratings is to some extent similar but not the same. For instance, Jose has the highest test score, but only the second-highest rating. Sue scored higher than Debbie on the test, but Debbie exceeds Sue on the ratings. Despite exceptions such as these, the overall ordering of individuals by the test is similar to their ordering in terms of supervisors' ratings.

Another way to look at a test's predictive validity is to compute its **validity coefficient**. A validity coefficient is a *correlation coefficient* used to express validity. Correlation coefficients are described in detail in Topic 57. At this point, only some basic properties of validity coefficients will be considered. In practice, the coefficients range from 0.00 to 1.00.[2] At the upper limit, a 1.00 indicates perfect validity. For practical purposes, this can be thought of as indicating that the ranks on the test are identical to the ranks on the criterion. At the lower limit, 0.00 indicates that there is no relationship between the ranks on the test and the ranks on the criterion, which indicates that knowing the test scores is of no benefit when predicting the criterion. For the data in Example 1, the value of the validity coefficient is .89, indicating a very high degree of validity—higher than is usually found in validity studies of this type.

So how high should predictive validity coefficients be? Of course, higher is better. But how high are they in practice? For an employment test validated against supervisors' ratings, a researcher would be surprised to obtain a coefficient greater than about .60 and would not be at all surprised to obtain one as low as .20 or less, indicating poor validity. Why are employment tests only modestly to poorly valid? For two reasons: First, success on the job is a complex construct involving many traits, such as interpersonal skills (e.g., getting along with coworkers), psychomotor skills (e.g., typing), work

---

[1] The definition of *empirical* that applies to this discussion is "relying on or based on observation rather than theory."

[2] It is also possible to obtain negative coefficients, but they are very rare in validity studies. Negative correlation coefficients are discussed in Topic 57.

habits (e.g., being punctual), and so on. It is not reasonable to expect a single test (especially a paper-and-pencil test) to predict all these traits successfully. Second, coefficients are not higher because criteria such as supervisors' ratings are themselves less than perfectly reliable and valid. Thus, even if a test, in truth, were perfectly valid, the coefficient would be less than 1.00 if the supervisors failed to put the employees in the correct order. (Note that human judgments are subject to biases and other sources of error.)

Sometimes, researchers determine the empirical validity of a test that is *not* designed to predict future behavior. For instance, a new self-administered version of the Addiction Severity Index (ASI) was validated by correlating scores on it with scores obtained using the expensive and time-consuming original version, which involves a lengthy, structured clinical interview. The original version, which had been widely accepted as being highly valid, was the *criterion* (or gold standard) by which the new version was judged. In this study, the Drug Domain subscale on the self-administered version of the ASI had a *validity coefficient* of .62, which is moderately high, indicating that to a reasonable extent the less expensive version of the ASI provided information similar to the more expensive original version.[3]

Another approach is to correlate scores on a test that is being validated with scores on a *different test* of the same trait. For instance, scores on the *Beck Depression Inventory* were correlated with scores on the *Revised Hamilton Psychiatric Rating Scale for Depression*, which resulted in a validity coefficient of .71. This relatively strong correlation indicates that to the extent that one of the measures is valid, the other one has a similar degree of validity.[4]

A validity coefficient that is obtained by administering the test and collecting the criterion data at about the same time is called a **concurrent validity coefficient** (as opposed to a **predictive validity coefficient**). The general term for both types of validity examined in this topic is **criterion-related validity**. Notice that in both predictive and concurrent validity, researchers validate by comparing scores with a criterion. The following table shows the relevant features of both.

Types of Criterion-Related Validity[*]	What is the **criterion**?	When is the **criterion** measured?
1. **Predictive Validity**	A measure of the outcome that the test is designed to predict.	After examinees have had a chance to exhibit the predicted behavior.
2. **Concurrent Validity**	An independent measure of the same trait that the test is designed to measure.	At about the same time that the test is administered.

[*]Both types of criterion-related validity employ the empirical approach. That is, they are based on data that have been collected (planned empirical data collection)—not subjective judgments or theory.

[3] Butler, S. F. et al. (2001). Initial validation of a computer-administered Addiction Severity Index: The ASI-MV. *Psychology of Addictive Behaviors, 15,* 4–12.

[4] Beck, A. T., Steer, R. A., & Brown, G. K. (1996). *Manual for the Beck Depression Inventory—Second Edition.* San Antonio, TX: The Psychological Corporation.

EXERCISE ON TOPIC 33

1. What is the term for the *standard* by which a test is judged?

2. How is *empirical* defined in this topic?

3. What question does predictive validity answer?

4. If a test is perfectly valid, what value will its validity coefficient have?

5. In light of this topic, should a researcher be surprised to get a validity coefficient of .95 for a paper-and-pencil employment test when validated against supervisors' job-performance ratings?

6. If a test has no validity whatsoever, what value will its validity coefficient have?

7. If a researcher collects the criterion data at about the same time the test is being administered, he or she is examining what type of empirical validity?

Questions for Discussion

8. Suppose a researcher validated a new multiple-choice reading test by correlating the test scores with teachers' ratings of students' reading abilities (i.e., the scores on the test were correlated with the ratings made by teachers). What is your opinion on using teachers' ratings for this purpose? Could teachers' ratings themselves be less than perfectly valid? Explain.

9. Suppose a researcher wanted to validate a new measure of self-esteem. Name a criterion that might be used in a criterion-related validity study. Be prepared to justify its use.

10. The validity of an achievement test might be validated by using either content validity (see Topic 32) *or* concurrent validity (e.g., correlating the scores with teachers' judgments of students' achievements). In your opinion, which approach to validity is more useful for achievement tests? Should both be used? Explain.

For Students Planning Research

11. Will you be evaluating the empirical validity of the measures you will be using in your research? Explain. (Note that if you use a published measure, information on empirical validity may already be available in the manual for the measure or in a research report in which the measure was used.)

NOTES

TOPIC 34 JUDGMENTAL-EMPIRICAL VALIDITY

The type of validity that relies on subjective judgments *and* empirical data (i.e., data based on observations) is **construct validity**.

A **construct** stands for a collection of related behaviors that are associated in a meaningful way. For instance, "depression" is a construct that stands for a personality trait manifested by behaviors such as lethargy, flat affect when speaking, loss of appetite, loss of sexual drive, preoccupation with suicidal thoughts, difficulty concentrating on tasks, and so on. Notice that each of these is an *indicator* of depression—the construct itself does not have a physical being outside of its indicators. That is, researchers infer its existence by observing the *collection* of related indicators. The emphasis on *collection* is important to notice because any one indicator may be associated with several constructs. For instance, although loss of appetite is an indicator of depression, it may also be an indicator of anxiety, fear, physical illness, and so on. Thus, loss of appetite is indicative of depression only when it is found in association with a number of other indicators of depression.

To determine the construct validity of a measure, researchers begin by hypothesizing about how the construct that the measure is designed to measure should affect or relate to other variables. For instance, a researcher might hypothesize that students who are depressed will earn lower grades and be more likely to drop out of college than students who are not depressed. Note that this is a *hypothesis* (see Topic 7) because it *predicts* a relationship between depression and grades earned in college. Also, note that the researcher arrived at the hypothesis by making a subjective judgment regarding the likely effects of the indicators of depression on grades. If a researcher tests the hypothesis using empirical methods, he or she is conducting a construct validity study.

Consider how this works for a new 50-question paper-and-pencil depression *scale*.[1] To determine its construct validity, the researcher could test the hypothesis stated above using a sample of college students as participants. First, suppose the researcher finds *no* relationship between the scores obtained on the depression scale and success in col-

lege. What does this mean? Either (1) the scale lacks validity for measuring depression (i.e., it measures something else that is not related to grades earned in college) or (2) the hypothesis is wrong. If the researcher holds firmly to his or her belief in the hypothesis, he or she will have to conclude that the empirical evidence argues against the validity of the scale.

Next, suppose the researcher finds a relationship between scores obtained on the new depression scale and success in college. What does this mean? Either (1) the depression scale is, to some degree, valid for measuring depression or (2) the depression scale measures a variable other than depression that is also related to grades earned in college. This other variable could be many things. For instance, maybe the scale is heavily loaded with signs of depression that are also signs of anxiety so that it is more a measure of anxiety than depression. Because debilitating anxiety may lead to poor grades in college, the scores on the scale may relate to success in college because it measures anxiety, not depression.

At this point, it should be clear that determining construct validity is a complex matter that involves both judgment and empirical data. Also, it should be clear that this method offers only *indirect* evidence regarding the validity of a measure. Notice that direct evidence on the validity of a depression scale could be obtained by determining *criterion-related validity* (see Topic 33). For instance, this could be done by correlating scores obtained on the depression scale with clinical psychologists' judgments on how depressed each participant is. This is direct evidence because the researcher would be comparing scores from a depression scale with some other established measure of depression, not with an entirely different variable such as grades earned in college.

Consider another example: the construct called *dependence on others*. A researcher might hypothesize that younger children are, on average, more dependent on adults than are older children. If the researcher tests the hypothesis and finds that the scores on a dependence scale fail to relate to age among children, this result would argue against the validity of the dependence scale. On the other hand, if the researcher finds the predicted relationship between the dependence scores and age, this empirical evidence would suggest that the scale might have validity.

---

[1] Measures of personality traits are often called *scales* so they can be distinguished from *tests* of cognitive skills, which have right and wrong answers.

Because the evidence generated by construct validity studies is indirect, researchers should be very cautious about declaring a measure to be valid on the basis of a single study. Instead, researchers hope to see a series of construct validity studies for a given measure—testing various hypotheses derived by considering how the construct should be related to other variables—before reaching firm conclusions.

From one perspective, the indirect nature of the evidence obtained in construct validity studies may be regarded as a weakness. However, when there are a series of construct validity studies on a given measure, researchers gain insight into how meaningful the scores are in various contexts. This gives richness to researchers' understanding of how well a measure works, which is a strength of this approach to validity.

Note that construct validity requires *judgments* about the nature of relationships as well as *empirical evidence* regarding whether a measure provides scores consistent with the judgments. Hence, construct validity is classified as *judgmental-empirical* in this book.

Historically, construct validity has been most closely associated with personality scales. However, its proper application can yield useful information about all types of measures.

It is often desirable to examine a given measure in several different types of validity studies. The types of validity considered in Topics 32, 33, and this topic are summarized in Table 1.

Table 1

A Comparison of Major Approaches to Validity

Approaches to Validity	Types	How Determined
Judgmental	Content	Make expert judgments on the appropriateness of the content.
	Face	Make judgments based on superficial appearance.
Empirical	Predictive	Correlate test scores with criterion scores obtained after examinees have had a chance to achieve the outcome that is supposedly predicted by the test.
	Concurrent	Correlate test scores with criterion scores obtained at about the same time the test is administered.
Judgmental-Empirical	Construct	Hypothesize a relationship between the test scores and scores on another variable. Then, test the hypothesis.

EXERCISE ON TOPIC 34

1. How is the term *construct* defined in this topic?

2. Is fear a construct?

3. To determine construct validity, researchers begin by hypothesizing what?

4. Does confirming a hypothesis in a construct validity study offer "direct" *or* "indirect" evidence on the validity of a test?

5. In Table 1, which two types of validity are classified as solely empirical?

6. In Table 1, which two types of validity are classified as solely judgmental?

7. Why is construct validity identified as judgmental-empirical in this book?

Questions for Discussion

8. In your opinion, what are some of the physical indicators of (or behaviors associated with) the construct called *industriousness*?

9. To determine the construct validity of a paper-and-pencil industriousness scale, a researcher hypothesized that scores earned on it should be correlated with the number of promotions employees received on the job. Do you think this is a good hypothesis for a construct validity study? Explain.

10. Consider the physical signs of *shyness*. Propose a hypothesis that might be tested in a construct validity study on a measure designed to measure this construct.

For Students Planning Research

11. Will you be considering the construct validity of any measures you will be using in your research? Explain.

NOTES

TOPIC 35 RELIABILITY AND ITS RELATIONSHIP TO VALIDITY

A test is said to be **reliable** if it yields *consistent* results. It is easy to see what this means by considering an extreme example. Suppose a professor writes a midterm exam on research methods that contains only four multiple-choice items. The items are on four different important concepts that were emphasized during instruction. Thus, the exam is valid in the sense that it covers appropriate content. Students who have thoroughly mastered the course content, however, should be concerned about taking such a test because it would be very easy to misinterpret a question or to miss a key term in it and get it wrong, yielding a score of 3 out of 4, or only 75% correct. On the other hand, students who have moved through the semester in a fog—not understanding even basic concepts—should be pleased at the prospect of taking this exam. With only four items, the odds of getting a few right by guessing, and thus passing the test, are reasonably high.

Now suppose some students complain about their scores on the midterm, so the professor writes four new multiple-choice items, and again, the items are all on appropriate content. After administering the test at the next class meeting (without announcing there would be a second test, so students are not motivated to study again), should the professor expect to obtain the same scores as he or she did the first time? In all likelihood, no. Some students who were lucky in guessing the first time will have their luck wash out. Other students who misinterpreted a key term in a question will not do so on the new set of items. Examining the scores from the two tests provides the professor with information on the *consistency of results* or *reliability*. In this case, he or she would probably find that the scores are rather inconsistent from one test to the other.

What can the professor do to increase the reliability of the midterm? Obviously, the professor can increase the length of the test. This reduces the effects of the occasional ambiguous item and the effects of guessing. After realizing this principle, the professor instructs a graduate assistant to prepare a 100-item test overnight. The assistant, being pressed for time, takes the easy route and pulls a standardized test off the shelf. Although it has 100 items, they are on educational psychology, which includes some research concepts but also much material not covered in the research methods class. Administering this test should give highly reliable results because it contains a large number of test items. If the professor administers it twice, for instance, students who have a good command of educational psychology should do well on both tests. Also, those who have little knowledge of educational psychology will have little chance of getting a good grade by guessing on such a large number of items and, thus, should do poorly on both administrations. However, the professor has a new problem: The test lacks **validity** because it covers the wrong content (see Topics 31 through 34 to review the concept of validity). This example illustrates an important principle: *A test with high reliability may have low validity*.

Here is another example of this principle: An employer wants to reward the best employees with end-of-year bonuses. The employer decides that to be perfectly fair, she should use a completely objective method for determining who should get the bonuses. To do this, the employer examines the employees' time cards and selects those who were never late for work during the previous year to receive bonuses. Notice that this method of measurement is highly reliable because of its high level of objectivity. Thus, another individual could independently perform the same measurement procedure and, if careful, identify exactly the same employees for bonuses, yielding consistent (reliable) results. But is the procedure valid? Probably only minimally so because the employer's measurement technique is limited to only one simple characteristic. Those who are outstanding in a number of other ways (such as identifying more effective ways to advertise products) but who were late to work even once are excluded from getting bonuses. Thus, the procedure is reliable, but it is of questionable validity.

This leads to the next principle: When evaluating measures, *validity is more important than reliability*. This should be clear from considering the example of the employer basing bonuses on employees' time cards. A complex measure involving subjective judgments of employees' performances that taps a variety of important types of behavior and achievement on the job would be much more valid (even if it turned out to be only modestly reliable) than a highly reliable measure that considers only punctuality measured by examining time cards.

Finally, there is a third principle: *To be useful, a measure must be both reasonably valid and reasonably reliable.*

To understand the complex relationship between reliability and validity, consider Figures 1 through 4.

In Figure 1, the gun is aimed in a valid direction (toward the target), and all the shots are consistently directed, indicating that they are reliable.

Figure 1. Reliable and valid.

In Figure 2, the gun is also aimed in the direction of the target, but the shots are widely scattered, indicating low consistency or reliability. The poor reliability makes it unlikely that most of the bullets will hit the target. Thus, poor reliability undermines the valid direction in which the gun is pointing.

Figure 2. Unreliable, which undermines the valid aim of the gun. Less useful than Figure 1.

In Figure 3, the gun is not pointing at the target, which makes it invalid, but there is great consistency in the shots, which indicates that it is reliable. (In a sense, it is very reliably invalid.)

Figure 3. Reliable but invalid. Not useful.

In Figure 4, the gun is not pointing at the target, which makes it invalid, and the lack of consistency in the direction of the shots indicates its poor reliability.

Figure 4. Unreliable and invalid. Not useful.

Of course, Figure 1 represents the ideal in measurement. For most measures in the social and behavioral sciences, however, researchers expect the direction of the gun to be off by at least a small amount, which would indicate less-than-perfect validity. They also expect some scatter in the shots, which would indicate less-than-perfect reliability.[1] Clearly, the first priority should be to point the gun in the correct *general direction*, which promotes validity. Then, researchers should work on increasing reliability.

---

[1] Examination of the technical manuals for published tests indicates that professional test makers usually are more successful in achieving high reliability than in achieving high validity. This is because it is relatively easy to increase reliability by increasing the number of objective-type test items, while the tasks that need to be undertaken to increase validity vary greatly from construct to construct and may not be obvious.

EXERCISE ON TOPIC 35

1. A test is said to be reliable if it yields what?

2. Should a researcher expect a very short, multiple-choice test to be highly reliable?

3. Is it possible for a test with high reliability to have low validity?

4. Overall, is "validity" *or* "reliability" more important when evaluating a measure?

5. If a test is highly reliable but highly invalid, is it useful?

6. In light of this topic, should a researcher expect most tests to be both perfectly reliable and perfectly valid?

7. Professional test makers tend to be more successful in achieving high validity than in achieving high reliability. Is this statement "true" *or* "false"?

Questions for Discussion

8. Consider the example of the employer who was trying to identify the best employees by using a measure of punctuality because it was reliable, even though it was not especially valid. Name one or two other traits that might be examined in evaluating employees. Comment on whether you think each of your suggestions can be measured reliably. Also, comment on whether you think each is more valid than punctuality for determining which employees should receive bonuses.

9. Suppose you were offered a choice between two midterm examinations for your research methods class. The first one contains eight short essay questions, and the second contains 38 multiple-choice questions. Both are on appropriate content. Which would you prefer to take? Why? In your opinion, which one is likely to be more reliable?

For Students Planning Research

10. Will you be evaluating the reliability of any measures you will be using in your research? Explain. (Note that reliability will be considered in more detail in the next topic.)

NOTES

How can a researcher determine reliability? The classic model is to measure twice and then check to see if the two sets of measurements are consistent with each other.

First, consider **interobserver reliability**. Suppose a researcher wants to test the hypothesis that tall individuals are waited on more quickly in retail stores than short individuals. To do this, the researcher could observe unobtrusively[1] to (1) classify each customer as tall, medium, or short; and then (2) count the number of seconds from the time each customer enters the store to the time a salesperson greets the customer.

Because judgments of height made from a distance might not be reliable, the researcher could check their reliability by having two observers independently observe. The researcher could then determine the *percentage* of participants that were put in the same height category (tall, medium, or short) *by both observers*. How high should the percentage be? Although there is no standard answer to this question, it is clear that if the percentage gets too low (let us say less than 60% agreement), the researcher has a serious problem: either one or both of the observers. Such a lack of consistency in their judgments would cast serious doubt on the meaningfulness of the results of the study.

Measurements of the number of seconds also might be unreliable if, for instance, the observers are distracted by other events, are inattentive to the measurement task, and so on. To check on this possibility, the researcher could compare the measurements reported by the two observers. When there are two quantitative scores per participant (such as the number of seconds for each customer, as indicated by each of the two observers), the researcher can check on the degree of relationship by computing a **correlation coefficient**.[2] As indicated in the discussion of empirical validity (see Topic 33), a correlation coefficient may vary in value from 0.00 to 1.00.[3] A 1.00 indicates perfect reliability. That is,

the rank order of the customers based on the observations of one observer is the same as the rank order based on the observations made by the other observer. When researchers use *correlation coefficients* to describe reliability, they call them **reliability coefficients**. When researchers use reliability coefficients to describe the agreement between observers, they are usually called **interobserver reliability coefficients**.

Notice that when studying interobserver reliability, researchers usually obtain the two measurements *at the same time* (i.e., the two observers observe the same participants at the same time). In contrast, in **test-retest reliability**, researchers measure at *two different points in time*. For instance, suppose a researcher wants to know the reliability of a new test designed to assess the ability to learn college-level math. The researcher might administer the test one week and then re-administer it two weeks later. Because the ability to learn college-level math should not change very much from week to week, the researcher would expect the scores from the two administrations to be consistent. Once again, for two sets of scores, the researcher would compute a correlation coefficient, which would indicate the *test-retest reliability* of the test.

Some published tests come in two parallel (or equivalent) forms that are designed to be interchangeable; they have different items that cover the same content. When they are available, **parallel-forms reliability** should be determined. This is usually done by administering one form of the test to examinees and then, about a week or two later, administering the other form to the same examinees, thus yielding two scores per examinee. When the sets of scores are correlated, the result indicates the *parallel-forms reliability* of the test.

How high should a reliability coefficient be? Most published tests have reliability coefficients of .80 or higher, so researchers should strive to select or build measures that have coefficients at least this high, especially if researchers plan to interpret the scores for *individuals*. For *group averages* based on groups of participants of about 25 or more, measures with reliability coefficients as low as .50 can be serviceable. To understand why researchers can

---

[1] Researchers attempt to measure unobtrusively to avoid changing participants' behavior. For instance, if salespeople know that researchers are observing them, the salespeople might modify their normal behavior toward customers.

[2] See Topic 57 for a detailed discussion of correlation.

[3] Correlation coefficients may also be negative, as discussed in Topic 57. In the unlikely event that a re-

searcher obtains a negative when studying reliability, it should be interpreted as representing no reliability.

tolerate rather low reliability coefficients in research in which they are examining averages, first keep in mind that reliability coefficients indicate the reliability of *individuals' scores*. Statistical theory indicates that averages are more reliable than the scores that underlie them because when computing an average, the negative errors tend to cancel out the positive errors. For instance, suppose a researcher wants to compare the average age of parents who read extensively with their sixth-grade children with the average age of parents who do not. Asking children their parents' ages is likely to be unreliable. However, a researcher might expect about half of the children to overestimate the ages and half to underestimate them. To the extent that this is true, the averages may be reasonably accurate because the underestimates will cancel out the overestimates.

EXERCISE ON TOPIC 36

1. Researchers need to use at least how many observers to determine interobserver reliability?

2. When there are two quantitative scores per participant, researchers can compute what statistic to describe reliability?

3. Do researchers usually measure at two different points in time to estimate interobserver reliability?

4. Do researchers usually measure at two different points in time to estimate test-retest reliability?

5. According to this topic, most published tests have reliability coefficients that are about how high?

6. According to this topic, serviceable reliability coefficients may be how low if researchers are examining group averages?

Questions for Discussion

7. In your opinion, which of the following variables mentioned in this topic would probably be easier to measure reliably: (1) height of customers based on observations made from a distance *or* (2) number of seconds from the time each customer enters a store until a salesperson greets him or her, also based on observations from a distance? Explain your choice.

8. For which of the following would test-retest reliability (with the measures administered two weeks apart) probably be more appropriate: (1) a questionnaire on voters' opinions on the honesty of two presidential candidates *or* (2) a questionnaire on prejudice against minority groups? Explain your choice.

For Students Planning Research

9. Will you be considering the reliability of any measures you will be using in your research? If so, which method(s) for examining reliability will you use? Explain.

TOPIC 37 INTERNAL CONSISTENCY AND RELIABILITY

Two methods for estimating the reliability of a test (such as an achievement test) or a scale (such as an attitude scale) were covered in the previous topic: test-retest reliability, in which a test[1] is administered twice, and parallel-forms reliability, in which two alternative forms of a test are administered. In both of these types of reliability, examinees must take a test twice, with a week or two intervening between the administrations. Thus, if a test is less than perfectly reliable (i.e., the scores are not perfectly consistent), which is usually the case, variables associated with time can be partly responsible. For instance, at the time of the first administration, an examinee might be emotionally upset and not do well on the test, while the same examinee might not be upset at the time of the second administration and perform much better. Such time-associated variables obviously reduce the consistency of the scores from one administration of the test to the other, reducing reliability (and the reliability coefficient).

A different approach to reliability is to use the scores from a single administration of a test to examine the consistency of test scores. One way to do this is to determine the **split-half reliability** of a test. To do so, a researcher administers a test but scores the items in the test as though they consisted of two separate tests. Typically, researchers do this by performing what is known as an odd-even split. Specifically, a researcher scores all the odd-numbered items and obtains a score for each examinee. Then, the researcher scores all the even-numbered items and obtains a second score for each examinee. This process results in two scores per examinee. Then, the researcher correlates the two sets of scores, yielding what is known as a *split-half reliability coefficient*. As with other types of reliability coefficients, these can range from 0.00, which indicates a complete absence of reliability (i.e., the scores on the odd-numbered items have no relationship to the scores on the even-numbered items), to 1.00, indicating complete consistency in the ordering of the two sets of scores.[2]

Note that the split-half method checks on the consistency of scores *within the test itself* (not across two test administrations). Hence, the split-half method belongs to a class of reliability estimates known as estimates of **internal consistency**.

An alternative to the split-half method for estimating internal consistency is **Cronbach's alpha**, whose symbol is α. While the computation of alpha is complex, the concept is relatively easy to understand. Like the split-half method, it is based on a single administration of a test. After the test has been administered, mathematical procedures are used to obtain the equivalent of the average of all possible split-half reliability coefficients. For instance, an odd-even split could be used, yielding a split-half reliability coefficient. Then, the split could be the first half of the test versus the second half of the test, and a second split-half reliability coefficient could be obtained. Yet another split (maybe items 1–5 and items 11–15 for one half of a 20-item test versus the remaining items) could be used to obtain a third split-half reliability coefficient. After continuing in this way until all possible splits have been used, a researcher could average all the split-half reliabilities and obtain a value equivalent to Cronbach's alpha. Fortunately, the formula devised by Cronbach makes it possible to obtain this value without physically rescoring various splits over and over.

Because computer programs can be used to easily compute alpha, it has become much more commonly used than the split-half method, which depends on only a single split. Thus, the split-half method is reported primarily in older literature.[3]

Having high internal consistency is desirable when a researcher has developed a test designed to measure a single unitary variable, which is usually the case. For instance, if a researcher builds a test on the ability to sum one-digit numbers, students who score high on some of the items should score high on the other items and vice versa. Thus, the researcher should expect high internal consistency (i.e., a high value of α such as .80 or more). In con-

---

[1] In this topic, the term *test* is being used to refer to both tests and scales.

[2] As indicated in Topic 35, the larger the number of items in a test, the more reliable it tends to be. However, the split-half method estimates the reliability of a test only half as long as the full test. To correct for this un-

derestimate, a correction using the Kuder-Richardson Prophecy Formula should be made.

[3] Other older methods for estimating internal consistency are obtained by using Kuder-Richardson's Formulas 20 and 21. Like the split-half method, these have given way to Cronbach's alpha.

trast, if the researcher builds a general achievement test with some math items, some social studies items, some vocabulary items, and so on, the researcher would expect less internal consistency (a lower value of α).

In review, test−retest reliability and parallel-forms reliability measure the consistency of scores over time, while internal consistency methods (split-half and alpha) measure consistency among the items within a test at a single point in time.

EXERCISE ON TOPIC 37

1. Which two methods for estimating reliability require two testing sessions?

2. Does the split-half method require "one" *or* "two" administrations of a test?

3. What is meant by an odd-even split?

4. If a split-half reliability coefficient equals 0.00, what does this indicate?

5. What is the highest possible value for a split-half reliability coefficient?

6. To obtain alpha, mathematical procedures are used to obtain the equivalent of what?

7. Does alpha estimate the consistency of scores over time?

Question for Discussion

8. Suppose a researcher prepares a poorly written test in which some items are ambiguous. Speculate on the effect of the ambiguous items on split-half reliability.

For Students Planning Research

9. Will you be considering the measures you will be using in your research? If so, which method (split-half or alpha) will you use? Explain.

TOPIC 38 NORM- AND CRITERION-REFERENCED TESTS

Tests designed to facilitate a comparison of an individual's performance with that of a norm group are called **norm-referenced tests (NRTs)**.[1] For instance, if an examinee takes a test and earns a *percentile rank* of 64, the examinee knows that he or she scored higher[2] than 64% of the individuals in the norm group. Often, the norm group is a national sample of examinees, but it also may be an entire local population (such as all seniors in a school district) or a sample of a local population (such as a random sample of all seniors in a state).

In contrast, tests designed to measure the extent to which individual examinees have met performance standards (i.e., specific criteria) are called **criterion-referenced tests (CRTs)**.[3] For instance, suppose a researcher wants to test student nurses on their ability to administer an injection. The researcher might draw up a list of 10 behaviors that must be performed correctly for a student to pass the test, such as measuring the correct amount of medication, using a sterile needle, and so on. In this case, performing all the behaviors correctly is the criterion (i.e., performance standard).[4] Notice that the interpretation of an examinee's test score is independent of how other students perform. For instance, an examinee with nine items right might be the best in a group, but he or she along with everyone else will have failed the test because the

standard is to perform all 10 behaviors correctly. Thus, being higher or lower than others who take the same criterion-referenced test is irrelevant to the interpretation.

Researchers who build norm-referenced tests approach the task differently from those who build criterion-referenced tests. NRTs are intentionally built to be of medium difficulty. Specifically, items that are answered correctly by about 50% of the examinees in tryouts during test development are favored in the selection of items for the final versions of the tests. It is essential that an NRT be of medium difficulty because this level of difficulty facilitates the comparison of an individual with a group. This can be seen most easily at the extremes. For instance, if a researcher foolishly built an NRT that was so easy that all participants in the norm group got every item right, the researcher could not interpret scores in terms of who has a higher or lower score than other examinees because everyone would have the same score. The same problem would occur if a researcher built an NRT that was so difficult that all the examinees got all the items wrong.

In contrast, when building CRTs, item difficulty typically is of little concern. Instead, expert judgment is used to determine the desired level of performance and how to test for it. These judgments are influenced very little by how difficult a task is. Certainly, this approach is often appropriate. For instance, it would be inappropriate for the professors at a nursing school to drop a test item on measuring the correct amount of medication before injecting it simply because it is too difficult for their students. Because of its importance, the item should be retained regardless of its difficulty.

The need to have items of medium difficulty in NRTs is the basis of a major criticism of this type of test. Specifically, the criticism is that building NRTs is primarily driven by statistical considerations (i.e., item difficulty) and not by content considerations. Of course, those who build NRTs do carefully consider the content that a test should cover, but essential content may be deleted if the items that measure it are very easy or very difficult in tryouts of the items.

Which type of test should be favored in research? The answer depends on the research purpose. Here are two general guidelines:

---

[1] Some individuals use the terms *norm-referenced tests* and *standardized tests* interchangeably. However, it is better to reserve the term *standardized* for describing tests that come with standard directions for administration and interpretation. Both *norm-referenced tests* and *criterion-referenced tests* may be standardized.

[2] Strictly speaking, a percentile rank indicates the percentage of those in a norm group that an examinee scored *as high as or higher than*.

[3] The term *criterion-related validity* is used in Topic 33. Note that the word *criterion* is being used here and in Topic 33 to mean a *standard*. In Topic 33, using a standard for validating tests is discussed. Here, the discussion concerns using a standard to interpret the scores of individuals. These are, of course, separate matters, even though the same adjective is used in both cases.

[4] Performance standards are established by expert judgments and may be less than 100% correct, depending on the trait being measured. For instance, on a typing test, a test administrator might require only 95% accuracy. Of course, performance standards are not always expressed as a percentage. Instead, descriptive labels such as *expert*, *novice*, and so on can be used.

Guideline 1:

If the purpose is to describe specifically what examinees know and can do, criterion-referenced tests should be used.

Example: To what extent can voters understand a ballot proposition?

Example: Have students mastered the essentials of simple addition?

Guideline 2:

If the purpose is to examine how a local group differs from a larger norm group, norm-referenced tests should be used.[5]

Example: How well are students in New York doing in reading in comparison with the national average?

EXERCISE ON TOPIC 38

1. A norm-referenced test is designed to facilitate a comparison of an individual's performance with what?

2. Are norm groups always national samples?

3. What is the definition of a criterion-referenced test?

4. In which type of test are items answered correctly by about 50% of the participants favored in item selection?

5. In which type of test are items typically selected on the basis of content they cover without regard to item difficulty?

6. Which type of test should be used in research where the purpose is to describe specifically what examinees can and cannot do?

Questions for Discussion

7. Assume you are a parent and your child's second-grade teacher offers to provide you with *either* scores on a "norm-referenced test" *or* a "criterion-referenced test" of your child's basic math ability. Which would you choose? Why?

8. For research on the percentage of students whose swimming skills are good enough for them to save themselves if they jump into the deep end of a pool, which type of test would you choose? Explain.

For Students Planning Research

9. Will you be using norm-referenced tests in your research? Criterion-referenced tests? Explain.

---

[5] To make predictions, researchers need tests that differentiate among participants. For instance, if all examinees earn the same score on a college admissions test, the scores cannot be used to predict who will and who will not succeed in college. Because norm-referenced tests are specifically built to make differentiations by being of medium difficulty, they are also useful in prediction studies.

TOPIC 39 MEASURES OF OPTIMUM PERFORMANCE

When researchers measure achievement, aptitude, and intelligence, they want examinees to strive to do their best—to perform at their optimum.

An **achievement test** measures *knowledge and skills individuals have acquired*. When researchers conduct research on the effectiveness of direct, planned instruction, they should use achievement tests designed to measure the objectives of that instruction. To the extent that the tests do that, they are *valid* (i.e., they measure what they should).

Multiple-choice tests of achievement are frequently used by researchers because they are easy to administer and score. Indeed, multiple-choice tests are often appropriate when a researcher wants a quick snapshot of participants' achievements. Researchers can also measure achievement by having participants write answers to open-ended questions (e.g., essay questions), by evaluating participants' overt performances (e.g., a musical performance), or by assessing products (e.g., a portfolio of watercolor paintings). Scoring of the latter types is more time-consuming than scoring multiple-choice tests and may be *unreliable* unless researchers make sure that the scorers know specifically what characteristics of the essays, performances, or products they are to consider and how much weight to give to each characteristic in arriving at the scores. For instance, to evaluate the ability of a student nurse to give an injection, a researcher could develop a list of desirable characteristics, such as "measures the appropriate amount of medication," "checks the patient's armband," and so on. These can be the basis for a *checklist* (a list of desirable characteristics of a product or performance, each of which is awarded a point) or a *rating scale* (e.g., "excellent," "above average," "average," "below average," "poor," terms that are applied in evaluating each characteristic).

An **aptitude test** is designed to *predict some specific type of achievement*. An example is the College Board's *Scholastic Aptitude Test* (SAT), which is used to predict success in college. The validity of an aptitude test is determined by correlating the scores participants earn (such as SAT scores determined while participants are in high school) with a measure of achievement obtained at a later date (such as freshman GPA in college). Other widely used aptitude tests are reading readiness tests (designed to predict reading achievement in the first grade by measuring whether examinees can discriminate among shapes, have basic concepts such as color names, etc.) and algebra prognosis tests (designed to predict achievement in algebra by measuring basic math skills that are used in algebra).

The most widely used aptitude tests are developed by commercial test publishers. Typically, they have low to modest validity (with validity coefficients of about .20 to .60). The modest predictive validity of aptitude tests is understandable because they measure only some of the skills needed for achievement in a particular area. For instance, many other skills such as persistence in the face of difficulty, study habits, and physical characteristics like being chronically ill can affect achievement but are not measured by aptitude tests. Published aptitude tests, however, usually have high reliability (with reliability coefficients of .80 or higher).

An **intelligence test** is designed to *predict achievement in general*, not any one specific type. The most popular intelligence tests (1) are culturally loaded and (2) measure knowledge and skills that can be acquired with instruction (with questions such as, "How far is it from New York to Los Angeles?"). The arguable assumption underlying intelligence tests is that all individuals are exposed to such information and more intelligent individuals are more likely to retain the information. Almost all contemporary experts on measurement, however, reject the notion that such tests measure innate (inborn) intelligence. At best, intelligence tests measure skills that have been acquired in some specific cultural milieu. Commercially available intelligence tests of this type have low to modest validity for predicting achievement in school—a degree of validity that can be achieved with less controversial aptitude tests.

Extensive efforts have been made to develop culture-free intelligence tests. Typical efforts in this area have concentrated on nonverbal tasks because of the high cultural load of language usage. These tests are usually less predictive of subsequent achievement than the more traditional intelligence tests, possibly because achievement is accomplished in a cultural context in which language is critical.

Research on intelligence can be controversial when, for instance, researchers assume that intelligence tests measure innate ability or that they measure all important aspects of intelligence. Issues such as racial and ethnic differences in innate intelligence, if worthy of study at all, cannot be satisfactorily investigated with the measures available at this time.

Because of increasing awareness of widespread misinterpretations of intelligence test scores and the structural limitations of intelligence tests (e.g., arguable assumptions underlying them), intelligence tests are used in research much less frequently now than they were several decades ago.

EXERCISE ON TOPIC 39

1. Which type of test is designed to predict achievement *in general*?

2. An algebra prognosis test is an example of what type of test?

3. A test designed to measure how much students learn in a particular course in school is what type of test?

4. A test designed to predict success in learning a new set of skills is what type of test?

5. A list of desirable characteristics of a product or performance is known as what?

6. How can researchers increase the reliability of scoring essays, products, and performances?

7. According to this topic, are intelligence tests good measures of innate ability?

8. According to this topic, how valid are commercially published aptitude tests?

Questions for Discussion

9. Did you ever take an achievement test on which you did not perform up to your optimum? If yes, briefly describe why. Was the test maker or test administrator responsible for your less-than-optimum performance? Were you responsible? Explain.

10. Name a specific type of achievement that can be most accurately measured using a checklist or rating scale. State why a scale or checklist would be better than a multiple-choice test.

For Students Planning Research

11. Will you be using an achievement test in your research? Have you selected it yet? Explain.

12. Will you be using an aptitude test? What will it be designed to predict? Explain.

13. Will you be using an intelligence test? Will it be one designed to be culture-free? If yes, do you believe it is fully culture-free? Explain.

TOPIC 40 MEASURES OF TYPICAL PERFORMANCE

As indicated in the previous topic, when researchers measure achievement, aptitude, and intelligence, they encourage examinees to perform their best. In contrast, when researchers measure deep-seated personality traits such as attitudes, interests, and dispositions, they want to determine participants' *typical* levels of performance. For instance, when selecting employees to work as salespeople, an employer might want to know how assertive each applicant typically is, not just how assertive they claim to be in their responses to an assertiveness scale (a series of questions that are scored to get an overall assertiveness score). When measuring such traits, a major concern is that applicants might indicate what is *socially desirable* rather than their true level of assertiveness in order to increase their chances of employment.

Individuals are often hesitant to reveal they have *socially undesirable* traits even when they have nothing directly to gain by being deceitful. Thus, the responses of participants in research projects may frequently be influenced by social desirability. Reducing the influence of social desirability increases the validity of personality measures.

There are three basic approaches to reducing social desirability in participants' responses. First, by administering personality measures anonymously, researchers may reduce this tendency. Another approach is to observe behavior unobtrusively (without the participants' awareness—to the extent that this is ethically possible) and rate selected characteristics such as aggressiveness.

A third approach is to use *projective techniques*. These provide loosely structured or ambiguous stimuli such as ink blots. As participants respond to these stimuli, such as by telling what they see, they are presumed to be projecting their feelings and beliefs and revealing them in their responses. For instance, a test administrator might infer that participants whose responses to ink blots contain numerous references to aggressiveness are themselves aggressive. When participants are unaware of the specific traits an investigator is looking for, the tendency to give socially desirable responses is reduced.

The literature on the validity and reliability of popular projective techniques is quite mixed, with some studies showing that they are remarkably deficient in these respects. Thus, they are best used only by those who have had formal training in their

administration and scoring. Furthermore, they are seldom used in personality research because (1) they are time-consuming to administer and score; (2) they do not naturally lend themselves to numerical results—instead, the interpretations are usually in words; and (3) their validity is highly suspect. Instead, researchers usually use objective-type personality measures in which participants respond to statements or questions with restricted choices such as true-false, "Strongly agree" to "Strongly disagree," and checklists in which respondents check off the characteristics they believe are true of themselves.

Scales that have choices from "Strongly agree" to "Strongly disagree" are known as **Likert-type scales**.[1] Each statement in a Likert-type scale should present a clear statement on a single topic. For instance, to measure attitudes toward school, a researcher might use statements such as, "In the mornings, I look forward to going to school" and "I get along well with my teacher." To reduce response bias (such as marking "Strongly agree" to all items without considering the individual items), it is a good idea to provide some positive and some negative statements and score them according to whether the associated statements are positive or negative. For instance, if five points are awarded for strongly agreeing to a positive statement toward school, a researcher would award five points for strongly disagreeing with a negative statement toward school. Researchers call this process **reverse scoring**.

Of course, the statements in a Likert-type scale should be derived from an analysis of the possible components of the attitude. For attitude toward school, a researcher might have several statements concerning attitudes in each of these areas: (1) learning in academic areas, (2) relationships with classmates, (3) relationships with teachers and staff, (4) participation in extracurricular activities, and so on. Such an analysis helps to assure that the contents of the attitude scale are comprehensive, which will contribute to its content validity (see Topic 32).

In short, when researchers measure personality traits, they want respondents to indicate what they are typically like, not how good they can make themselves look. This is quite different from measurement of cognitive skills with achievement, apti-

---

[1] Named for Rensis Likert, who popularized the format.

tude, and intelligence tests on which researchers
want respondents to show their best.

EXERCISE ON TOPIC 40

1. Do researchers usually want participants to show their best when measuring personality traits?

2. In this topic, what is the main reason for administering personality measures anonymously?

3. What do researchers reduce by observing behavior unobtrusively?

4. Loosely structured stimuli are used in which type of personality measure?

5. According to this topic, which type of personality measure is seldom used in personality research?

6. What is the range of choice in a Likert-type scale?

7. Is content validity a relevant concern when assessing the validity of a Likert-type scale for measuring attitudes?

Questions for Discussion

8. Have you ever given a socially desirable response that was not true of you when being interviewed or answering a questionnaire? If yes, briefly describe why. Is there anything the interviewer or questionnaire writer could have done to increase the odds that you would have been more forthright?

9. Write three statements that could be used with a Likert-type scale to measure attitudes toward your research methods class. Each should be on a different aspect of the class, such as the textbook, the instructor, and so on. Two should be positive statements and one should be negative. Explain how they would be scored.

For Students Planning Research

10. Will you be using a measure of typical performance in your research? If so, to what extent might it be subject to the influence of social desirability? Explain.

11. Will you be measuring attitudes? If yes, will you use a Likert-type scale? Explain.

PART F

EXPERIMENTAL DESIGN

In experiments, researchers give treatments in order to observe their effects on participants' behavior. In this part of the book, various designs for experiments are described. Specifically, designs for true experiments, preexperiments, and quasi-experiments are explained and illustrated. The external validity of experiments (which answers the question, "Can a researcher generalize beyond the experimental setting?") and their internal validity (which answers the question, "Did the treatments, in fact, cause the observed differences?") are considered.[1]

---

[1] This part highlights some of the main ideas in the classic work of Campbell, D. T., & Stanley, J. C. (1963). *Experimental and quasi-experimental designs for research.* Chicago, IL: Rand McNally.

NOTES

As indicated in earlier topics, the purpose of an experiment is to explore cause-and-effect relationships. In this discussion, the terminology and symbols first suggested by Campbell and Stanley (1963) are used.

First, consider a classic design for exploring cause-and-effect relationships:

Design 1:

Assign participants at random to groups.	Group A: (Experimental Group)	Pretest	Experimental Treatment	Posttest
	Group B: (Control Group)	Pretest	Control Condition	Posttest

Design 1 is the **pretest-posttest randomized control group design**. By assigning participants at random to groups, researchers are assured that there are no biases in the assignment.[1] That is, the two groups of participants are equal except for random differences.

In Design 1, if the experimental group makes greater gains from pretest to posttest than the control group *and* if the two groups have been treated the same in all respects except for the experimental treatment, the difference is attributable to only one of two causes: (1) the treatment or (2) random errors. As indicated in Part G of this book, researchers can use inferential statistics to assess the role of random errors in creating any observed differences. Thus, researchers can tolerate random errors because the results can be interpreted in light of their possible effects. There are no generalizable statistical techniques for assessing the influence of bias. Hence, researchers prefer to avoid bias in the assignment to the two conditions (i.e., experimental and control conditions) by using random assignment.

Researchers can simplify the representation of Design 1 by using symbols suggested by Campbell and Stanley (1963): R (which stands for random assignment to groups), O (which stands for observation or measurement, whether pretest or posttest), and X (which stands for experimental treatment). There is no symbol for control condition, so it is

represented by a blank. Note that a control condition may include some type of treatment (in education, it might be a traditional form of instruction; in medicine, it might be a placebo—a sugar pill). Thus, the control condition is the standard by which the effectiveness of the experimental treatment is judged. Using symbols, Design 1 looks like this:

R   O   X   O
R   O   O

The advantage of using a pretest is that it permits researchers to determine how much each group has *gained*, not just whether they are different at the end of the experiment. However, sometimes having a pretest causes a problem because it can sensitize participants to the experimental treatment and, in effect, become part of the treatment. For instance, by taking a pretest at the beginning of an experimental course of instruction, participants can gain an overview of what will be covered, the depth to which the material will be covered, and so on. Thus, changes observed in the experimental group may be the result of a *combination of the pretest and the treatment*. This problem is called **pretest sensitization** (also called the **reactive effect of testing**). It can be overcome by conducting an experiment without a pretest, as shown in Design 2, which is the **posttest-only randomized control group design**.

Design 2:

R   X   O
R   O

At first, the lack of a pretest may seem to be a flaw, but remember that the comparability of the two groups in Design 1 was achieved by assigning participants at random to the two groups. This initial comparability is also achieved in Design 2 above by this random assignment. In other words, it is not the pretest that makes the two groups comparable. Rather, it is the random assignment that does this.

Researchers can have the best of both designs by using the **Solomon randomized four-group design**, which is a combination of Designs 1 and 2. Solomon's design is shown in Design 3. Because it has four rows of symbols, it has four groups. The first two rows are the same as Design 1, while the bottom two rows are the same as Design 2. In ef-

---

[1] See Topic 25 for a discussion of how to select participants at random. If half of them are selected at random to be the experimental group and the rest are designated as the control group, the researcher has used random assignment to groups.

fect, the Solomon design is two experiments conducted at the same time.

Design 3:

$$
\begin{array}{cccc}
R & O & X & O \\
R & O & & O \\
R & & X & O \\
R & & & O \\
\end{array}
$$

The advantage of Design 3 above is that researchers can compare the first two groups to determine how much gain is achieved and can also compare the last two groups to determine whether the treatment is more effective than the control condition in the absence of a pretest (without pretest sensitization). The only potential drawback to Design 3 is that a researcher must begin with a reasonably large pool of participants so that when they are divided into four groups, each of the groups will have a sufficient number to yield reliable results.

How many is enough? The answer is complex, but generally speaking, it probably would be unwise to use the four-group design instead of a two-group design if the total pool of participants is less than 48.

All three of the preceding designs are called **true experimental designs**. True experimental designs are easy to spot because they are all characterized by random assignment to treatments.

Note that sometimes it is not possible to assign participants at random. For instance, for ethical and legal reasons, a researcher might not be able to withhold a particular treatment from individuals. In such a case, the researcher might treat an entire group with a treatment mandated by law and use another group that is not required to have the treatment as the control group. Because the participants were *not* assigned at random to treatments, such experiments are *not* true experiments.

EXERCISE ON TOPIC 41

1. What is the purpose of an experiment?

2. In an experiment, how can researchers ensure that there are no biases when they assign participants to groups?

3. In a diagram for an experimental design, the symbol O stands for what?

4. In a diagram for an experimental design, the symbol X stands for what?

5. What is the name of the potential problem caused by the pretest in the pretest-posttest randomized control group design?

6. What is the name of the true experimental design that has no pretests?

7. What is a potential drawback to the Solomon randomized four-group design?

8. True experimental designs are easy to spot because they are all characterized by what?

Question for Discussion

9. Briefly describe an experimental problem for which a researcher probably would not be able to assign participants at random to conditions.

For Students Planning Research

10. Will you be conducting an experiment? If so, will you be using a true experimental design? Explain.

Suppose a researcher observes major changes in participants' behavior in an experiment. Is it reasonable to attribute these changes to the effects of the treatment(s)? Depending on the design of the experiment, there may be explanations for the changes other than the treatment. These alternative explanations are called **threats to internal validity**. It is easiest to understand them in the context of a poor experiment with no control group (specifically, one in which a researcher pretests, treats, and then posttests one group of participants). Using the symbols described in the previous topic, the design looks like this:

O X O

Suppose the treatment (X) was designed to improve participants' self-concept, and the researcher observed an average gain of 9 points in self-concept from pretest (the first O) to posttest (the second O). Of course, the treatment could be responsible for the increase. Another possibility is the internal threat called **history** (i.e., other environmental influences on the participants between the pretest and posttest). For instance, perhaps some of the participants read a new self-help book that improved their self-concepts during the same period of time that the treatment was being administered. Thus, the gain could have resulted from reading the book and not from the treatment.

Another threat in this design is **maturation**. Perhaps the participants matured (e.g., became older, wiser, or smarter) during the period between the pretest and posttest, and the increase is due to maturation and not to the treatment.

Instrumentation is another threat. This refers to possible changes in the measurement procedure (sometimes called *instrumentation*) from the time it was used as a pretest to the time it was used as a posttest. For instance, the particular observers who made the pretest observations may have been less astute at noticing signs of good self-concept than the observers who made the posttest observations.

Another threat is **testing**, which is defined as the effects of the pretest on the performance exhibited on the posttest. For instance, while taking the pretest self-concept scale, the participants may have learned how to interpret the questions. Their posttest performance might be affected by this learning experience that occurred while they took the pretest.

Statistical regression is another threat that occurs only if participants are selected on the basis of their extreme scores. For instance, perhaps a large group of students was administered a self-concept scale, and those in the lowest 20% were selected for treatment in the experiment. A fundamental principle of measurement is that those who are extremely low on a screening test will, on average, tend to have a higher score when tested again, purely because of the nature of random errors created by the less-than-perfect reliability of the measures researchers use—whether or not the treatment is effective.[1]

The next threat to internal validity can occur when researchers use two comparison groups that are *not* formed at random. Suppose, for instance, that a researcher uses the students in one school as the experimental group and those in another as the control group. Because students are not assigned to schools at random, the researcher is using **intact groups** (i.e., previously existing groups). This is diagrammed by putting a dashed line between the symbols for the groups, which indicates that the groups were intact, as shown here:

O X O
―――――
O   O

Notice that when researchers do not assign participants to the two groups at random, there is a very strong possibility that the two groups are not initially the same in all important respects, which is the threat called **selection**. Selection can *interact* with all the other threats to internal validity. For instance, consider **selection-history interaction**. Because the selection of participants for the two groups was not at random, they may be systematically subjected to different life experiences. For instance, it may be that the teachers in the school with the experimental group took a self-concept workshop, which was not part of the treatment, and applied what they learned to their students. Thus, the improvement in self-concepts may be the result

---

[1] Statistical regression is difficult to grasp without a solid background in measurement theory. However, some students may recall the principle of *regression toward the mean* from their study of other sciences. Those who are very low will, on average, tend to be higher on retesting (closer to the mean—on average), and those who are very high will tend to be lower on retesting.

Another example is **selection-maturation interaction**. Perhaps the two groups, on average, were at somewhat different developmental stages at the time of the pretest, which would have led to different rates of maturation in the two groups, which could affect self-concept.

Selection can also interact with a threat called **mortality** (i.e., differential loss of participants from the groups to be compared). For instance, those in an experimental school may have a higher dropout rate than those in a control school. If those who drop out have lower self-concepts, the posttest mean for the experimental group will be higher than the pretest mean, resulting in a statistical change in the average that is not the result of the treatment. At the same time, the control group will not exhibit as much change because it has a lower dropout rate.

All threats to internal validity can be overcome by using a **true experimental design** (see Topic 41), in which participants are assigned at random to experimental and control conditions. Because random assignment has no bias (or favorites), both the experimental and the control group are equally likely to experience the same environmental events (have the same history), mature at the same rates, drop out at the same rates, and so on.

EXERCISE ON TOPIC 42

1. What is the name of the threat that indicates that taking a pretest may affect performance on a posttest?

2. Suppose an experimental group is being taught letters of the alphabet as a treatment. At about the same time, the students are watching an educational program on television, from which they learn the names of the letters. What is the name of the threat that this problem illustrates?

3. If observers are more tired and less astute when making posttest observations than when making pretest observations, what threat is operating?

4. What is the name of the threat posed by nonrandom assignment of participants to experimental and control groups?

5. If infants naturally improve in visual acuity and thus perform better at the end of an experiment than at the beginning, what threat is operating?

6. Under what circumstance will statistical regression operate?

7. How can researchers overcome all the threats to internal validity?

Question for Discussion

8. Suppose a researcher gave a series of wellness workshops over a six-month period and then determined that five of the participants had quit smoking during the six-month period. The researcher's interpretation was that the workshops caused the decrease in smoking. Is this interpretation flawed? Explain.

For Students Planning Research

9. If you will be conducting an experiment, which threats, if any, will it be subject to? Explain.

TOPIC 43   THREATS TO EXTERNAL VALIDITY

Consider this example: A researcher drew a sample from a population and divided it into an experimental group and a control group. To conduct the experiment, the researcher administered the experimental treatment and control condition in a laboratory on a college campus. Suppose the results of the experiment showed that the experimental group improved significantly more than the control group. Can the researcher accurately **generalize** from the sample to the population (i.e., is it accurate to assume that the treatment administered to the experimental group will work as well in the population as it did in the sample)? Also, will the treatment be as effective in the population's natural setting as it was in the artificial laboratory setting? The answers depend on the extent to which the experiment is subject to what researchers call **threats to external validity**.

The first threat is **selection bias** and its interaction with the experimental (independent) variable. As indicated in Part D of this book, if a sample is biased, a researcher's ability to generalize to a population is greatly limited. In a strict scientific sense, no generalizations should be made when this is the case. This threat reminds researchers that if a biased sample of participants is used in an experiment (such as using the students who happen to be in one professor's class), a researcher will not know whether the effects of the treatment (observed in that class) can be expected if the treatment is administered to the entire population. Of course, the way to control this threat is to select the participants for an experiment at random from a population because a random sample is, by definition, unbiased.

Another threat is the **reactive effects of experimental arrangements**. This threat reminds researchers that if the experimental setting is different from the natural setting in which the population usually operates, the effects that are observed in the experimental setting may not generalize to the natural setting. For instance, if a treatment is administered in a laboratory to fifth graders, the responsiveness of the students may be different from the responsiveness of the population of fifth graders when the treatment is used in public school classroom settings. In other words, it can be risky to generalize from an experimental setting to a natural setting. The way to control this threat is to conduct experiments under natural conditions when possible.

The possible **reactive effect of testing** (also called **pretest sensitization**) is another threat. This threat refers to the possibility that the pretest might influence how the participants respond to the experimental treatment. For instance, if a researcher gives a pretest on racial prejudice and then administers a treatment designed to lessen prejudice, participants' responses to the treatment may be affected by the experience of taking the pretest. That is, having to think about prejudice (while taking the pretest) might change participants' sensitivity to the treatment. This is a problem when researchers want to generalize about how well the treatment will work in the population *if* the population will not be given a pretest. As indicated in Topic 41, researchers can conduct true experiments without pretests, thereby eliminating this threat.

Multiple-treatment interference is a threat that occurs when a group of participants is given more than one treatment. For instance, at first a researcher might give participants no praise for correct answers, then start giving them moderate amounts of praise, and finally give them large amounts of praise. Suppose the researcher finds that large amounts of praise work best. Will it work in the same way in the population? The generalization will be risky if those in the population will *not* first be given the no-praise condition, then the moderate-praise condition, and, finally, the large-praise condition. In other words, the fact that these participants first received small and then moderate amounts of praise might make their responses to large amounts of praise different from the responses of a population that will receive *only* large amounts of praise. To put it a different way, treatment(s) given earlier in an experiment might affect the effectiveness of treatments given later to the same participants.

Take care to distinguish between **internal validity** (see Topic 42) and **external validity**. As indicated in this topic, the external validity of an experiment is concerned with "To whom and under what circumstances can the results be generalized?" Internal validity is concerned with the question, "Is the treatment, *in this particular case*, responsible for the observed change(s)?" Thus, threats to internal validity are potential explanations for the observed changes. That is, they are possible explanations that become confounded with the treatment as an explanation for any observed changes. Threats to internal validity are controlled by using true experimental designs (see Topic 41).

Note that internal and external validity are separate considerations. Even if an experiment has excellent internal validity, it may not be appropriate to generalize the results to other populations because of the threats to external validity discussed in this topic. Likewise, a study with high external validity might have poor internal validity because the threats to internal validity have confounded a researcher's understanding of what caused the observed changes. Thus, each one of these two types of threats should be considered and evaluated independently.

EXERCISE ON TOPIC 43

1. Which type of validity deals with the question of whether a researcher can generalize with confidence to a larger population in a natural setting?

2. Which type of validity deals with whether the treatment is directly responsible for any changes observed in the experimental setting?

3. What is the name of the threat that warns researchers to be careful in generalizing the results to a population when an experiment is conducted on a nonrandom sample?

4. Suppose a random sample of workers in a factory is exposed to five different reward systems, with each system being used for one month. What is the name of the threat that reminds researchers that the results may not generalize to the population of workers if the population is to be exposed to only the last reward system tried in the experiment?

5. Suppose an experimental classroom has research observers present at all times. What is the name of the threat that reminds researchers that the results may not generalize to other classrooms without observers?

6. If a pretest causes a change in participants' sensitivity to a treatment, what threat is operating?

Question for Discussion

7. Briefly describe a hypothetical experiment that has high internal validity but low external validity.

For Students Planning Research

8. If you will be conducting an experiment, which threats to external validity, if any, will it be subject to? Explain.

TOPIC 44 PREEXPERIMENTAL DESIGNS

The three designs discussed in this topic are of very limited value for investigating cause-and-effect relationships because of their poor internal validity. Thus, they are called **preexperimental designs**. One of the designs was introduced in Topic 42: the **one-group pretest-posttest design**. Its diagram is shown here as Design 4.[1]

Design 4:

O X O

As indicated in Topic 42, changes from pretest to posttest in Design 4 may be attributable to *history*, *maturation*, *instrumentation*, *testing*, and, if the participants were selected on the basis of extreme scores, *statistical regression*[2] (see Topic 42 for a discussion of these threats to internal validity). These threats are possible explanations for any changes observed from the pretest to the posttest. Of course, researchers want to determine what changes, if any, the treatment (X) caused. Thus, the interpretation of pretest to posttest change is *confounded* by multiple explanations.

Design 5 is called the **one-shot case study**. In it, one group is given a treatment (X) followed by a test (O). This is its diagram:

Design 5:

X O

If a teacher provides instruction on a unit of material and follows it with an achievement test, he or she is using Design 5. For instructional purposes, there is nothing wrong with this design. For instance, the posttest will help the teacher to determine what grades to assign for students' achievements on the unit of instruction. However, if a teacher wants to know whether the instruction *caused* whatever achievements are seen on the test, the design is of no value because it fails to make comparisons. The teacher cannot determine whether

the students achieved anything as a result of the instruction without a pretest (or a randomly selected control group). In other words, it is quite possible that the achievement the students display on the posttest is at the same level they might have displayed on a pretest if there had been one.[3]

Design 6, the **static-group comparison design**, has two groups, but participants are not assigned to the groups at random. The dashed line between the two groups indicates they are **intact groups** (i.e., previously existing groups that were not formed at random).

Design 6:

X O

O

The obvious problem with Design 6 is the threat to internal validity called *selection* (the selection of the two groups was not made in such a way that a researcher can have confidence that they are initially the same in all important respects).[4] Furthermore, without a pretest, a researcher does not have a basis for knowing whether the two groups were similar at the beginning of the experiment. For instance, the treatment might have been totally ineffective, but the experimental group might have been superior to the control group at the beginning of the experiment and may have retained the same amount of superiority throughout the experiment. This initial superiority would produce a difference in favor of the experimental group in the posttest results, which might lead to the risky assumption that the treatment caused the difference.[5]

Because of their weaknesses, the three preexperimental designs are of very limited value in exploring cause-and-effect relationships. However,

---

[1] Each of the designs in this part is given a number for reference in class discussions. The numbering system is not a universal one. Thus, in discussions outside class, refer to the names of the designs given in boldfaced type, not to the design numbers.

[2] Campbell and Stanley (1963) note that this design is also subject to the *interaction of selection with history, maturation*, etc. See Campbell, D. T., & Stanley, J. C. (1963). *Experimental and quasi-experimental designs for research*. Chicago, IL: Rand McNally.

[3] Campbell and Stanley (1963) note that this design is subject to the internal threats of history, maturation, selection, and mortality.

[4] Campbell and Stanley (1963) note that this design is also subject to the internal threats of mortality and the interaction of selection with history, maturation, etc.

[5] As indicated in Topic 41, a pretest is not essential in a two-group design *if* the participants are assigned at random to the groups. This is because the random assignment assures that the two groups are initially the same *except for random differences*, which can be assessed with inferential statistics. See the discussion of Design 2 in Topic 41.

they are sometimes useful in *preliminary pilot studies* in which a researcher's goal is to try out potential treatments and measuring tools to learn more about their acceptability and accuracy, not to obtain definitive information on causal relationships. For instance, a researcher might administer a new drug to a small group of participants in order to observe for side effects, to determine the maximum tolerable dosage, to explore different routes of administration, and so on. The results could be used in planning a subsequent true experiment on the effects of the drug, using a design that has a randomized control group (see Topic 41).

EXERCISE ON TOPIC 44

1. Are preexperimental designs valuable for identifying cause-and-effect relationships?

2. Suppose a researcher administered a new program to all students in a school. At the end of the school year, the researcher administered a standardized test to the students in the school as well as to students in another school who were serving as a control group. Is the comparison of the average scores for the two groups of students useful for determining the effects of the program?

3. What is the name of the preexperimental design used in Question 2?

4. If a researcher gives a pretest on knowledge of child abuse to a group of social workers, then gives them a series of seminars on child abuse followed by a posttest, what is the name of the preexperimental design the researcher used?

5. Is the design used in Question 4 useful for determining cause-and-effect relationships?

Questions for Discussion

6. Suppose a researcher selected participants at random from a population and then used the one-group pretest-posttest design. Would random selection make this design good for exploring cause-and-effect relationships?

7. Have you ever used a preexperimental design in any of your professional or everyday activities (e.g., have you ever tried doing something in a new way and observing for its effects without a control group)? If so, briefly describe it. Discuss whether your activity shed light on a cause-and-effect relationship.

For Students Planning Research

8. If you will be conducting an experiment, will you be using a preexperimental design? If yes, explain why you will be using such a design given that it has serious weaknesses.

TOPIC 45 QUASI-EXPERIMENTAL DESIGNS

As indicated in Topic 41, true experimental designs, which involve random assignment to treatment conditions, are excellent for exploring cause-and-effect relationships. Often, however, it is not possible to assign participants at random. When this is the case, preexperimental designs (see Topic 44) should be avoided. Instead, **quasi-experimental designs**, which are of intermediate value for exploring cause and effect, should be used.[1]

Design 7 was first discussed in Topic 42, where threats to internal validity were addressed. It is a widely used, quasi-experimental design that has two intact groups (not assigned at random, as indicated by the dashed line). This is the **nonequivalent control group design**.

Design 7:

$$O \quad X \quad O$$
$$\overline{}$$
$$O \quad \quad O$$

As indicated in Topic 42, this design is subject to the threats of *mortality*, *selection*, and *interaction of selection* with other threats such as *history*. Thus, it is far from ideal but is superior to the preexperimental designs, which are not directly interpretable in terms of causal effects. When random assignment to groups is not possible, Design 7 above may provide useful results.

Even though participants are not assigned at random to the two groups in Design 7, researchers often use some form of matching to increase the internal validity of the results. For instance, in studying the effects of patients' satisfaction with their experiences in hospitals, the patients in a hospital that is undergoing organizational change might be designated as the experimental group, while the patients in a hospital that is not undergoing organizational change might be designated as the control group. To form matched groups, a researcher might select a sample of individuals from the first hospital and determine their status on these demographics: medical condition, age, gender, and socioeconomic status. Then, the researcher could handpick participants from the other hospital who are similar in terms of the same demographics. Although this is better than using unmatched samples from both hospitals, there is still the danger that the two groups may not have been matched on all relevant variables. For instance, in this example, the researcher has not taken into account whether the patients have insurance or not. Those with insurance and those without insurance may be fundamentally different in their views of patient satisfaction. Obviously, assigning participants at random to the two conditions (using a true experimental design) would be vastly superior because the random assignment would assure the researcher that the two groups were initially the same on *all variables* except for random differences, whose effects can be assessed with inferential statistics. Inferential statistics is a topic that is considered in detail in Part G of this book.

Design 8, which is known as the **equivalent time-samples design**, has only one group (or possibly only one participant). Treatment conditions are alternated (preferably on a random basis), as indicated in the design by alternating X_1 (an experimental treatment) with X_o (a control condition or comparison treatment).

Design 8:

$$X_oO \quad X_1O \quad X_oO \quad X_1O$$

The participants in Design 8 are, in effect, serving as both the control participants (when they are receiving X_o) and the experimental participants (when they are receiving X_1). This is a major advantage because researchers know that the experimental participants and control participants (who are actually the same individuals) are identical in their genetic characteristics, income level, attitudes, and beliefs—in fact, in all ways—at the beginning of the experiment. A major disadvantage of this design is the strong possibility of *multiple-treatment interference*. In this case, the second time the participants receive X_1, they have already been exposed to and possibly changed by the earlier exposure to X_1.

Notice that giving the treatments repeatedly in Design 8 above strengthens internal validity because it is unlikely that the threats to internal validity are operating only at the times when X_1 is given but not when X_o is given. For instance, it is unlikely that participants mature only at X_1 and not at X_o. Similarly, it is unlikely that *history* confounds the

---

[1] Only the two most widely used quasi-experimental designs are presented in this topic. For a discussion of others, see Campbell, D. T., & Stanley, J. C. (1963). *Experimental and quasi-experimental designs for research*. Chicago, IL: Rand McNally.

interpretation by causing changes only when X_1 is given.

In psychology, a single-group design in which treatments are alternated is often called an ABAB design, where A and B indicate alternating treatments. Typically, when this design is used, there are multiple initial observations before any treatment is given. These initial observations constitute the **baseline**, which determines the typical variation in the behavior of participants over time before any intervention. For instance, perhaps a researcher plans to give rewards for in-seat behavior in a classroom to a hyperactive child. The researcher could measure the amount of out-of-seat behavior on a daily basis for a number of days to determine the natural amount of variation from day to day without treatment. Then, when the researcher introduces the rewards, any changes observed during treatment can be evaluated in terms of the natural variation before treatment. In other words, the researcher would ask: Is the decrease in out-of-seat behavior after treatment greater than the natural day-to-day decreases (and increases) observed during the baseline?

EXERCISE ON TOPIC 45

1. What is the name of the design diagrammed immediately below?

O X O

O   O

2. In the design shown in Question 1, what indicates that the participants were not assigned at random to the groups?

3. If a researcher uses matching to form the two groups in the design in Question 1, would the resulting experiment be superior to a true experiment?

4. What is a major advantage of the equivalent time-samples design?

5. What is a major disadvantage of the equivalent time-samples design?

6. In psychology, what is an ABAB design?

Question for Discussion

7. Suppose a researcher observed two classes for baseline data on calling-out behavior (i.e., calling out in class when it is inappropriate). In Class A, the researcher observed much variation in the amount of calling out from day to day. In Class B, there was little variation (i.e., there was about the same amount from one day to the next). In your opinion, for which class would it be desirable to have a longer baseline? Why?

For Students Planning Research

8. If you will be conducting an experiment, will you be using a quasi-experimental design? If yes, which one? Why are you using a quasi-experimental design instead of a true experimental one? (See Topic 41.)

In experimental research, a **confound** is a source of confusion regarding the explanation for a given difference. Suppose, for instance, a researcher gave an experimental group instruction in algebra using a new software program and, at the same time, a student teacher taught the same algebra skills to the participants using manipulative devices. Furthermore, suppose the control group received no algebra instruction. If the experimental group outperformed the control group, the results would be said to be confounded because there would be no way to sort out the relative influence of the software versus the manipulatives. Unfortunately, not all sources of confounding are as obvious as the one in this example.

An important source of confounding is the **Hawthorne Effect**, which can be thought of as the *attention effect*. This source was discovered in a series of industrial psychology studies at the Hawthorne Plant of Western Electric. In the studies, worker productivity went up when the lighting was increased. Oddly, however, when the lighting was decreased, productivity also went up. This was interpreted to mean that participants were responding to the attention they were receiving from the researchers (knowing they were being observed in an experiment) in addition to (or in spite of) the treatments with varying illumination. Thus, there were two intertwined explanations for the differences observed (i.e., the amount of illumination and the amount of attention participants received).

To control for the Hawthorne Effect, some researchers use three groups: (1) an experimental group, (2) a control group that receives attention, and (3) a control group that receives no special attention. For instance, an experimental group could be shown a film containing aggressive behaviors to determine whether students' aggressiveness on the playground increased after they saw the film. The attention control group could be shown a film with no aggression (thus, giving attention to this control group), while the no-attention control group could be shown no film. Comparing the aggressiveness of the three groups on a playground would yield information on how much attention contributed to any changes as well as how much the film with aggressive behaviors contributed.

A related confound is the **John Henry Effect**. This effect refers to the possibility that the control group might become aware of its "inferior" status

and respond by trying to outperform the experimental group. Thus, researchers should try to conceal the control group's knowledge of its status whenever possible. For ethical reasons, participants usually need to be informed that they will be participating in an experiment, but it is often sufficient to inform them that they may be in either the experimental or the control group, without revealing the group to which they were assigned.

Researchers who study the effectiveness of medications usually are concerned with the potentially confounding effects of the **placebo effect**. The placebo effect refers to the tendency of individuals to improve (or at least feel that they are improving) simply because they know they are being treated. Suppose, for instance, a new drug was given to a group of individuals suffering from a certain condition. Because of the placebo effect, some individuals might report that they feel better (or might have real improvement) even if the drug was totally ineffective.

To control for the placebo effect, researchers use a control group that is given a **placebo**. In drug studies, for instance, a placebo could be a pill that contains only inert ingredients (e.g., a sugar pill), which provides a treatment for the control group. Comparing the experimental group with a placebo-control group indicates how much more effective the new medication is than treatment with an inactive substance.

When administering a placebo, researchers say they are using a **blind** procedure when they do not disclose to the participants whether they are receiving an active or inactive substance. (For ethical reasons, participants are told that they will be receiving *either* an active or an inactive drug.) In a **double-blind** experiment, neither the participants nor the individual dispensing the drug know which is the active drug and which is the placebo. This is done to prevent the possibility that the individual dispensing the drug will subtly communicate to the participants their status as either control or experimental participants.[1] For instance, the packaging of the drug and placebo could be color-coded; the individual who is dispensing might know only that

---

[1] Note that those who dispense the drugs in these experiments might also subconsciously communicate their *expectations* (i.e., that those receiving the active drug will improve).

the blue package should be dispensed to a random half while the yellow package should be dispensed to the other half, without knowing which color package contains the active drug.

Demand characteristics can also be a source of confounding. A demand characteristic is a cue that lets participants know the expected outcome of an experiment. This can be a problem if participants attempt to please the experimenter by reporting or acting in a way they believe is expected. To the extent possible, researchers should try to conceal their expectations from the participants (i.e., the researchers' hypotheses).

EXERCISE ON TOPIC 46

1. A confound is a source of confusion regarding what?

2. What is the name of the effect that refers to the possibility that the control group might become aware of its "inferior" status and respond by trying to outperform the experimental group?

3. What is the formal name of what is characterized as the *attention effect* in this topic?

4. In addition to an experimental and a traditional control group (with no treatment), what other group can be used to control for the Hawthorne Effect?

5. The term *placebo effect* refers to what tendency?

6. In what type of experiment do neither the participants nor the individuals dispensing the drug know which is the active drug and which is the placebo?

7. A *demand characteristic* is a cue that lets participants know what?

Question for Discussion

8. If you were a participant in an experiment, did you try to guess what the researcher's hypothesis was? If yes, do you think that your guess(es) influenced your behavior in the experiment? Explain.

For Students Planning Research

9. If you will be conducting an experiment, will you be taking measures to try to prevent any of the potential sources of confounding discussed in this topic?

PART G

UNDERSTANDING STATISTICS

This part of the book begins by examining the differences between the two major branches of statistics: (1) *descriptive statistics*, which help to summarize and describe data that have been collected, and (2) *inferential statistics*, which help in making inferences from samples to the entire populations from which the samples were drawn. Then, the use of statistical techniques for analyzing the results of research are described.

Because this part of the book is designed to prepare readers to comprehend statistics reported in research reports, the emphasis is on understanding their meanings—not on computations.

Important Note

The topics in this part of the book are highly interrelated. Therefore, students are strongly advised to read them in the order in which they are presented.

NOTES

TOPIC 47 DESCRIPTIVE AND INFERENTIAL STATISTICS

Descriptive statistics summarize data so they can easily be comprehended. For instance, suppose a researcher administered a test to all 362 freshmen enrolled in a university. It would be difficult to see even the major trends in an unordered list of such a large number of scores. However, if the researcher prepares a **frequency distribution** such as the one in Table 1, he or she can easily see how the scores are distributed. For instance, the frequency distribution clearly indicates that a majority of the freshmen had scores from 14 through 16, with a scattering above and below these levels.

Table 1
Frequency Distribution with Percentages

Score (X)	Frequency (f)	Percentage
20	5	1.4
19	9	2.5
18	24	6.6
17	35	9.7
16	61	16.9
15	99	27.3
14	68	18.8
13	29	8.0
12	21	5.8
11	11	3.0
Totals	362	100.0%

The **frequencies** in Table 1 are descriptive statistics. They describe how many students earned each score. The **percentages** in the table are also descriptive. They describe how many students *per one hundred* had each score. For instance, 3.0% had a score of 11. This means that for each 100 freshmen, three of them have a score of 11. These and other descriptive statistics, such as averages, are described in this part of the book.

Now, suppose that in order to economize, a researcher sampled at random (by drawing names out of a hat) only 100 freshmen to be tested (instead of testing all 362). Would the researcher obtain exactly the same results that he or she would if the researcher tested all freshmen? The answer is, in all likelihood, *no*. As indicated in Topics 24 through 26, random sampling produces random errors that statisticians call *sampling errors*. The purpose of **inferential statistics** is to help researchers draw inferences about the effects of sampling errors on the results that are described with descriptive statistics. More specifically, inferential statistics help researchers to make generalizations about the char-acteristics of populations on the basis of data obtained by studying samples.

An inferential statistic widely reported in the mass media is a **margin of error**. When reporting the results of public opinion polls, for instance, reporters frequently cite margins of error to help readers interpret results in light of sampling error. Let us say that a recent poll indicated that approval of the president was at 45%, with a margin of error of ±2 (i.e., plus/minus 2) percentage points. This indicates that readers can be highly confident that the level of approval in the population is between 43% and 47% (i.e., within two points of the 45% observed in the sample).

An important family of inferential statistics consists of *significance tests*, which help researchers decide whether the differences in descriptive statistics they identify (such as differences in the reading achievement between samples of boys and girls) are reliable. In the next topic, the general purpose of significance testing is considered in more detail, and in later sections, three popular tests of significance are considered.

Because inferential statistics help researchers to evaluate results in light of sampling errors, it follows that if researchers do *not* sample, they do *not* need inferential statistics. For instance, if a researcher conducts a *census* (a study in which all members of a population are included), the descriptive statistics the researcher obtains (such as percentages) are values that are free of sampling errors. Because margins of error, for instance, are designed to help interpret results in light of sampling errors, and because there are no sampling errors in the results obtained in a census, margins of error are not needed to assist in interpreting the results.

Researchers distinguish between values obtained from a sample and values obtained from a census by using the terms **parameters** (for values from a census) and **statistics** (for values from studies in which samples were examined). Thus, statistical values are referred to as parameters when they are derived from a census, but they are classified as statistics when they are based on the results obtained from a sample. As a mnemonic device, remember the first letters shown here in italics:

Samples yield *Statistics*, and
Populations yield *Parameters*.

Exercise on Topic 47

1. Which branch of statistics ("inferential" *or* "descriptive") helps researchers to summarize data so they can be easily comprehended?

2. According to Table 1 in this topic, how many participants had a score of 19?

3. What is the name of the statistic that describes how many participants per 100 have a certain characteristic?

4. Which branch of statistics helps researchers to draw inferences about the effects of sampling errors on their results?

5. If a researcher tests a random sample instead of all members of a population, is it likely that the sample results will be the same as the results the researcher would have obtained by testing the population?

6. Is a margin of error a "descriptive" *or* an "inferential" statistic?

7. Are significance tests associated with "descriptive" *or* "inferential" statistics?

8. By studying populations, do researchers obtain "statistics" *or* "parameters"?

9. By studying samples, do researchers obtain "statistics" *or* "parameters"?

Question for Discussion

10. Try to locate a report of a poll in which a margin of error is reported. Copy it and bring it to class for discussion.

For Students Planning Research

11. Will you be reporting descriptive statistics? (Note that statistics often are not reported in qualitative research. See Topics 9 and 10.) Explain.

12. Will you be reporting inferential statistics? Explain.

TOPIC 48   INTRODUCTION TO THE NULL HYPOTHESIS

Suppose a researcher drew random samples of engineers and psychologists, administered a self-report measure of sociability, and computed the mean (the most commonly used average) for each group. Furthermore, suppose the mean for engineers was 65.00 and the mean for psychologists was 70.00. Where did the five-point difference come from? There are three possible explanations:

1. Perhaps the population of psychologists is truly more sociable than the population of engineers, and the samples correctly identified the difference. (In fact, the *research hypothesis* may have been that psychologists are more sociable than engineers, which now appears to be supported by the data the researcher collected.)

2. Perhaps there was a bias in procedures. By using random sampling, the researcher has ruled out sampling bias, but other procedures, such as measurement, may be biased. For instance, maybe the psychologists were contacted during December, when many social events take place, and the engineers were contacted during a gloomy February. The only way to rule out bias as an explanation for the difference between the two means is to take *physical steps* to prevent it. In this case, the researcher would want to make sure that the sociability of both groups was measured in the same way at the same time.

3. Perhaps the populations of psychologists and engineers are the same in their sociability, but the samples are unrepresentative of the populations because of random sampling errors. For instance, the random draw may have provided a sample of psychologists who are more sociable, on average, than their population purely by chance (at random).

The third explanation has a name: the **null hypothesis**. The general form in which it is stated varies from researcher to researcher. Here are three versions, all of which are consistent with each other:

Version A of the null hypothesis:

The observed difference was created by sampling error. (Note that the term *sampling error* refers only to *random errors*, not errors created by a bias. Note that there is no bias in sampling

in the example because the researcher sampled at random.)

Version B of the null hypothesis:

There is no true difference between the two groups. (The term *true difference* refers to the difference a researcher would find in a census of the two populations. That is, the *true difference* is the difference a researcher would find if there were no sampling errors.)

Version C of the null hypothesis:

The true difference between the two groups is zero.

Significance tests determine the probability that the null hypothesis is true. (The use of specific significance tests is covered in Topics 51–52 and 58–60.) Suppose the researcher in the example being considered conducted a significance test and found that the probability that the null hypothesis is a correct hypothesis is less than 5 in 100. This would be stated as $p < .05$, where p stands for the word *probability*. If the odds that something is true are less than 5 in 100, it seems likely that it is *not* true. Thus, the researcher would *reject the null hypothesis* and be left with only the first two explanations listed earlier in this topic.

There is no rule of nature that dictates at what probability level the null hypothesis should be rejected. However, conventional wisdom suggests that .05 or less (such as .01 or .001) is reasonable because they are low probabilities. Of course, researchers should state in their reports the probability level they used to determine whether to reject the null hypothesis.

Note that when researchers fail to reject the null hypothesis because the probability is greater than .05, they do just that: They fail to reject the null hypothesis, and it remains on the list of possible explanations for the difference. Note that it is *not* possible to accept the null hypothesis as the only explanation for a difference based on inferential statistics because there are three possible explanations for a difference. In other words, failing to reject one possible explanation (the null hypothesis) does *not* mean researchers are accepting it as the only explanation (because there are two additional explanations on the list).

An alternative way to say that a researcher has rejected the null hypothesis is to state that the difference is **statistically significant**. Thus, if a researcher states that a difference is statistically significant at the .05 level (meaning .05 or less), it is equivalent to stating that the null hypothesis has been rejected at that level.

In research reports in academic journals, the null hypothesis is seldom stated by researchers, who assume that readers know that the sole purpose of a significance test is to test the null hypothesis. In-stead, researchers report which differences were tested for significance, which significance test they used, and which differences were found to be statistically significant. It is more common to find null hypotheses stated in theses and dissertations because committee members may want to make sure the students they are supervising understand the reason they have conducted a significance test.

The most commonly used significance tests are described later in this part of the book.

EXERCISE ON TOPIC 48

1. How many explanations were there for the difference between psychologists and engineers in the example in this topic?

2. What does the null hypothesis say about sampling error?

3. Does the term *sampling error* refer to "random errors" *or* to "bias"?

4. The null hypothesis says the true difference equals what numerical value?

5. Significance tests are designed to determine the probabilities regarding the truth of what hypothesis?

6. The expression $p < .05$ stands for what words?

7. Do researchers reject the null hypothesis when the probability of its truth is "high" *or* when the probability is "low"?

8. What do researchers do if the probability is greater than .05?

9. What is an alternative way of saying a researcher has rejected the null hypothesis?

10. Are null hypotheses more likely to be explicitly stated in a "journal article" *or* in a "dissertation"?

Question for Discussion

11. All individuals use probabilities in everyday activities to make decisions. For instance, when deciding whether to cross a street with traffic, individuals estimate the odds, before beginning to cross, that they will get across the street safely. Briefly describe one other specific use of probabilities in everyday decision making.

For Students Planning Research

12. Will you be testing the null hypothesis in your research? Explain.

TOPIC 49 SCALES OF MEASUREMENT

There are four scales (or levels) at which researchers measure. The lowest level is the **nominal** level (also called the *nominal scale*). This may be thought of as the *naming* level. For instance, when researchers ask participants to name their marital status, participants will respond with *words*—not numbers—such as *married, single, divorced*, and so on. Notice that nominal data do not put participants in any particular mathematical order. There is no logical basis for saying that one category, such as *single*, is higher or lower mathematically than any other category.

The next level is **ordinal**. At this level, the measurements place participants in order from high to low. For instance, an employer might rank applicants for a job on their professional appearance. Traditionally, researchers give a rank of 1 to the participant who is highest, 2 to the next highest, and so on. It is important to note that ranks do not indicate the amount by which participants differ. If a researcher knows that Janet has a rank of 1 and Frank has a rank of 2, the researcher does not know if Janet's appearance is greatly superior to Frank's or only slightly superior. To measure the *amount* of difference among participants, researchers use the next two levels of measurement.

Measurements at the **interval** and **ratio** levels have equal distances among the scores they yield. For instance, when researchers say that Jill weighs 120 pounds and Sally weighs 130 pounds, they know by *how much* the two participants differ. Also, note that a 10-pound difference represents the same amount regardless of where participants are on the scale. For instance, the difference between 120 and 130 pounds is the same as the difference between 220 and 230 pounds.

The ratio scale is at a higher level than the interval scale because the ratio scale has an absolute zero point that researchers know how to measure. Thus, *weight* is an example of the ratio scale because it has an absolute zero.

The interval scale, while having equal intervals like the ratio scale, does not have an absolute zero. The most common examples of interval scales are scores obtained through the use of objective measures such as attitude scales and multiple-choice tests of achievement. For achievement tests, it is widely assumed that each multiple-choice test item measures a single point's worth of the trait being measured and that all points are equal to all other points, making it an interval scale (just as all pounds are equal to all other pounds of weight). However, such tests do not measure at the ratio level because the zero on such tests is arbitrary, not absolute. To see this, consider someone who gets a zero on a multiple-choice final examination. Does the zero mean that the student has absolutely no knowledge of or skills in the subject area? Probably not. He or she probably has some knowledge of simple facts, definitions, and concepts, but the test was not designed to measure at the low skill level at which the student is operating. Thus, a score of zero indicates only that the student knows nothing *on that test*, not that the student has zero knowledge of the content domain. Thus, the scores are at the interval level, not the ratio level.

Here is a summary of the levels:

Lowest Level	Scale	Characteristic
	Nominal	*naming*
	Ordinal	*ordering*
⬇	**Interval**	*equal interval without an absolute zero*
	Ratio	*equal interval with an absolute zero*
Highest Level		

For those who like to use mnemonics, remember this environmentally friendly phrase:

No Oil In Rivers

The first letters—**NOIR**—are the first letters of the scales in order from lowest to highest.

At which level should researchers measure? There is no simple answer. First, some variables are inherently nominal in nature. For instance, when researchers need to know participants' gender or state of residence, nominal data are the natural choice. Second, many novice researchers overuse the ordinal scale. For instance, if a researcher wants to measure reading ability, it would usually be much better to use a carefully constructed standardized test (which measures at the interval level) than to have teachers rank students in terms of their reading ability. Remember, measuring at the interval level provides more information than measuring at the ordinal level because the interval-level measurements indicate the amount by which participants differ. Thus, when possible, researchers prefer to measure at the interval or the ratio level instead of the ordinal level.

The choice between interval and ratio depends solely on whether it is possible to measure with an absolute zero. When it is possible, researchers usually do so. For the purposes of applied statistical analyses, however, interval and ratio data are treated in the same way.

The level at which researchers measure has important implications for data analysis, so there are references to scales of measurement throughout the discussion of statistics in subsequent topics in this part of the book.

EXERCISE ON TOPIC 49

1. If a researcher asks participants to name the country in which they were born, the researcher is using which scale of measurement?

2. Which two scales of measurement have equal distances among the scores they yield?

3. If a researcher assigns a teacher to rank students according to their oral-language skills, the researcher is using which scale of measurement?

4. Which scale of measurement has an absolute zero?

5. Which scale of measurement is at the lowest level?

6. Objective, multiple-choice achievement tests are usually assumed to measure at what level?

7. If a researcher measures in such a way that he or she finds out which participant is the most honest, which is the next most honest, and so on (without measuring to determine how much honesty each one has), the researcher is measuring with what scale of measurement?

8. The number of minutes of overtime work that employees perform is an example of which scale of measurement?

9. Weight measured in pounds is an example of which scale of measurement?

Question for Discussion

10. Name a trait that inherently lends itself to nominal measurement. Explain your answer.

For Students Planning Research

11. List the measures you will be using in your research, and name the scale of measurement for each one.

TOPIC 50 DESCRIPTIONS OF NOMINAL DATA

As indicated in the previous topic, researchers obtain *nominal data* when they classify participants according to names (words) instead of quantities. For instance, suppose a researcher asked each member of a population of 540 teachers which candidate he or she prefers for a school board vacancy and found that 258 preferred Smith and 282 preferred Jones. (Because Smith and Jones are names, the data are at the nominal level.) The 258 and 282 are *frequencies*, whose symbol is *f*. Researchers also may refer to them as **numbers of cases**, whose symbol is *N*.

The numbers of cases can be converted to *percentages* by dividing the number who prefer each candidate by the number in the population and multiplying by 100. Thus, for Smith, the calculations are:

$$258 \div 540 = 0.478 \times 100 = 47.8\%$$

When reporting percentages, it is desirable to also report the underlying numbers of cases, which is done in Table 1.

Table 1
Teachers' Preferences

Candidate	Percentage
Jones	52.2% (N = 282)
Smith	47.8% (N = 258)
Total	100.0% (N = 540)

Table 1 is an example of what is called a **univariate analysis**. The researcher is analyzing how participants *vary* (thus, researchers use the root *variate*) on only *one* variable (hence, researchers use the prefix *uni-*).

Researchers can examine a relationship between two nominal variables by conducting a **bivariate analysis**. Perhaps a researcher wants to know whether there is a relationship between teachers' genders and their preferences for candidates. Table 2 shows the results of a bivariate analysis of these variables.

The data in Table 2 clearly indicate that there is a relationship between gender and the preferences for the two candidates because a larger percentage of males than females prefers Jones, but a larger percentage of females than males prefers Smith. In general, teachers' genders are predictive of their preferences. For instance, by knowing a teacher is male, a researcher would predict that the teacher is more likely to vote for Jones than to vote for Smith.

Table 2
Teachers' Preferences by Gender

Gender	Jones	Smith	Total
Male	66.4% (N = 85)	33.6% (N = 43)	100.0% (N = 128)
Female	47.8% (N = 197)	52.2% (N = 215)	100.0% (N = 412)

Note that in this population of teachers, there are many more female teachers than male teachers. When this is the case, examining only the numbers of cases (e.g., 85 males for Jones versus 197 females for Jones) can be misleading. For instance, in Table 2, a *majority* of the population of males (the smaller population) is in favor of Jones, but only a *minority* of the larger population of females is in favor of him. With percentages, legitimate comparisons of groups of unequal size are possible. This is because percentages convert numbers of cases to a common scale, with a base of 100. (The percentage of 66.4% of males for Jones indicates that *for every 100 males*, 66.4 of them are in favor of Jones, while the percentage of 47.8% of females for Jones indicates that *for every 100 females*, only 47.8 of them are in favor of Jones.)

In academic writing, some researchers report **proportions** instead of *percentages*. For instance, a percentage of 47.8% in favor of Smith in Table 1 corresponds to a proportion of 0.478 or 0.48. (Proportions are calculated in the same way percentages are except that the multiplication by 100 is not performed. For instance, $258 \div 540 = 0.478 = 0.48$.) Because a proportion has a base of 1, a proportion of 0.48 means that for every *one* participant, 48 hundredths of each participant favors Smith. Clearly, proportions are more difficult to comprehend than percentages. When consumers of research encounter proportions in reports, it is a good idea to convert them mentally to percentages. That is, think of the proportion of 0.48 as 48% (i.e., the percentage obtained by multiplying 0.48 by 100).

In the next topic, a method for analyzing univariate nominal data in studies in which researchers have sampled at random and need to take account of random sampling errors is considered. In Topic

52, the analysis of bivariate nominal data in light of sampling errors is described.

Note that researchers use an uppercase N when they study an entire population, as in the example in this topic. They use a lowercase n when they study only a sample, as in the example in the next topic.

Exercise on Topic 50

1. If 600 individuals in a population of 1,000 are Democrats, what is the corresponding percentage of Democrats?

2. When reporting a percentage, is it a good idea to also report the underlying number of cases?

3. Do researchers use "univariate" *or* "bivariate" analyses to examine relationships between two nominal variables?

4. Percentages for different groups are expressed on a common scale with what base?

5. What is the base for a proportion?

6. Are "percentages" *or* "proportions" easier for most individuals to comprehend?

7. When consumers of research encounter proportions in research reports, it is a good idea to do what?

Question for Discussion

8. Try to locate a report in the popular press in which percentages are reported. Bring a copy to class. Be prepared to discuss whether the frequencies are also reported and whether the analysis is univariate *or* bivariate.

For Students Planning Research

9. Will you be measuring one or more variables at the nominal level? Explain.

10. Will you be reporting percentages?

11. Will you do a univariate analysis? A bivariate analysis? Explain.

TOPIC 51   INTRODUCTION TO THE CHI-SQUARE TEST

Suppose a researcher drew at random a sample of 200 members of an association of sociologists and asked them whether they were in favor of a proposed change to their bylaws. The results are shown in Table 1. Note that these *observed results* are not necessarily the *true results*[1] that the researcher would have obtained if he or she had questioned the entire population. Remember that the null hypothesis (see Topic 48) asserts that any observed difference was created by random sampling errors (i.e., in the population, the true difference is zero). Put another way, the null hypothesis states that the observed difference ($n = 120$ vs. $n = 80$) is an *illusion* created by random errors created by random sampling (i.e., created by sampling errors).

Table 1
Members' Approval of a Change in Bylaws

Response	Percentage
Yes	60.0% ($n = 120$)
No	40.0% ($n = 80$)
Total	100.0% ($n = 200$)

The usual test of the null hypothesis for differences between frequencies (i.e., number of cases or *n*) is **chi-square**, whose symbol is:

$$\chi^2$$

After some computations for the data in Table 1 (which are beyond the scope of this book), the results are:

$$\chi^2 = 4.00, df = 1, p < .05$$

What does this mean for a consumer of research who sees this in a report? The values of chi-square and **degrees of freedom** (*df*) were calculated solely to obtain the probability that the null hypothesis is correct. In other words, chi-square and degrees of freedom are *not* descriptive statistics that a typical consumer of research should attempt to interpret. Rather, they should be thought of as substeps in the mathematical procedure for obtaining the value of

---

[1] The term *true results* stands for the results that would be obtained by conducting a census of the entire population. The results of a census are *true* in the sense that they are free of *sampling errors*.

p. Thus, a consumer of research should concentrate on the fact that *p* is *less than* .05. As indicated in Topic 48, when the probability (*p*) that the null hypothesis is correct is .05 or less, researchers reject the null hypothesis. (Remember, when the probability that something is true is less than 5 in 100, which is a low probability, conventional wisdom suggests it should be rejected.) Thus, the difference observed in Table 1 was probably not created by random sampling errors. Therefore, a researcher can say that the difference is *statistically significant* at the .05 level.

At this point, the conclusion has been reached that the difference observed in the sample was *probably not* created by sampling errors. So where did the difference come from? These two possibilities remain:

1. Perhaps there was a bias in procedures, such as the interviewer leading the respondents by talking enthusiastically about the proposed change in the bylaws. Thus, the sample would no longer be representative of the population because the interviewer biased the respondents.

    If consumers of research are convinced that adequate measures were taken to prevent procedural bias, they are left with only the next possibility as a viable explanation.

2. Perhaps the *population* of sociologists is, in fact, in favor of the proposed change, and this fact has been correctly identified by studying the random sample.

Now, consider some results from a survey in which the null hypothesis was *not* rejected. Table 2 shows the numbers and percentages of participants in a random sample from a population of teachers who prefer one of three methods for teaching reading.

Table 2
Teachers' Preferences for Methods

Method A	Method B	Method C
$n = 30$	$n = 27$	$n = 22$
(37.97%)	(34.18%)	(27.85%)

In Table 2, there are three differences: (1) 30 preferring A versus 27 preferring B, (2) 30 preferring A versus 22 preferring C, and (3) 27 preferring B versus 22 preferring C. The null hypothesis states that this *set of three differences* was created by random sampling errors. In other words, it says that there is no true difference in the population—that a difference has been observed only because of sampling errors. The results of the chi-square test for the data in Table 2 are as follows:

$$\chi^2 = 1.241, df = 2, p > .05$$

Note that *p* is *greater than* (>) .05. According to the decision rule that *p* must be equal to or less than .05 for the rejection of the null hypothesis, the null hypothesis should *not* be rejected (i.e., fail to reject), which is called a *statistically insignificant* result. In other words, the null hypothesis must remain on the

list as a viable explanation for the set of differences observed by studying a sample. Put another way, the probability that sampling error created the difference is too great for it to be rejected as a possible explanation for the differences.

In this topic, the use of chi-square in a *univariate analysis*, in which each participant is classified in only one way (such as which candidate each prefers), has been considered. In the next topic, the use of chi-square in a *bivariate analysis* (in which each participant is classified in two ways, such as which candidate each prefers *and* the gender of each) is considered.

EXERCISE ON TOPIC 51

1. When researchers study a sample, are the results called the "true results" *or* the "observed results"?

2. According to the null hypothesis, what created the difference in Table 1?

3. What is the name of the test of the null hypothesis used in this topic?

4. According to this topic, should the typical consumer try to interpret the value of *df*?

5. What is the symbol for *probability*?

6. If a researcher found that a chi-square test of a difference yielded a *p* of less than 5 in 100, on the basis of conventional wisdom, what should the researcher conclude about the null hypothesis?

7. Does "*p* < .05" *or* "*p* > .05" usually lead a researcher to declare a difference statistically significant?

8. If a researcher fails to reject a null hypothesis, is the difference in question statistically significant?

9. If a researcher has a statistically significant result, should the null hypothesis remain on the list of viable explanations for an observed difference?

Question for Discussion

10. Briefly describe a hypothetical study in which it would be appropriate to conduct a chi-square test for univariate data.

For Students Planning Research

11. Will you be conducting a univariate chi-square test in your research? Explain.

TOPIC 52 A CLOSER LOOK AT THE CHI-SQUARE TEST

This topic concerns the use of the chi-square test in a *bivariate analysis* (i.e., an analysis in which each participant is classified in terms of two variables in order to examine the relationship between them). Consider an example. Suppose a researcher conducted an experiment in which three methods of job training were tried with welfare recipients. Random samples of recipients were drawn for each method, and the number who obtained jobs by the end of the training sessions was determined. The resulting data are shown in Table 1.

Table 1
Training Methods and Job Placement

Job?	Method A	Method B	Method C
Yes	$n = 20$	$n = 15$	$n = 9$
	(66.7%)	(51.7%)	(31.0%)
No	$n = 10$	$n = 14$	$n = 20$
	(33.3%)	(48.3%)	(69.0%)

Clearly, the statistics in Table 1 suggest there is a relationship between the method of job training and whether or not participants got jobs. Specifically, the researcher has observed that Method A is superior to Methods B and C, and that Method B is superior to Method C. A stumbling block in the interpretation of these results is the *null hypothesis*, which states there is no true difference (i.e., if all members of the population had been studied, the researcher would have found no differences among the three methods). For instance, quite by luck of the random draw, recipients who were more employable to begin with (before treatment) were assigned to Method A, while the less employable were assigned by chance to the other two methods. A researcher can test this null hypothesis by using the chi-square test.

For the data shown in Table 1 above, this result would be shown in a report on the experiment:

$$\chi^2 = 7.54, df = 2, p < .05$$

As indicated in previous topics in this part of the book, the null hypothesis is rejected when the odds that it is true are equal to or less than .05 (i.e., $p < .05$). Thus, for these data, the researcher should reject the null hypothesis and declare the result to be significant at the .05 level. In other words, the researcher should conclude that the observed differences are too great to be attributed to random errors (i.e., sampling errors). Thus, it is unlikely that the observed relationship is merely a result of random sampling errors.

Now consider more carefully what is meant by the term "the .05 level." When a researcher rejects the null hypothesis at exactly the .05 level (i.e., $p = .05$), there are 5 chances in 100 that the null hypothesis is correct. Thus, the researcher is taking 5 chances in 100 of being *wrong* by rejecting the null hypothesis at this level. Note that a researcher can never be certain that he or she has made the correct decision when rejecting the null hypothesis. It is always possible that the null hypothesis is true (in this case, there are 5 in 100 chances that it is true). The possibility that a null hypothesis is rejected when it is, in fact, a correct hypothesis is called a **Type I Error**. When researchers use the .05 level, the odds of making a Type I Error are 5 in 100; when they use the .01 level, the odds of making this type of error are 1 in 100; and when they use the .001 level, the odds of making it are 1 in 1,000.

When researchers fail to reject the null hypothesis, as in Topic 51 for the data in Table 2, they are also taking a chance of making an incorrect decision. That is, perhaps the null hypothesis should have been rejected, but the significance test failed to lead the researchers to the correct decision. This mistake is called a **Type II Error**.

In review, these are the two types of errors that researchers can make:

Type I Error: Rejecting the null hypothesis when it is in fact a correct hypothesis.

Type II Error: Failing to reject the null hypothesis when it is in fact an incorrect hypothesis.

At first, this discussion of errors may make significance tests such as chi-square seem weak because a researcher can be wrong regardless of the decision made. However, the usefulness is clear in light of the full context. Specifically, once one has decided to sample at random (the desirable way to sample because it is free from bias), it is likely that random error will affect the results—at least to some extent. In light of this, researchers can never be *certain* about decisions based on the observed differences. Instead, researchers must use *probabilities* to make decisions. Researchers use probabilities in such a way as to *minimize* the probabilities that erroneous decisions are being made. To do this, researchers usually emphasize minimizing the probability of a Type I Error by using a low probability such as .05 or less. By using a low probability, researchers will infrequently be in error when rejecting the null hypothesis.

EXERCISE ON TOPIC 52

1. Which type of analysis classifies participants in terms of two variables in order to examine the relationship between the two variables?

2. What decision should researchers make about the null hypothesis if a chi-square test leads to the conclusion that the observed differences are unlikely to be due to random errors?

3. If $p = .05$ for a chi-square test, chances are how many in 100 that the null hypothesis is true?

4. When a researcher uses the .01 level, what are the odds of making a Type I Error?

5. What is the name of the error researchers make when they fail to reject the null hypothesis when, in fact, it is an incorrect hypothesis?

6. What is the name of the error researchers make when they reject the null hypothesis when, in fact, it is a correct hypothesis?

7. Why is random sampling desirable even though it creates errors?

Questions for Discussion

8. Are both variables in Table 1 nominal? Explain.

9. Briefly describe a hypothetical study in which it would be appropriate to conduct a chi-square test on bivariate data.

For Students Planning Research

10. Will you be using a chi-square test in a bivariate analysis? Explain.

TOPIC 53 SHAPES OF DISTRIBUTIONS

One way to describe quantitative data is to prepare a *frequency distribution* such as the one shown in Topic 47. It is easier to see the shape of a distribution if the data in a frequency distribution are used to construct a figure called a **frequency polygon**. Figure 1 is a frequency polygon for the data in Topic 47.

Figure 1. Frequency polygon for data on page 113.

A frequency polygon is easy to read. For instance, a score of 20 has a frequency (*f*) of 5, which is why the curve is low at a score of 20. A score of 15 has a frequency of 99, which is why the curve is high at 15.

Notice that the curve in Figure 1 above is fairly symmetrical, with a high point in the middle and a drop off on the right and left. When very large samples are used, the curve often takes on an even smoother shape, such as the one shown in Figure 2.

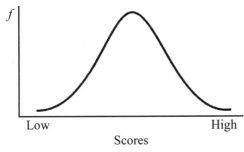

Figure 2. The normal curve.

The smooth, bell-shaped curve in Figure 2 above has a special name: the **normal curve**. Many variables in nature are normally distributed, such as the weights of grains of sand on a beach, the heights of women (or men), the annual amounts of rainfall in most areas, and so on. The list is almost limitless.

Many social and behavioral scientists also believe that mental traits of humans are also normally distributed.[1]

Some distributions are **skewed** (i.e., they have a tail on one side and not the other). Figure 3 shows a distribution that is *skewed to the right* (i.e., the tail is to the right), which is called a **positive skew**. An example of a distribution with a positive skew is income. Most individuals earn relatively small amounts, so the curve is high on the left. Small numbers of rich and very rich individuals create a tail to the right.

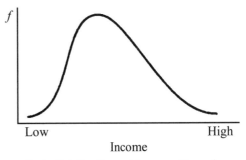

Figure 3. A distribution with a positive skew.

Figure 4 is *skewed to the left*; it has a **negative skew**. A researcher would get a negative skew, for instance, if he or she administered a test of basic math skills to a large sample of college seniors. Almost all would do very well and get almost perfect scores, but a small scattering would get lower scores for a variety of reasons, such as misunderstanding the directions for marking their answers, not feeling well the day the test was administered, and so on.

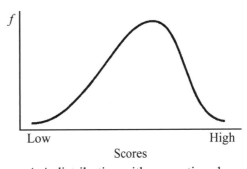

Figure 4. A distribution with a negative skew.

---

[1] Because measures of mental traits are far from perfect, it is not possible to show conclusively that mental traits are normally distributed.

While there are other shapes, the three shown here are the most common. Whether a distribution is normal (or close to normal) or skewed affects how quantitative data at the interval and ratio levels are analyzed (see Topic 49). This issue is considered in the next topic.

To make the proper associations with the names *positive skew* and *negative skew*, consider a number line on which zero is in the middle. The negative values are to the left of zero. Thus, when the tail of a curve points to the left, researchers say it has a *negative skew*. Because the positive values on a number line are to the right, when the tail points to the right, researchers say the curve has a *positive skew*. Sometimes, researchers merely say "skewed to the left" to indicate a negative skew and "skewed to the right" to indicate a positive skew.

EXERCISE ON TOPIC 53

1. According to Figure 1, about how many participants had a score of 16?

2. In Figure 1, are the frequencies on the "vertical" *or* the "horizontal" axis?

3. What is the name of the curve that is symmetrical?

4. If a distribution has some extreme scores on the right (but not on the left), it is said to have what type of skew?

5. If a distribution is skewed to the left, does it have a "positive" *or* a "negative" skew?

6. In most populations, income has what type of skew?

7. Does a distribution with a tail to the right have a "positive" *or* a "negative" skew?

Question for Discussion

8. Name a population and a variable you think might have a positive skew.

For Students Planning Research

9. Do you anticipate that any of your distributions will be highly skewed? Explain.

Topic 54   The Mean, Median, and Mode

The most frequently used average is the **mean**, which is the *balance point* in a distribution. Its computation is simple: Add up the scores and then divide by the number of scores. The most common symbols for the mean in academic journals are M (for the mean of a population) and m (for the mean of a sample). The symbol preferred by statisticians is:

$\overline{X}$, which is pronounced "X-bar."

Consider the formal definition of the mean: It is *the value around which the deviations sum to zero*. This definition is illustrated in Table 1, in which the mean of the scores is 4.0. When the mean is subtracted from each of the other scores, the *deviations* (whose symbol is lowercase x) are obtained. Notice that the sum of the deviations equals zero, as shown in the last column of Table 1.

Table 1
Scores and Deviation Scores

X	minus	M	equals	x
1	–	4.0	=	–3.0
1	–	4.0	=	–3.0
1	–	4.0	=	–3.0
2	–	4.0	=	–2.0
2	–	4.0	=	–2.0
4	–	4.0	=	0.0
6	–	4.0	=	2.0
7	–	4.0	=	3.0
8	–	4.0	=	4.0
8	–	4.0	=	4.0
Sum of the deviations (x) = 0.0				

Note that for *any set of scores*, if the steps in Table 1 are followed, the sum of the deviations will equal zero.[1] In other words, the mean always has this defining characteristic. If the deviations do not sum to zero, the statistic is not the mean (or a mistake was made in the computation of the mean).

Considering the formal definition, it is possible to see why the mean is also informally defined as the *balance point* in a distribution. This is because the positive and negative deviations *balance* each other out, causing the deviations to balance out to zero.

A major drawback of the mean is that it is drawn in the direction of extreme scores (i.e., in the direc-

tion of the skew). Consider the following two sets of scores and their means.

Scores for Group A: 1, 1, 1, 2, 3, 6, 7, 8, 8
$M = 4.11$

Scores for Group B: 1, 2, 2, 3, 4, 7, 9, 25, 32
$M = 9.44$

Notice that there are nine scores in both sets of scores, and the two distributions are very similar except for the scores of 25 and 32 in Group B, which are much higher than the others and thus create a skewed distribution. (To review skewed distributions, see Topic 53.) Also, notice that the two very high scores (25 and 32) have greatly pulled up the mean for Group B. In fact, the mean for Group B is more than twice as high as the mean for Group A just because of the two high scores. Because seven of the nine scores for Group B are 9 or less, a mean of 9.44 is not a good descriptor of the typical or center score.

While the mean is the most frequently used average, when a distribution is highly skewed, researchers use a different average: the **median**. The median is defined as the *middle score*. To get an *approximate median*, put the scores in order from low to high as they are for Groups A and B (from low on the left to high on the right), and then count to the middle. Because there are nine scores in Group A, the median (middle score) is 3 (five scores up from the bottom score of 1). For Group B, the median (middle score) is 4 (also five scores up from the bottom score of 1). For Group B, an average of 4 is more representative of the center of this skewed distribution than the mean, which is 9.44. Thus, an important use of the median is to describe the averages of skewed distributions. Another use is to describe the average of ordinal data, which will be explored in Topic 56.

A third average, the **mode**, is the *most frequently occurring score*. For Group B, there are more scores of 2 (i.e., two 2s) than any other score. Thus, 2 is the mode. The mode is sometimes used in informal reporting but is very seldom reported in formal reports of research. Note that the mode does not always have a unique value. For instance, if one individual with a score of 3 joined Group B, there would be two modes: (1) 2 because there are two 2s and (2) 3 because there would also be two 3s. Note that the mean and median, unlike the mode, always

---

[1] It might be slightly off from zero if a rounded mean such as 20.33 is used instead of its precise value, 20.3333333333.

have just one value for a given set of scores (i.e., they have unique values).

Because there is more than one type of average, it is vague to make a statement such as, "The *average* is 4.11." Instead, researchers indicate the specific type of average being reported with statements such as, "The *mean* is 4.11."

A synonym for the term **averages** is **measures of central tendency**. Although this term is seldom used in reports of scientific research, it is often used in research and statistics textbooks when averages are discussed.

EXERCISE ON TOPIC 54

1. Which average is defined as the *most frequently occurring score*?

2. Which average is defined as the *balance point* in a distribution?

3. Which average is defined as the *middle score*?

4. What is the formal definition of the mean?

5. How is the mean calculated?

6. Should the mean be used for highly skewed distributions?

7. Should the median be used for highly skewed distributions?

8. Which one of the three averages is very seldom used in formal reports of research?

9. What is a synonym for the term *averages*?

Question for Discussion

10. Suppose a fellow student gave a report in class and said, "The average is 25.88." For what additional information should you ask? Why?

For Students Planning Research

11. Do you anticipate calculating measures of central tendency? If so, name the one(s) you expect to report. Explain your choice(s).

TOPIC 55   THE MEAN AND STANDARD DEVIATION

Often, a set of scores is described with only two statistics: the **mean** to describe its *average* and the **standard deviation** (whose symbol is *S* or *SD* for a population, and *s* or *sd* for a sample) to describe its *variability*. The term **variability** refers to the amount by which participants *vary* or differ from each other. Consider what this means by considering the scores of three groups, all of which have the same mean but different standard deviations.

Group A: 0, 5, 10, 15, 20, 25, 30
$M = 15.00, S = 10.00$

Group B: 14, 14, 14, 15, 16, 16, 16
$M = 15.00, S = 0.93$

Group C: 15, 15, 15, 15, 15, 15, 15
$M = 15.00, S = 0.00$

Although Groups A, B, and C are the same on average, as indicated by the mean, they are very different in terms of variability. Notice that the differences among the scores of Group A (a score of 0 vs. a score of 5 vs. a score of 10 vs. a score of 15, and so on) are much greater than the differences among the scores of Group B (a score of 14 vs. a score of 14 vs. a score of 14 vs. a score of 15, and so on). At the extreme, when all the scores are the same, as in Group C, there is no variability. As a result, the standard deviation equals zero. Thus, as a rule, the smaller the variability is, the smaller the standard deviation is.[1]

The standard deviation has a special relationship to the normal curve (see Topic 53). *If a distribution is normal, 68% of the participants in the distribution lie within one standard-deviation unit of the mean.*[2] For example, if a consumer of research reads in a report that $M = 70$ and $S = 10$ for a normal distribution, the consumer would know that 68% of the participants have scores between 60 and 80 (i.e., $70 - 10 = 60$ and $70 + 10 = 80$). This is illustrated in Figure 1.

In Figure 2, the mean is also 70, but the standard deviation is only 5. The smaller standard deviation in Figure 2 is reflected by the fact that the curve is narrower than in Figure 1. Yet in both distributions,

68% of the cases lie within one standard deviation unit of the mean because they are both normal.

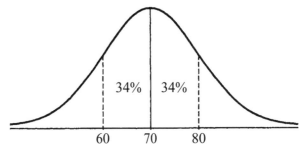

Figure 1. Normal curve with a mean of 70 and a standard deviation of 10.

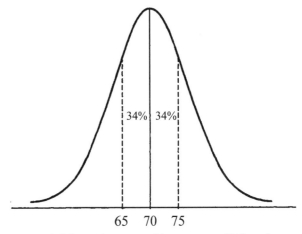

Figure 2. Normal curve with a mean of 70 and a standard deviation of 5.

Note that the middle area of Figure 2 is narrower *but taller* than the middle area of Figure 1. This additional height in Figure 2 makes it possible for it to have the same percentage (68%) of cases that the middle area of Figure 1 has.

At first, it may seem contradictory that, regardless of the value of the standard deviation, 68% of the cases lie within one standard-deviation unit of the mean in a normal curve. Actually, it is not a contradiction but a property of the normal curve. When a researcher is calculating the standard deviation, he or she is actually calculating the number of points that one must go out from the mean to capture 68% of the cases.

Note that the 68% rule of thumb does *not* strictly apply if the distribution is *not* normal. The less normal it is, the less accurate the rule is. Put another way, if the middle area of a distribution does not

---

[1] The computation of the standard deviation is illustrated in Appendix D. Considering the method of computation provides a more precise indication of its meaning.

[2] Note that *within* means on *both sides of the mean* (i.e., the mean plus/minus the standard deviation).

contain approximately 68% of the cases, the distribution is not normal.

Note that the normal curve (see Topic 53) is not an invention of statisticians. Instead, it is a curve that has been observed with great frequency in nature. Statisticians derived the standard deviation in order to have a standardized method for describing the variability of normal distributions.

EXERCISE ON TOPIC 55

1. Which average is usually reported when the standard deviation is reported?

2. What is meant by the term *variability*?

3. Is it possible for two groups to have the same mean but different standard deviations?

4. If all individuals in a group have the same score, what is the value of the standard deviation for the scores?

5. What percentage of the participants lies within one standard-deviation unit of the mean (i.e., on both sides of the mean) in a normal distribution?

6. The middle 68% of the participants in a normal distribution have scores between what two values if the mean equals 100 and the standard deviation equals 15?

7. If the mean of a normal distribution equals 50 and the standard deviation equals 5, what percentage of the participants have scores between 45 and 50?

8. Does the 68% rule strictly apply if a distribution is *not* normal?

9. If the standard deviation for Group X is 14.55 and the standard deviation for Group Y is 20.99, which group has less variability in its scores?

10. Refer to Question 9. Does "Group X" *or* "Group Y" have a narrower curve?

Question for Discussion

11. Locate a journal article in which the researcher reports a mean and standard deviation. Does the researcher indicate whether the underlying distribution being described is normal in shape? Do you think the 68% rule strictly applies? Explain.

For Students Planning Research

12. Will you be reporting means and standard deviations? Explain.

TOPIC 56 THE MEDIAN AND INTERQUARTILE RANGE

As indicated in Topic 54, the **median** is the *middle score* in a distribution. Being in the middle, it always has 50% of the scores above it and 50% of the scores below it. For the scores in Figure 1, the median is 6.5 (halfway between the middle two scores of 6 and 7).

1, 1, 1, 2, 3, 4, 5, 6, 7, 8, 8, 9, 10, 11, 11, 12

⇧

6.5

Figure 1. Scores for Group A and their median.

The median is used instead of the mean when a distribution is highly skewed (see Topic 53). It also is used to describe the average when the data are *ordinal* (i.e., data that put participants in *order* from high to low but do not have equal intervals among them; see Topic 49).[1]

When the **median** is reported as the average, it is customary to report the **range** or **interquartile range** as a measure of variability. As indicated in Topic 55, *variability* refers to the amount by which participants *vary* or differ from each other.

The *range* is simply the highest score minus the lowest score. For the scores shown above, it is 12 – 1 = 11. Thus, the range is 11, or a researcher might state that the scores *range from 1 to 12*. For reasons that are beyond the scope of this discussion, measurement theory indicates that the more extreme the score, the more unreliable it is. In other words, the more extreme the score is, the more likely that it has errors in it. (This is true in the natural sciences as well as the social and behavioral sciences.) Because the range is based on the two most extreme scores, it is an unreliable statistic. To get around this problem, researchers often use a modified version of the range, which is called the *interquartile range*. Because *inter-* means *between* and *-quartile* refers to *quarters*, *interquartile range* refers to the *range between quarters*. Specifically, it is the range of the middle two quarters. To calculate it, first divide the distribution into quarters, as shown in Figure 2 (e.g., the first quarter consists of scores 1, 1,

1, and 2). Thus, the middle 50% of the participants are between the values of 2.5 and 9.5. Because the formal definition of the *interquartile range (IQR)* is the *range of the middle 50% of the participants*, it is calculated as follows: 9.5 – 2.5 = 7.0. Thus, *IQR* = 7.0.[2]

1, 1, 1, 2, 3, 4, 5, 6, 7, 8, 8, 9, 10, 11, 11, 12

⇧   ⇧   ⇧

2.5   6.5   9.5

Figure 2. Scores for Group A divided into quarters.

To see how the *IQR* helps to describe the variability in sets of data, compare Figure 2 above (for Group A) with Figure 3 (for Group B). In Figure 3, the median is 43.0 and the interquartile range is 71.0 (i.e., 83.5 – 12.5 = 71.0). The larger interquartile range for Group B indicates greater variability.

0, 5, 7, 10, 15, 22, 30, 41, 45, 57, 67, 78, 89, 92, 95, 99

⇧   ⇧   ⇧

12.5   43.0   83.5

Figure 3. Scores for Group B divided into quarters.

Thus, for Groups A and B, the findings might be presented in a research report as illustrated in Table 1.

Table 1
Medians and Interquartile Range for Two Groups

Group	Median	Interquartile Range
A	6.5	7.0
B	43.0	71.0

Table 1 indicates two things. First, Group A has a lower average than Group B (as indicated by the median of 6.5 for Group A vs. the median of 43.0 for Group B). Second, Group A has less variability (as indicated by an interquartile range of 7.0 for Group A vs. 71.0 for Group B). Consideration of the scores shown in Figures 2 and 3 indicates that these results make sense. The middle score for Group A is much lower than the middle score for

---

[1] It is inappropriate to use the *mean* to describe ordinal data because the mean is the point around which the differences sum to zero. If the differences are unequal in size (as they are with ordinal data), it makes no sense to use a statistic based on the values of the differences. See Topics 49 and 54.

[2] Some researchers report the value of the *semi-interquartile range*. Because *semi-* means *half*, the semi-interquartile range is half of the interquartile range. In this example, the semi-interquartile range for Group A equals half of 7.0 (i.e., 7.0/2 = 3.5).

Group B, and the differences among the scores for Group A (1 vs. 1 vs. 1 vs. 2 vs. 3, etc.) are much smaller than the differences among the scores for Group B (0 vs. 5 vs. 7 vs. 10 vs. 15, etc.), indicating less variability in Group A than Group B.

In summary, the median describes the average (i.e., the central tendency) of a set of scores, while the interquartile range describes their variability. When the median is reported as the average (or measure of central tendency), it is customary to report the interquartile range as the measure of variability.

EXERCISE ON TOPIC 56

1. If the median for a group of participants is 25.00, what percentage of the participants has scores above a score of 25.00?

2. Should the "mean" *or* the "median" be used with ordinal data?

3. How is the range of a set of scores calculated?

4. Is the "range" *or* the "interquartile range" a more reliable statistic?

5. The *interquartile range* is the range of what?

6. Suppose a researcher reported that for Group X, the median equals 55.1 and the *IQR* equals 30.0, while for Group Y, the median equals 62.9 and the *IQR* equals 25.0. Which group has the higher average score?

7. On the basis of the information in Question 6, the scores for which group are more variable?

8. Which statistics discussed in this topic are measures of variability?

9. Which two statistics mentioned in this topic are averages (i.e., measures of central tendency)?

10. When the median is reported as the measure of central tendency, it is customary to report which measure of variability?

Question for Discussion

11. Name two circumstances under which the median is preferable to the mean.

For Students Planning Research

12. Do you anticipate reporting medians and interquartile ranges? Explain.

TOPIC 57   THE PEARSON CORRELATION COEFFICIENT

When researchers want to examine the relationship between two quantitative sets of scores (at the interval or ratio levels; see Topic 49), they compute a correlation coefficient. The most widely used coefficient is the **Pearson product-moment correlation coefficient**, whose symbol is r (usually called the **Pearson r**).

Consider the scores in Table 1. Note that the employment test scores put participants in *roughly* the same order as the ratings by supervisors. In other words, those who have high employment test scores (e.g., Joe and Jane) have high supervisors' ratings, *and* those who have low test scores (e.g., Jake and John) have low supervisors' ratings. This illustrates what is meant by a **direct relationship** (also called a **positive relationship**).

Table 1
Direct Relationship; r = .89

Employee	Employment Test Scores	Supervisors' Ratings
Joe	35	9
Jane	32	10
Bob	29	8
June	27	8
Leslie	25	7
Homer	22	8
Milly	21	6
Jake	18	4
John	15	5

Notice that the relationship in Table 1 is not perfect. For instance, although Joe has a higher employment test score than Jane, Jane has a higher supervisors' rating than Joe. If the relationship were perfect, the value of the Pearson r would be 1.00. Being less than perfect, its actual value is .89. As indicated in Figure 1, this value indicates a strong, direct relationship.

In an **inverse relationship** (also called a **negative relationship**), those who are high on one variable are low on the other. Such a relationship exists between the two sets of scores in Table 2. Individu-

als who are high on self-concept (such as Joe and Jane) are low on depression, while those who are low on self-concept (such as Jake and John) are high on depression. However, the relationship is not perfect. The value of the Pearson r for the relationship in Table 2 is –.85.

Table 2
Inverse Relationship; r = –.85

Employee	Self-Concept Scores	Depression Scores
Joe	10	2
Jane	8	1
Bob	9	0
June	7	5
Leslie	7	6
Homer	6	8
Milly	4	8
Jake	1	9
John	0	9

The relationships in Tables 1 and 2 are strong because they are near 1.00 and –1.00, but in each case there are exceptions, which make the Pearson rs less than 1.00 and less than –1.00. As the number and size of the exceptions increase, the values of the Pearson r become closer to 0.00. A value of 0.00 indicates the complete absence of a relationship. (See Figure 1.)

It is important to note that a Pearson r is *not* a proportion and *cannot* be multiplied by 100 to get a percentage. For instance, a Pearson r of .50 does not correspond to 50% of any characteristic of the data. To represent correlation in terms of percentages, values of Pearson r need to be converted to another statistic called the **coefficient of determination**, whose symbol is r^2, which indicates how to compute it: Simply square r. Thus, for an r of .50, r^2 equals .25. Multiplying .25 by 100% gives a result of 25%. What does this mean? Simply this: A Pearson r of .50 is 25% better than a Pearson r of 0.00. Table 3 shows selected values of r, r^2, and the corresponding percentages that should be considered when one is interpreting a value of r.[1]

−1.00		INVERSE RELATIONSHIP		0.00		DIRECT RELATIONSHIP		1.00
⇧	⇧	⇧	⇧	⇧	⇧	⇧	⇧	⇧
perfect	strong	moderate	weak	none	weak	moderate	strong	perfect

Figure 1. Values of the Pearson r.

---

[1] Note that the procedure for computing a Pearson r is beyond the scope of this book.

Table 3
Selected Values of r and r²

r	r²	Percentage better than zero[1]
.90	.81	81%
.50	.25	25%
.25	.06	6%
−.25	.06	6%
−.50	.25	25%
−.90	.81	81%

[1]Also called *percentage of variance accounted for* or *percentage of explained variance.*

EXERCISE ON TOPIC 57

1. "Pearson *r*" stands for what words?

2. When the relationship between two variables is perfect and inverse, what is the value of *r*?

3. Is it possible for a negative relationship to be strong?

4. Is an *r* of −.90 stronger than an *r* of .50?

5. Is an *r* of .75 stronger than an *r* of −.35?

6. Is a relationship "direct" *or* "inverse" when those with high scores on one variable have high scores on the other *and* those with low scores on one variable have low scores on the other?

7. What does an *r* of 1.00 indicate?

8. For a Pearson *r* of .60, what is the value of the coefficient of determination?

9. What must be done in order to convert a coefficient of determination into a percentage?

10. A Pearson *r* of .70 is what percentage better than a Pearson *r* of 0.00?

Question for Discussion

11. Name two variables between which you would expect to get a strong, positive value of *r*.

For Students Planning Research

12. Will you be reporting Pearson *r*s? If so, name the two variables that will be correlated for each value of *r*.

Suppose a researcher had a *research hypothesis* that said, "Homicide investigators who take a short course on the causes of HIV will be less fearful of the disease than investigators who do not take the course." The researcher tested the hypothesis by conducting an experiment in which a random sample of investigators was assigned to take the course and another random sample was designated as the control group that did not take the course.[1] At the end of the experiment, the experimental group had a mean of 16.61 on a fear-of-HIV scale, and the control group had a mean of 29.67 (where the higher the score, the greater the fear of HIV). These means support the research hypothesis. However, can the researcher be certain that the research hypothesis is correct? The answer is "no" because of the *null hypothesis*, which says that there is no *true* difference between the means. In other words, it says the difference was created merely by the chance errors created by random sampling. (These errors are known simply as *sampling errors*.) Put another way, unrepresentative groups may have been assigned to the two conditions quite at random, creating the difference between the two means.

The *t* **test** is often used to test the null hypothesis regarding the observed difference between two means.[2] For the example being considered, a series of computations, which are beyond the scope of this book, would be performed to obtain a value of *t* (in this case, it is 5.38) and a value of degrees of freedom (which, in this case, is $df = 179$). The values of *t* and *df* are not of any special interest to typical consumers of research because they are only substeps in the mathematical procedure used to get the *probability* (*p*) that the null hypothesis is true. In this particular case, *p* is less than .05. Thus, in a research report, the following statement could be made.

The difference between the means is statistically significant ($t = 5.38$, $df = 179$, $p < .05$).[3]

---

[1] Random sampling is preferred because (1) it precludes any bias in the assignment of participants to the groups and (2) the effect of random errors produced by random sampling can be assessed with significance tests.

[2] To test the null hypothesis between two *medians*, the *median test* is used. It is a specialized form of the chi-square test, which was covered in Topics 51 and 52.

[3] Sometimes, researchers leave out the abbreviation *df* and present the result as $t(179) = 5.38$, $p < .05$.

As indicated in Topic 48, the term *statistically significant* indicates that the null hypothesis has been rejected. When the probability that the null hypothesis is true is .05 or less (such as .01 or .001), the null hypothesis is rejected. (When something is unlikely to be true because it has a low probability of being true, it is rejected.)

Having rejected the null hypothesis, the researcher is in a position to assert that the research hypothesis is probably true (assuming no procedural bias was allowed to affect the results, such as testing the control group immediately after a major news story on a famous individual with AIDS while testing the experimental group at an earlier time).

What causes a *t* test to yield a low probability? Three interrelated factors:

1. *Sample size.* The larger the sample, the less likely that an observed difference is due to sampling errors. (As indicated in the previous topics on sampling, larger samples provide more precise data.) Thus, other things being equal, the larger the sample, the lower the value of *p*.

2. *The size of the difference between means.* The larger the difference, the less likely that the difference is due to sampling errors. Thus, other things being equal, the larger the difference between the two means, the lower the value of *p*.

3. *The amount of variation in the population.* As indicated in Topic 30, when a population is very homogeneous (has little variability), there is less potential for sampling error. Thus, other things being equal, the smaller the variability (as indicated by the standard deviations of the samples), the lower the value of *p*.

A special type of *t* test is also applied to correlation coefficients. Suppose a researcher drew a random sample of 50 students and correlated their hand size with their GPAs and got an *r* of 0.19 on the Pearson *r* scale, with possible values ranging from 1.00 to –1.00. The null hypothesis says that the *true* correlation in the population is 0.00. In other words, it says that a value of 0.19 was obtained merely as the result of sampling errors. For this example, the *t* test indicates that $p > .05$. Because the probability that the null hypothesis is true is greater than 5 in 100, the researcher would *not* reject the null hypothesis. In other words, the researcher would have a statistically insignificant correlation coefficient because the t test indicated that for $n = 50$, an r of 0.19 is not significantly different from an r of 0.00. When reporting the results of the t test for the significance of a correlation coefficient, it is conventional *not* to mention the value of t. Rather, researchers usually indicate only whether or not the correlation is significant at a given probability level.

EXERCISE ON TOPIC 58

1. What does the null hypothesis say about the difference between two sample means?

2. Are the values of t and df of any special interest to typical consumers of research?

3. Suppose you read that $t = 2.000$, $df = 20$, $p > .05$ for the difference between two means. Using conventional standards, should you conclude that the null hypothesis should be rejected?

4. Suppose you read that $t = 2.859$, $df = 40$, $p < .01$ for the difference between two means. Using conventional standards, should you conclude that the null hypothesis should be rejected?

5. On the basis of the information in Question 4, should you conclude that the difference between the means is statistically significant?

6. When a researcher uses a large sample, is he or she "more likely" *or* "less likely" to reject the null hypothesis than when a researcher uses a small sample?

7. When the size of the difference between means is large, is a researcher "more likely" *or* "less likely" to reject the null hypothesis than when the size of the difference is small?

8. If a researcher found that for a sample of 92 participants, $r = .41$, $p < .001$, would the researcher reject the null hypothesis?

9. Is the value of r in Question 8 statistically significant?

Question for Discussion

10. Of the three factors that lead to a low probability when t tests are conducted, which one is most directly under the control of a researcher?

For Students Planning Research

11. Will you be conducting t tests? Explain.

TOPIC 59 ONE-WAY ANALYSIS OF VARIANCE

In the previous topic, the use of the *t* test for testing the null hypothesis for the observed difference between two sample means was covered. An alternative test for this problem is **analysis of variance** (often called **ANOVA**). Instead of *t*, it yields a statistic called *F*, [1] as well as degrees of freedom (*df*), sum of squares, mean square, and a *p* value, which indicates the probability that the null hypothesis is correct. As with the *t* test, the only value of interest to the typical consumer of research is the value of *p*. By convention, when *p* equals .05 or less (such as .01 or .001), researchers reject the null hypothesis and declare the result to be *statistically significant.*

Because the *t* test and ANOVA are based on the same theory and assumptions, when two means are compared, both tests yield exactly the same value of *p* and, hence, lead to the same conclusion regarding significance. Thus, for two means, both tests are equivalent. Note, however, that a single *t* test can compare only two means, but a single ANOVA can compare a number of means, which is a great advantage.

Suppose, for example, a researcher administered three drugs designed to treat depression in an experiment and obtained the means in Table 1.

Table 1
Posttest Means: Depression Scores for Three Drugs

Group X Drug A	Group Y Drug B	Group Z Drug C
M = 6.00	*M* = 5.50	*M* = 2.33

Note that the higher the score, the greater the depression. Inspection of the means shows that there are three observed differences:

1. Drug C is superior to Drug A.
2. Drug C is superior to Drug B.
3. Drug B is superior to Drug A.

The null hypothesis asserts that this *entire set* of three differences was created by sampling error. Through a series of computations that are beyond the scope of this book, an ANOVA for these data was conducted and this is the result: $F = 10.837$, $df = 2, 15$, $p < .05$. This result might be stated in a sentence or presented in a table such as Table 2, which is called an ANOVA table.

Table 2
ANOVA for Data in Table 1

Source of Variation	df	Sum of Squares	Mean Square	F
Between Groups	2	47.445	23.722	10.837*
Within Groups	15	32.833	2.189	
Total	17	80.278		

* $p < .05$

While Table 2 contains many values, which were used to arrive at the probability in the footnote to the table, the typical consumer of research is only interested in the end result, which is the value of *p*. As indicated in previous topics, when the probability is .05 or less (as it is here), researchers reject the null hypothesis. This means that the *entire set* of differences is statistically significant at the .05 level. Note that the ANOVA does *not* indicate which of the three differences are significant. It could be that only one, only two, *or* all three are significant. This needs to be explored with additional tests known as *multiple comparisons tests.* There are a number of such tests based on different assumptions, which usually yield the same result. (There is still some controversy over which multiple comparisons test is most appropriate.) For the data being considered, application of Scheffé's test (a popular multiple comparisons test) yields these probabilities:

1. for Drug C versus A, $p < .05$
2. for Drug C versus B, $p < .05$
3. for Drug B versus A, $p > .05$

Thus, the multiple comparisons test has indicated that Drug C is significantly better than Drugs A and B because the probabilities are less than .05, but Drugs B and A are not significantly different from each other because the probability is greater than .05.

In review, an ANOVA indicates whether a set of differences is significant *overall*. If so, researchers can use a multiple comparisons test to determine which individual pairs of means are significantly different from each other.

In this topic, the **one-way ANOVA** (also known as a **single-factor ANOVA**) has been considered. An ANOVA is called "one-way" when the participants have been classified in only one way. In this case, they were classified only in terms of which

---

[1] Because it yields a value of *F*, it is sometimes called an *F* test.

drug they took (A, B, or C). In the next topic, the two-way ANOVA is considered.

EXERCISE ON TOPIC 59

1. ANOVA stands for what words?

2. If a researcher compares two means for significance, will ANOVA and the t test yield the same probability?

3. If an ANOVA yields $p < .05$, should the null hypothesis be rejected?

4. If an ANOVA yields $p > .05$, is/are the difference(s) statistically significant?

5. If a researcher has four means on an achievement test for samples of students in four states, can he or she determine whether the set of differences, overall, is statistically significant by using a t test? Explain.

6. For the information in Question 5, could a researcher use an ANOVA for the same purpose?

7. Should the typical consumer of research be concerned with the values of the degrees of freedom?

8. In an ANOVA table, which statistic is of greatest interest to the typical consumer of research?

9. If an overall ANOVA for three or more means is significant, it can be followed by what type of test to determine the significance of the differences among the individual pairs of means?

Questions for Discussion

10. Very briefly describe a hypothetical study in which it would be appropriate to conduct a one-way ANOVA but it would *not* be appropriate to conduct a t test.

11. If there are means for four groups (named A, B, C, and D), there are how many individual pairs of means to be compared with a multiple comparisons test?

For Students Planning Research

12. Will you be conducting a one-way ANOVA? Explain.

TOPIC 60 TWO-WAY ANALYSIS OF VARIANCE

The previous topic considered the use of **ANOVA** to test for the overall significance of a set of means when participants have been classified in only one way. Often, however, researchers use a two-way classification, such as (1) which drug was taken and (2) how long participants have been depressed. Table 1 shows the means for such a study.[1] Because higher depression scores indicate more depression, a low mean is desirable.

Table 1
Means for a Study of Depression: Drugs and Length of Depression Comparisons

Length of depression	Drug A	Drug B	Row mean
Long term	$M = 8.11$	$M = 8.32$	$M = 8.22$
Short term	$M = 4.67$	$M = 8.45$	$M = 6.56$
Col. mean	$M = 6.39$	$M = 8.38$	

Although the participants are classified in two ways, the statistics in the table answer *three* questions. First, by comparing the column means of 6.39 and 8.38, a researcher can see that overall, those who took Drug A are less depressed than those who took Drug B. It is important to notice that the mean of 6.39 for Drug A is based on both those who have long-term *and* those who have short-term depression. The same is true of the column mean of 8.38 for Drug B. Thus, by comparing the column means, a researcher is answering this question: Which drug is more effective *in general without regard to how long participants have been depressed?* In a two-way analysis of variance, this is known as a **main effect**.

Each way in which participants are classified yields a main effect in analysis of variance. Because participants were also classified in terms of their length of depression, there is a main effect for short-term versus long-term depression, which can be seen by examining the row means of 8.22 and 6.56. This main effect indicates that overall, those with short-term depression were less depressed at the end of the experiment than those with long-term depression.

In this example, the most interesting question is the question of an **interaction**. This is the interaction question: Is the effectiveness of the drugs de-

pendent, in part, on the length of depression? By examining the individual cell means (those *not* in bold in Table 1), it becomes clear that the answer is "yes." Drug A is more effective for short-term than for long-term depression (4.67 vs. 8.11), while Drug B is about equally effective for both types of depression (8.32 vs. 8.45). What is the practical implication of this interaction? The overall effectiveness of Drug A is almost entirely attributable to its effectiveness for short-term depression. In other words, if an individual has short-term depression, Drug A is indicated, but if an individual has long-term depression, either drug is likely to be about equally effective. Thus, the two classification variables *interact*: The best drug to take is dependent on the length of the depression.

For the data in Table 1, it turns out that $p < .05$ for both main effects and the interaction. Thus, the researcher can reject the null hypothesis, which asserts that the differences are the result of random errors. Of course, it does not always turn out this way. It is possible for one or two of the main effects to be significant but the interaction to be insignificant. It is also possible for neither main effect to be significant while the interaction is significant, which is the case for the data in Table 2.

Table 2
Means for a Study of Depression: Drugs and Gender Comparisons

Gender	Drug C	Drug D	Row mean
Female	$M = 8.00$	$M = 5.00$	$M = 6.50$
Male	$M = 5.00$	$M = 8.00$	$M = 6.50$
Col. mean	$M = 6.50$	$M = 6.50$	

In Table 2, notice that the column means (6.50 vs. 6.50) indicate no main effect for Drug C versus Drug D. Likewise, the row means (6.50 vs. 6.50) indicate no main effect for gender. However, there is one very interesting finding: There is an interaction of drug type and gender, which indicates that for females, Drug D is superior, while Drug C is superior for males. (Keep in mind that higher scores indicate more depression.) Note that if the researcher had compared the two drugs in a one-way ANOVA without also classifying the participants according to gender (as was done here in a two-way ANOVA), he or she would have missed this important interaction. By examining interactions using ANOVA, researchers are one step closer to examin-

---

[1] For instructional purposes, only two types of drugs are shown. However, ANOVA may be used when there are more than two.

ing the effects of various traits in complex ways
(not just one at a time).

EXERCISE ON TOPIC 60

1. Suppose a researcher drew random samples of urban, suburban, and rural children, tested them for creativity, and obtained three means. Should the researcher use a "one-way" *or* a "two-way" ANOVA to test for significance? Explain.

2. Do the following means on a performance test indicate an interaction between type of reward and age?

Age level	Praise reward	Monetary reward	Row mean
Young adults	$M = 50.00$	$M = 60.00$	$M = 55.00$
Older adults	$M = 60.00$	$M = 50.00$	$M = 55.00$
Col. mean	$M = 55.00$	$M = 55.00$	

3. Do the means for Question 2 indicate a main effect for type of reward?

4. Do the following means on an achievement test indicate an interaction between the method of instruction (A vs. B) and the aptitude of the students (high vs. low)?

Aptitude	Method A	Method B	Row mean
High aptitude	$M = 100.00$	$M = 85.00$	$M = 92.50$
Low aptitude	$M = 100.00$	$M = 85.00$	$M = 92.50$
Col. mean	$M = 100.00$	$M = 85.00$	

5. Do the means for Question 4 indicate a main effect for method of instruction?

6. Do the means for Question 4 indicate a main effect for aptitude?

7. If $p > .05$ for an interaction in an analysis of variance, should the researcher reject the null hypothesis?

Question for Discussion

8. Very briefly describe a hypothetical study in which it would be appropriate to conduct a two-way ANOVA but it would *not* be appropriate to conduct a one-way ANOVA.

For Students Planning Research

9. Will you be conducting a two-way ANOVA? Explain.

TOPIC 61 PRACTICAL SIGNIFICANCE OF RESULTS

As indicated in previous topics, **statistical significance** deals with the question of whether a difference is reliable in light of random errors. Assume, for instance, that a researcher assigned students at random to two groups: one that was taught a mathematics lesson with new instructional software (the experimental group) and one that was taught using a traditional lecture/textbook approach (the control group). Furthermore, assume that use of the instructional software *in truth* is very slightly superior to the lecture/textbook approach (i.e., it really produces a superior outcome in math achievement, but the superiority is quite small). With a very large sample, randomization should yield experimental and control groups that are very similar at the beginning of the experiment (i.e., on the pretest). Because larger samples have less sampling error than smaller ones, a significance test such as a *t* test for the difference between the two posttest means may be able to detect the reliability of the small difference and allow the researcher to declare it to be *statistically significant* at some probability level, such as $p < .05$. This illustrates an important principle: Even a small difference can be a statistically significant difference.[1] This is true because statistical significance determines only the likelihood that a difference is due to random errors, not whether it is a large difference.

Determining the statistical significance of a difference is the first step; determining the **practical significance** is the next step. Determining practical significance involves five considerations.

The first consideration is the cost in relation to the benefit, which is often referred to as a **cost-benefit analysis**. While there are mechanical, statistical means for conducting such an analysis, for most purposes, common sense and good judgment can give a good answer to the question of whether the results are of practical significance in terms of cost. Consider the preceding example. Suppose all

students already have access to computers for their math lessons and the software is being donated (or is highly subsidized by a foundation). In this case, the low cost might make the small difference of practical significance. On the other hand, if expensive computers and software would need to be purchased and the teachers would need extensive (and, therefore, expensive) training in its use, educators might forgo using the experimental method in everyday instruction because the small increase in performance would come at a high cost.

The example being considered illustrates that even a small difference can be of both statistical and practical significance if the cost is low. In addition, a small, statistically significant difference can be of practical significance—even if it is costly—if it is a crucial difference (the second consideration). A crucial difference is one that results in a crucial increase or decrease. Consider an extreme example. Suppose an experiment in which very expensive computerized simulations teaching how to conduct a delicate form of surgery reduces the death rate from such surgery from 2 in 100,000 to 1.8 in 100,000. In this case, a surgeon might decide that even this small difference is worth the high cost because saving even a very small number of lives during surgery is crucial. The following is a less extreme example: If a school needs an increase of just a few points (on the average) to cross a crucial threshold, such as having the average student score at or above the 50th percentile rank on a standardized math test in order to obtain substantially increased state funding for instruction, crossing this threshold might be considered crucial by teachers, parents, and students.

The third consideration in determining practical significance is **client acceptability**. In school settings, students are clients. If students greatly dislike a statistically superior computerized technique for improving math achievement, using the technique might cause students to develop negative attitudes toward math. If so, the statistically significant difference might be of little practical significance because of the *negative side effect* (i.e., development of negative attitudes).

The fourth consideration is **public and political acceptability**. For instance, studies suggest that stem cell research might be fruitful in curing a number of debilitating and deadly diseases. Yet some segments of the public (at the time of this

---

[1] As indicated in Topic 58, the *t* test is more likely to lead to significance if the difference between the two means is large. However, if there is little variation among the participants and if a large enough sample is used, even small differences can be reliably detected and declared statistically significant. Note that in some circumstances, a small difference can be of great practical importance. For instance, in a national election, having only one vote more than the competing candidate out of millions of votes can lead to victory.

writing) are opposed to it, calling into question its practical significance as a line of research that scientists should continue to pursue.

Fifth, the **ethical and legal implications** of statistically significant results should be considered. No matter how much benefit and no matter how low the cost, some treatments that have been shown to produce statistically superior results may violate the ethical standards of a profession or impinge on legal requirements such as the laws that govern the operation of schools and other institutions.

It should be clear that determining practical significance should not be done mechanically. If there is any question as to the practical significance of the results of a study, representative groups of potential providers of the treatments (such as teachers or psychologists, their clients, the public, and politicians) may need to be consulted. In addition, legal counsel may be needed to help in the determination of practical significance.

EXERCISE ON TOPIC 61

1. Is it possible for a small difference to be statistically significant?

2. This topic describes *how many* types of considerations for determining practical significance?

3. If the cost is very low, might a very small statistically significant difference be of practical significance?

4. Does a crucial difference need to be numerically large to be of practical significance?

5. According to this topic, should client acceptability of a treatment be considered when determining practical significance?

6. According to this topic, ethical considerations should play no role in the interpretation of the results of a study. Is this statement "true" *or* "false"?

7. Should determining the practical significance of a study's results be a mechanical process?

Questions for Discussion

8. In addition to the two examples in this topic, name a hypothetical result that you would favor implementing, even if it were costly, because it might make a *crucial difference*.

9. Consider the last research report you read that had statistically significant results. Did the researcher who wrote the article discuss the practical significance of his or her results? Explain.

For Students Planning Research

10. Can you anticipate any considerations that might limit the practical significance of the results you hope to obtain in your study? Explain.

PART H

EFFECT SIZE AND META-ANALYSIS

The statistical tool effect size is described in this part of the book. Effect size helps evaluate the size of a difference, such as the difference between two means. Also considered is the statistical technique meta-analysis. Meta-analysis is used to combine results across diverse studies on a given topic.

NOTES

TOPIC 62 INTRODUCTION TO EFFECT SIZE (d)

To understand the need to consider the **effect size** of a difference, consider a practical problem in interpreting research. Suppose that Experimenter A administered a new treatment for depression (Treatment X) to an experimental group, while the control group received a standard treatment. Furthermore, suppose that Experimenter A used a 20-item true-false depression scale (with possible raw scores from 0 to 20) and obtained the results on the posttest shown in Table 1.[1] Note that the difference between the two means is 5 raw-score points.

Table 1
Statistics Obtained in Experiment A (Treatment X)

Group	m	sd
Experimental group ($n = 50$)	12.00	4.00
Control group ($n = 50$)	7.00	4.00
Difference between two means	5.00	

Suppose that Experimenter B administered Treatment Y to an experimental group while treating the control group with the standard treatment. Furthermore, suppose Experimenter B used a 30-item scale with choices from "Strongly agree" to "Strongly disagree" (with possible scores from 0 to 120) and obtained the results in Table 2, which show a difference of 10 raw-score points in favor of the experimental group.

Table 2
Statistics Obtained in Experiment B (Treatment Y)

Group	m	sd
Experimental group ($n = 50$)	80.00	14.00
Control group ($n = 50$)	70.00	14.00
Difference between two means	10.00	

Which treatment is superior? Treatment X, which resulted in a 5-point raw-score difference between the two means, *or* Treatment Y, which resulted in a 10-point raw-score difference between the two means? The answer is not clear because the two experimenters used different measurement scales (0 to 20 versus 0 to 120).

For the results of the two studies to be comparable, they need to be *standardized* so that both differences can be expressed on the same scale. The most straightforward way to do this is to express both differences in terms of their *standard-deviation units* (instead of their raw-score units).[2] In Experiment A, *one standard-deviation unit* equals 4.00 raw-score points. Dividing the difference between the means (5.00) by the size of the standard-deviation unit for Experiment A (4.00 points) yields an answer of 1.25. This value is known as d and is obtained by applying the following formula, in which m_e stands for the mean of the experimental group, and m_c stands for the mean of the control group:

$$d = \frac{m_e - m_c}{sd} = \frac{12.00 - 7.00}{4.00} = 1.25$$

The result indicates that the experimental group exceeded the control group by 1.25 (one and one-quarter) standard-deviation units. For all practical purposes, there are only three standard-deviation units on each side of the mean. Thus, d is expressed in standard-deviation units and has an effective range from 0.00 (no difference between the means) to 3.00 (the maximum difference between the means).[3] Thus, for Experiment A, the experimental group is one and one-quarter standard deviations above no difference (0.00) on a standardized scale that ranges from 0.00 to 3.00. On such a limited scale, a value of d of 1.25 indicates that the difference is substantially above 0.00.

Using the formula for Experiment B, the difference between the means is divided by the standard deviation (10.00/14.00), yielding $d = 0.71$, which is almost three-quarters of the way above 0.00 on the three-point scale. The following is what is now known about the differences in the two experiments when both are expressed on a common (i.e., standardized) scale called d. Clearly, the difference in Experiment A (1.25) is greater than the difference in Experiment B (0.71).

```
0.00  0.50  0.75  1.00  1.50  1.75  2.00  2.50  2.75  3.00
            ↑           ↑
          Exp. B      Exp. A
```

Table 3 summarizes the differences. Remember that the two raw-score differences are not directly comparable because different measurement scales

---

[1] Note that in the experiments in this topic, the researchers used measures that yield *higher* scores when there is *less* depression.

[2] See Topic 55 to review the meaning of the standard deviation.

[3] If a control group has a higher mean than the experimental group, the value of d will be negative.

were used (0 to 20 points versus 0 to 120 points). By examining the standardized values of d, which range from 0.00 to 3.00, a meaningful comparison of the results of the two experiments can be made.

Within each of the two examples in this topic, the two standard deviations are equal. When they are unequal, a special averaging procedure that results in the pooled standard deviation should be used. See Appendix E for more information.

Now for an important definition: *Effect size* refers to the *magnitude* (i.e., size) of a difference when it is expressed on a standardized scale. The statistic d is one of the most popular statistics for

describing the effect size of the difference between two means. In the next topic, the interpretation of d is discussed in more detail. In Topic 64, an alternative statistic for expressing effect size is described.

Table 3
Differences Expressed in Raw Scores and in Values of d

Group	Raw-score difference	Standardized differences (d)
Experimenter A	5 points	1.25
Experimenter B	10 points	0.71

EXERCISE ON TOPIC 62

1. In this topic, which experimenter had the smaller range of possible raw scores? Explain.

2. In this topic, the raw-score differences between the means (5 for Experimenter A and 10 for Experimenter B) were standardized by dividing each of them by what statistic?

3. When comparing the results of two experiments, is it possible for the experiment with the smaller raw-score difference to have a larger difference when the differences are expressed as d?

4. Suppose a researcher obtained a value of d of 2.95. Should this be characterized as representing a large difference? Explain.

5. Suppose you read that the mean for an experimental group is 20.00 and the mean for the control group is 22.00. On the basis of this information alone, can you calculate the value of d? Explain.

6. Suppose a researcher conducted an experiment on improving algebra achievement, and the experimental posttest raw-score mean equaled 500.00 ($sd = 100.00$), and the control group raw-score mean equaled 400.00 ($sd = 100.00$). What is the value of the effect size for the experiment?

7. What is the definition of *effect size*?

Question for Discussion

8. In your own words, briefly explain why it is desirable to compute d when comparing the results of two experiments that use different measurement scales.

For Students Planning Research

9. Do you plan to report value(s) of d in the results section of your research report? Explain.

TOPIC 63 INTERPRETATION OF EFFECT SIZE (*d*)

In the previous topic, effect size expressed as *d* was introduced. The two examples in that topic had values of *d* of 0.71 and 1.25. Obviously, the experiment with a value of 1.25 had a larger effect than the one with a value of 0.71.

While there are no universally accepted standards for describing values of *d* in words, many researchers use Cohen's (1992)[1] suggestions: (1) a value of *d* of about 0.20 (one-fifth of a standard deviation) is "small," (2) a value of 0.50 (one-half of a standard deviation) is "medium," and (3) a value of 0.80 (eight-tenths of a standard deviation) is "large." (Keep in mind that in terms of values of *d*, an experimental group can rarely exceed a control group by more than 3.00 because the effective range of standard-deviation units is only three on each side of the mean. Thus, for most practical purposes, 3.00 [or –3.00] is the maximum value of *d*.)[2]

Extrapolating from Cohen's suggestions, a value of 1.10 might be called "very large," and a value of 1.40 or more might be called "extremely large." Values this large are rarely found in social and behavioral research.

Table 1 summarizes the new material covered so far in this topic.

Table 1
Labels for Values of d

Value of *d*	Label
0.20	Small
0.50	Medium
0.80	Large
1.10	Very Large
1.40+	Extremely Large

Using the labels in Table 1, the value of *d* of 0.71 in the previous topic would be described as being closer to large than medium, while the value of 1.25 would be described as being between very large and extremely large.

Cohen (1992), who proposed the labels for the first three values in Table 1, noted that he originally established them subjectively but that they subsequently have been found to be useful by other researchers in various fields of study.

The labels being discussed should not be used arbitrarily without consideration of the full context in which the values of *d* were obtained and the possible implications of the results. This leads to two principles: (1) a small effect size might represent an important result, and (2) a large effect size might represent an unimportant result.

Consider the *first principle*. Suppose that researchers have been frustrated by consistently finding values of *d* well below 0.20 when trying various treatments for solving an important problem (such as treatments for a new and deadly disease). If a subsequent researcher finds a treatment that results in a value of about 0.20, this might be considered a very important finding. At this low level (0.20), the effect of the treatment is small, but it might be of immense importance to ill individuals helped by the treatment—however small the effect size. In addition, the results might point the scientific community in a fruitful direction for additional research on treatments for the problem in question.

The *second principle* is that a large value of *d*—even one above 1.40—might be of limited importance. This is most likely when the results lack practical significance in terms of cost, public and political acceptability, and ethical and legal concerns. (See Topic 61 for considerations in determining the practical significance of research results.)

Here are three steps for interpreting the difference between two means. First, determine whether the difference is statistically significant at an acceptable probability level, such as $p < .05$. If it is not, the difference should usually be regarded as unreliable and should be interpreted as such. Second, for a statistically significant difference, consider the value of *d* and consider the labels in Table 1 for describing the magnitude of the difference. Third, consider the implications of the difference for validating any relevant theories as well as the practical significance of the results.

Of course, before the researchers begin to follow the three steps outlined in the previous paragraph, the adequacy of the research methodology that they employed should be considered. Woefully inadequate sampling (such as a very biased sample), clearly invalid measures (such as a test that measures a variable other than the one the researcher

---

[1] Cohen, J. (1992). A power primer. *Psychological Bulletin, 112*, 155–159.

[2] A negative is obtained when the control group's mean is higher than the experimental group's mean. Note that less than one-half of one percent of a normal distribution lies above +3.00 and below –3.00, which means that it is technically possible—but highly unlikely—to obtain values larger than +3.00 and –3.00.

wanted to study), and/or a very poor research design (such as a design that will not answer the research question) would lead to very serious questions regarding the validity of the results. In such cases, consideration of values of d might be meaningless.

EXERCISE ON TOPIC 63

1. Are there universally accepted standards for describing effect sizes?

2. What is the "effective range" of standard deviation units on both sides of the mean? Explain.

3. If the value of d for the difference between two means equals 1.00, the experimental group's mean is how many standard-deviation units higher than the control group's mean?

4. What value of d is associated with the label "extremely large"?

5. According to Cohen, what label should be attached to a value of d of 0.80?

6. Under what circumstance will a negative value of d be obtained?

7. Should a test of statistical significance be conducted "before" *or* "after" computing d and interpreting its value using labels?

Questions for Discussion

8. As noted in this topic, a small value of d might be associated with an important result. Name a specific problem that is currently confounding researchers and for which even a small value of d might indicate a result of great practical importance.

9. Is it possible for a large value of d to be associated with a difference that is unimportant? Explain.

For Students Planning Research

10. Will you be comparing the difference between two means in your analysis? If so, do you expect to find a statistically significant difference? Do you expect to find a large value of d? Explain.

TOPIC 64   EFFECT SIZE AND CORRELATION (*r*)

Cohen's *d* is so widely used as a measure of effect size that some researchers use the term *effect size* and *d* interchangeably—as though they are synonyms. However, effect size refers to any statistic that *describes the size of a difference on a standardized metric*. For instance, *d* describes the size of the difference between two means.[1] Furthermore, *d* is *standardized* because regardless of what variables are being studied and regardless of what raw-score scale is being used to express the difference, the value of *d* is always expressed on a standard-deviation scale that almost always ranges only from –3.00 to +3.00.[2] (See the previous topic to review *d*.)

In addition to *d*, a number of other measures of effect size have been proposed. One that is very widely reported is *effect-size r*, which is simply the Pearson correlation coefficient (*r*), which was described in Topic 57. As outlined in that topic, *r* indicates the direction and strength of a relationship between two variables expressed on a scale that ranges from –1.00 to +1.00, where 0.00 indicates no relationship. Values of *r* are interpreted by first squaring them (r^2). For instance, when *r* = 0.50, r^2 = 0.25 (i.e., 0.50 × 0.50 = 0.25). Then, the value of r^2 should be multiplied by 100 to make it a percent. Thus, 0.25 × 100 = 25%. This indicates that the value of *r* of 0.50 is 25% greater than 0.00 on a scale that extends up to a maximum possible value of 1.00.

In basic studies, the choice between reporting *means* and the associated values of *d* (which can range from –3.00 to 3.00) and reporting *correlation coefficients* and the associated values of r^2 (which can range from 0.00 to 1.00)[3] is usually quite straightforward. If a researcher wants to determine which of two groups is superior *on average*, a comparison of means using *d* is usually the preferred method of analysis. On the other hand, if there is one group of participants with two scores per participant, and if the goal is to determine the *degree of relationship between the two sets of scores*, then *r* and r^2 should be used. For instance, if a vocabulary knowledge test and a reading comprehension test were administered to a group of students, it would not be surprising to obtain a correlation coefficient as high as 0.70, which indicates a substantial degree of relationship between two variables (i.e., there is a strong tendency for students who score high on vocabulary knowledge to score high on reading comprehension). As described in Topic 57, for interpretative purposes, 0.70 squared equals 0.49, which is equivalent to 49%. Knowing this allows a researcher to say that the relationship between the two variables is 49% higher than a relationship of 0.00.

When reviewing a body of literature on a given topic, some studies present means and values of *d* while other studies on the same topic present values of *r*, depending on the specific research purposes and research designs. When interpreting such a set of studies, it can be useful to think in terms of the equivalence of *d* and *r*. Table 1 shows the equivalents for selected values.

Table 1
Equivalent Values of d, r, and r^2

d	*r*	r^2	% for r^2
0.20	0.100	0.010	1.0%
0.50	0.243	0.059	5.9%
0.80	0.371	0.138	13.8%
1.20	0.514	0.264	26.4%
1.50	0.600	0.360	36.0%
2.00	0.707	0.500	50.0%

Consider an example that illustrates the usefulness of Table 1. Suppose a researcher was examining the literature on anxiety and depression and found a study in which one group was administered scales that measured the two variables, and *r* = 0.37 was obtained. Suppose that in another study, an experimental group was administered a treatment designed to induce anxiety while the control group received a neutral treatment. Then, all participants were administered a depression scale (to see whether anxiety induces depression). Further, suppose that the experimenter reported that *d* = 0.80 for the difference between the posttest means for the two groups. From Table 1 above, it can be seen that the effect sizes (i.e., magnitude of the differences) in the two studies are the same (i.e., for a value of *d*

---

[1] If the means of two groups are identical, *d* = 0.00.

[2] Note that it is mathematically possible for *d* to exceed 3.00 because a very small percentage of the cases lies above three standard deviations above the mean. Such values are seldom seen in the social and behavioral sciences.

[3] Note that all values of r^2 are positive because squaring a negative correlation coefficient results in a positive product. Thus, the bottom of the range for values of r^2 is 0.00, not –1.00.

of 0.80 in the first column, the corresponding value of r in the second column is 0.371).

For values not shown in Table 1, it is often sufficient to locate the closest values and make approximations. To obtain more precise equivalent values of d and r, use the formulas provided near the end of Appendix E.

EXERCISE ON TOPIC 64

1. According to this topic, what are the two measures of effect size that are very widely reported?

2. Correlation coefficients are expressed on a standard scale that always ranges from –1.00 up to what value?

3. A value of r should be interpreted by doing what?

4. A value of r equal to 0.40 is what percentage of the distance above zero?

5. If there is one group of participants and a researcher wants to determine the strength of the relationship between two sets of test scores, which measure of effect size would typically be the more appropriate?

6. A value of d of 1.20 corresponds to what value of r^2?

7. A value of r of 0.600 corresponds to what value of d?

Question for Discussion

8. Briefly describe a hypothetical study in which it would be more appropriate to compute a value of d instead of a value of r as a measure of effect size.

For Students Planning Research

9. In this topic, there is an example of an experiment and an example of a correlational study. Will you be conducting either type of study? Explain.

Meta-analysis is a set of statistical methods for combining the results of previous studies.[1] To understand its basic premise, consider the following example. Suppose a researcher (named W) randomly assigned 50 students to an experimental group that received one-on-one remedial tutorial reading instruction. The remaining 50 children were the controls. At the end of the experiment, the experimental group had a mean of 22.00, and the control group had a mean of 19.00 on a standardized reading test. Subsequently, three other experimenters conducted strict replications of the first experiment using the same research methods, the same type of tutorial reading instruction, and the same number of second grade students drawn at random from the same pool of students (e.g., second-graders in a particular school district). The posttest means of the four experiments are shown in Table 1.

Table 1
Results of a Meta-Analysis of Two Experiments

	Experimental Group	Control Group	Mean Difference
Researcher W	$m = 22.00$	$m = 19.00$	$m_{difference} = 3.00$
Researcher X	$m = 20.00$	$m = 18.00$	$m_{difference} = 2.00$
Researcher Y	$m = 23.00$	$m = 17.00$	$m_{difference} = 6.00$
Researcher Z	$m = 15.00$	$m = 16.00$	$m_{difference} = -1.00$

In Table 1, there are differences in the results from study to study. The differences could be caused by one or more of the following types of errors:

1. Random sampling errors created by assigning participants at random to the two groups, such as having more motivated students assigned (quite at random) to the experimental group in one or more of the experiments.
2. Random errors of measurement such as participants guessing on the multiple-choice test, and some students not feeling well on the day the test was administered.
3. Systematic errors known to one or more of the researchers, such as the unavailability of experienced tutors for one or more of the experiments.
4. Systematic errors of which one or more of the researchers are unaware, such as tutors not following the curriculum when the researcher or researchers were not present.

All four types of errors are possible in any experiment. Hence, the results of any one experiment should be interpreted with caution. However, in this particular example, there are four experiments, which should provide more confidence in any overall conclusions than any single study could provide. In a *traditional, subjective narrative review of these studies*, it would be reasonable to synthesize these four experiments with a statement such as, "Three of the four experiments on the tutorial instruction showed positive results, with one experiment showing a six-point difference in favor of the experimental group. However, the one negative case in which the control group exceeded the experimental group by one point reduces confidence in the effectiveness of this program."

In a *meta-analysis*, a reviewer might also make comments such as the one in the previous paragraph. However, the main thrust of the conclusions in a meta-analysis is based on a *mathematical synthesis* of the statistical results of the previous studies. To obtain the synthesis, average the results by summing the four mean differences (3.00 + 2.00 + 6.00 − 1.00 = 10.00) and then dividing the sum by four because there were four studies (10.00/4.00 = 2.50). Thus, in a meta-analysis, the author would state that the best estimate of the effectiveness of the program is 2.50 points.[2]

At this point, it should be clear that a meta-analysis estimate of 2.50 points has two important characteristics. The first one is that the statistical result (e.g., 2.50) is based on a sample of 400 students. (Note that each of the four individual studies had 50 in each group for a total of 100 in each

---

[1] The prefix *meta* means occurring later and/or being later and more highly organized. Meta-analysis is conducted on previous results and mathematically synthesizes them.

[2] For reasons discussed in the next topic, those who conduct meta-analyses usually convert their results to one or more measures of effect size (such as *d* or *r*), which were discussed in the previous three topics.

study.) Statistics based on larger samples (such as 400 versus 100) yield more *reliable* results.

It is important to note that *reliable results* are not necessarily *valid results*. A systematic bias that skews the results (such as the experimental group having access to the answer key for the test) will yield invalid results no matter how large the sample is.

The second important characteristic of meta-analysis is that it typically synthesizes the results of studies conducted by *independent* researchers (i.e., researchers who are not working together). Thus, if one researcher makes a *systematic error* (such as using poorly trained tutors), the effects of his or her erroneous results will be moderated when they are averaged with the results obtained by other independent researchers who have not made the same error.

In short, the process of averaging when conducting a meta-analysis tends to decrease the effects of both the random and the systematic errors listed earlier in this topic.

EXERCISE ON TOPIC 65

1. What is the meaning of the prefix *meta* as used in this topic?

2. For what purpose is a set of statistical methods called meta-analysis used?

3. Two types of random errors tend to be canceled out in the process of conducting a meta-analysis. What are the two types of random errors discussed in this topic?

4. In the report of a meta-analysis, the main thrust of the conclusions is based on what?

5. Very briefly state the second important characteristic of meta-analysis.

Question for Discussion

6. On the basis of what you have learned about meta-analysis in this topic, to what extent do you think that it is a good method for advancing knowledge on a topic? Explain.

For Students Planning Research

7. Some institutions (and journals) consider a meta-analysis to be a work of original research even though it is based on a reanalysis of the research results created by others. If you are planning to conduct research, would you be interested in conducting a meta-analysis as your research project (on the basis of what you know about it at this point)? Explain. (Note: After reading the next two topics, reconsider your answer to this question.)

TOPIC 66 META-ANALYSIS AND EFFECT SIZE

For instructional purposes, the example in the previous topic illustrated a meta-analysis on four studies that were as similar as possible (i.e., a study by Researcher W plus three strict replications). In practice, it would be difficult to find even one perfectly strict replication of a study. One very important way that various studies on a given topic often differ is that various researchers frequently use different measures of the same variable. To see the importance of this issue when conducting and interpreting a meta-analysis, consider the values in Table 1, which are based on a study in which Experimenter A used a test with possible score values from 200 to 800 (like the SAT), while Experimenter B used a test with possible score values from 0 to 50.

Table 1
Results Used in Conducting a Meta-Analysis

	Experimental Group	Control Group	Mean Difference
Exp. A $n = 50$	$m = 500.00$ $sd = 200.00$	$m = 400.00$ $sd = 200.00$	$m_{difference}$ $= 100.00$
Exp. B $n = 50$	$m = 24.00$ $sd = 3.00$	$m = 22.00$ $sd = 3.00$	$m_{difference}$ $= 2.00$

If the average of the mean differences is computed (100.00 + 2.00 = 102.00/2 = 51.00), the average lacks meaning because the results are expressed on different scales. In other words, the answer of 51.00 does *not* refer specifically to the scale that goes from 200 to 800 *nor* does it refer specifically to the scale that goes from 0 to 50. When locating additional studies on the same topic, other tests with other score-point ranges are likely to be found, making a simple average of the mean differences entirely uninterpretable.

The solution to the problem being considered is to use a measure of *effect size*. One of the most popular is Cohen's *d*, which is expressed on a standardized scale that typically ranges from –3.00 to +3.00. (This statistic was discussed in Topics 62 through 64.) Calculating *d* for all studies to be included in a meta-analysis permits the averaging of the values of *d* to get a meaningful result.

As indicated in Topic 62, to obtain *d*, divide the difference between the means by the standard deviation. For Experiment A, $d = 100.00/200.00 = 0.50$. For Experiment B, $d = 2.00/3.00 = 0.67$. When the results of the two experiments are expressed on a common scale (*d*), it becomes clear that Experiment B (with a *d* of 0.67) had a larger effect than Experiment A (with a *d* of 0.50), which was not clear by a simple inspection of Table 1.

To proceed with the meta-analysis, the two values of *d* can be averaged to get a mathematical synthesis of the results [(0.67 + 0.50)/2 = 0.58]. Thus, **0.58** is the best estimate of the overall effect. Referring to Table 1 in Topic 63, a researcher can say that the overall result of the meta-analysis is somewhat above medium in strength.

In the example in this topic, the standard deviations for both groups in each experiment were the same. In reality, they will almost always differ. Those who plan to conduct a meta-analysis and want more information on several possible solutions to this problem should consult Appendix E.

Also in the example in this topic, the two experiments had the same number of participants ($n = 50$ in each). Suppose an additional published experiment (Experiment C) is located in which 300 participants were used. A researcher would, of course, calculate *d* for this experiment (assume that $d = 0.90$, which is "large" according to Table 1 in Topic 63). By summing the three values of *d* and dividing by 3 (the number of studies), each study is given equal weight. In other words, the three values of *d* are being treated as though they were equally important even though the value of *d* for Experiment C is based on a much larger sample than that of the other two experiments. Using statistical methods that are beyond the scope of this book, researchers can weight the average value of *d* to take into account the varying numbers of participants, giving more weight to those studies with more participants in the final average. Thus, consumers of research should look to see whether a meta-analysis is based on weighted averages, which is almost always desirable.

As indicated in Topic 64, *r* is also a measure of effect sizes. Like *d*, it is expressed on a standardized scale. However, the scale for *r* has values that can range from –1.00 to 1.00. Like *d*, values of *r* reported in various studies can be averaged while weighting the average to take into account varying sample sizes. (The mathematics of the weighting procedure for *r* are beyond the scope of this book.)

In this topic and the previous one, very simple examples were used to illustrate the purposes of meta-analysis and its interpretation. These simple examples may have failed to fully convey the importance of meta-analysis, so briefly consider two published meta-analytic studies. First, in one meta-analysis, researchers located 162 studies that reported on the gender differences in smiling. Combined, these studies contained a total of 109,654 participants. By averaging the effect sizes across the 162 studies, the researchers found that women smiled more than men, with an overall weighted mean value of d of 0.41. This is close to medium in strength according to Table 1 in Topic 63.[1] Note that this result is based on a large number of studies and a very large combined sample size.

In another meta-analysis, researchers reported a weighted average value of r of 0.48 for the relationship between posttraumatic stress disorder and anger, based on 29 studies involving 7,486 participants. With such a large sample, the result of this meta-analysis is highly reliable.[2]

In conclusion, meta-analysis provides a statistical method that can synthesize multiple studies on a given topic. Thus, meta-analytic studies are an important adjunct to traditional, more subjective narrative reviews of literature, which are largely non-mathematical (i.e., reviews of literature in which some particular statistics may be mentioned but the results of the studies being reviewed are not mathematically synthesized).

EXERCISE ON TOPIC 66

1. According to this topic, is it easy to find perfectly strict replications of previous studies?

2. What is one very important way that various studies on a given topic differ?

3. Computing a mean difference across studies that used measurement scales with different possible numbers of score points is meaningless. What is suggested in this topic to overcome this problem?

4. What should usually be done when the studies to be used in a meta-analysis have different sample sizes?

5. Is d the only standardized measure of effect size used in meta-analytic studies? Explain.

Question for Discussion

6. In this topic, a meta-analytic study that reported a weighted average value of r of 0.48 for the relationship between posttraumatic stress disorder and anger is cited. On the basis of what you know about correlation, how would you interpret the direction and strength of this relationship?

For Students Planning Research

7. Reconsider your answer to Question 7 in the previous topic in light of what you learned in this topic. Has your answer changed? Explain.

[1] LaFrance, M., Hecht, M. A., & Paluck, E. L. (2003). The contingent smile: A meta-analysis of sex differences in smiling. *Psychological Bulletin, 129*, 305–334.

[2] Orth, U., & Wieland, E. (2006). Anger, hostility, and posttraumatic stress disorder in trauma-exposed adults: A meta-analysis. *Journal of Consulting and Clinical Psychology, 74*, 698–706.

TOPIC 67 META-ANALYSIS: STRENGTHS AND WEAKNESSES

Meta-analysis has both strengths and weaknesses. A major strength mentioned in the previous topic is that it produces results based on large combined samples—sometimes very large samples. The previous topic cited a meta-analysis of 162 studies that produced a mathematical synthesis involving 109,654 participants, which is a lot larger than the typical number in research reports in academic journals. Such very large samples yield very reliable (although not necessarily valid) results. However, if the studies subjected to a meta-analysis have serious methodological flaws (resulting in a lack of validity), then the mathematical synthesis of their results will also lack validity.

As indicated in Topic 65, a strength of meta-analysis is that it can be used to synthesize the results of studies conducted by *independent* researchers (i.e., researchers who are not working together). Whether or not meta-analysis is used, independent confirmation of results is an important standard that is applied when one is assessing the validity of the results.

An additional strength of meta-analysis is the objectivity of its conclusions.[1] After making subjective judgments regarding how to define a topic, how to search for relevant studies, and what criteria should be used to select studies from the available pool of potential studies, the remaining steps in a meta-analysis are mathematical, leading to an objectively obtained result (such as an average value of *d* or *r*). Note that in a traditional qualitative literature review (i.e., a review that consists of a narrative discussion without averaging measures of effect size), the conclusions are expressed in words. The phrasing, emphasis, and other characteristics of written communication used to express the conclusions in a nonmathematical, traditional review are not objective from a mathematical point of view.

A potential weakness occurs if a researcher is not careful in the selection of studies to include in a meta-analysis. Poor selection might produce results that are difficult to interpret (at best) or meaningless (at worst). For instance, a meta-analysis involving all studies of tutoring in reading regardless of grade

level (from first grade through high school) would not be very helpful in reaching conclusions that have implications for program implementation at any given grade level. This is because different types of results might be obtained at different levels (e.g., tutoring might be more helpful at the primary level than at the high school level). When combined into one grand mean, the poor effectiveness at the high school level might cancel out much of the effectiveness at the primary level (by pulling the grand mean down).

One way to handle the problem of diversity across a set of studies is to establish criteria for the inclusion of studies on a topic in a meta-analysis. For instance, a researcher might include only those that meet criteria such as employment of teachers as tutors, use of tutoring sessions that last at least 30 minutes per session, and tutoring of only primary-grade students.

Another solution to the problem of diversity is to conduct multiple meta-analyses within a single meta-analytic project. For instance, a researcher might conduct three separate analyses: one for studies involving primary-grade students, one for those involving middle-school students, and a third for high school students. Comparing results of the three analyses would provide insights into the effectiveness of the programs at different grade levels.

In a report in which separate analyses are conducted for various subgroups, the variable on which the studies were divided into subgroups (e.g., the various grade levels) is called a *moderator variable* because it may moderate the results so that the results for subgroups are different from the grand combined result. The use of moderator variables is very common in published reports of meta-analyses.

A final potential weakness of meta-analysis stems from what is known as *publication bias*. Typically, researchers are looking for significant differences (and relationships). When they fail to find them, they may be inclined *not* to write reports on such studies for submission for publication. It is also possible that some journal editors may have a bias such that they tend to reject studies with insignificant results. Hence, the body of published research available on a topic for a meta-analysis might be biased toward studies that have statistically significant results. (A researcher conducting a meta-analysis, of course, wants to include all rele-

---

[1] Quantitative researchers value and strive for objectivity, while qualitative researchers tend to question whether objectivity is obtainable. Thus, qualitative researchers challenge the feasibility and desirability of seeking complete objectivity in scientific research.

vant studies, whether the differences are significant or not, in order to get an *overall* estimate of effectiveness.) A partial solution to this problem is for those conducting meta-analyses to search for studies that might be reported in dissertations, convention papers, government reports, and other nonjournal sources where there might not be as much bias against studies with statistically insignificant results.

Despite the potential weaknesses, meta-analysis is an important tool for gaining mathematical perspectives on the results of the studies on a research topic. It shows what can be obtained "objectively," which can be compared and contrasted with more subjective qualitative literature reviews on the same research topic.

EXERCISE ON TOPIC 67

1. What was the sample size for the meta-analysis of the 162 studies mentioned in this topic?

2. According to this topic, is a "meta-analysis" *or* a "review" consisting of a narrative discussion of the literature more objective?

3. Even if a meta-analysis yields highly reliable results based on objective mathematical procedures, are its results necessarily valid? Explain.

4. What is the name of the final potential weakness of meta-analysis?

5. What is a partial solution to the problem you named in your response to Question 4?

Question for Discussion

6. Is meta-analysis completely objective? Explain.

For Students Planning Research

7. On the basis of what you know about meta-analysis, would you be interested in conducting one in the near future? At some later point in your professional career? Explain.

PART I

QUALITATIVE RESEARCH

Topics 9 and 10 in the first part of this book describe some of the major distinctions between quantitative and qualitative research. In this part, techniques used by qualitative researchers are explored in more detail. Topics 68 and 69 describe sampling in qualitative research, Topics 70 and 71 describe methods used to collect data, and Topic 72 describes specific techniques qualitative researchers use to ensure the quality of their research. Finally, Topics 73 and 74 describe two frequently used general approaches to the analysis of qualitative data.

NOTES

In Part D of this book (i.e., Topics 24 through 30), the emphasis was on sampling from the point of view of quantitative researchers. However, Topic 27 briefly described **purposive sampling**, which is widely used by qualitative researchers. To select a purposive sample, a researcher must first identify a research topic of interest and then seek individuals who are likely to have relevant information. This is sometimes described as seeking individuals who will be rich sources of information. In other words, qualitative researchers make subjective judgments regarding the individuals to select based on the likelihood that they will be able to provide the needed information. Example 1 illustrates purposive sampling in which department chairs are asked to nominate potential participants. In the example, notice that the department chairs were asked to use their "judgment" rather than some objective criteria such as GPAs.

EXAMPLE 1
Purposive sampling: To identify a sample of Asian American college students majoring in clinical psychology who have the potential to become highly successful clinicians, letters were sent to chairs of departments of psychology soliciting nominations. The letters asked the chairs to nominate Asian American students who, in the chairs' judgment, had the greatest potential for success as clinical psychologists, without regard to the students' grades or test scores.

Purposive sampling is the correct term to use when the researchers seek participants who fit into a broad category such as "Asian American students with the greatest potential to succeed as clinical psychologists." In contrast, when there are a number of criteria to be applied in the selection of a sample, the sampling technique is more properly called **purposive criterion sampling**. This is illustrated in Example 2.

EXAMPLE 2
Purposive criterion sampling: To identify a sample of distinguished elementary school teachers, a list of all elementary school teachers in a school district who had received merit raises in the past five years was obtained. From those on the list, teachers were selected who met these criteria: (1) at least three years of teaching experience at the elementary school level, (2) hold full credentials issued by the state in which they taught, (3) hold master's de-grees in education, and (4) had supervised at least one student teacher in the past three years. The last criterion was included because student teachers are typically assigned only to experienced teachers whom school administrators believe to be master teachers.

Sometimes, qualitative researchers seek diversity in their samples. Thus, for instance, in Example 2, the researchers might purposively select teachers who are diverse in their ages, ethnic/racial backgrounds, and in their majors as undergraduates in college. Using a diverse sample introduces additional variables that might need to be accounted for during the analysis of participants' responses (e.g., analyze separately the data from older versus younger teachers). Hence, some qualitative researchers seek fairly homogeneous samples in order to simplify their research.

Regardless of whether diversity is sought during sampling, qualitative researchers should collect **demographic information** that will help consumers of research to "see" the participants. Example 3 lists the demographics collected for a qualitative study of American Indians with alcohol dependence. Note that these demographics were *not* a basis for selecting the participants. The demographic data were collected after the participants were selected so that the sample could be described in detail for consumers of the research.

EXAMPLE 3
Measure used to collect demographics in a qualitative study: The Demographics Questionnaire is a standard assessment instrument used at the Center on Alcoholism, Substance Abuse, and Addictions (CASAA; http://casaa.unm.edu). Relevant questions included age, gender, tribal affiliation, marital and employment status, annual income, and education. (p. 354.)[1]

Sometimes, qualitative researchers are silent on the issue of how their samples were selected and provide little demographic information in their research reports. For instance, they might simply say, "Fifteen male students who were en-

---

[1] Venner, K. L., Greenfield, B. L., Vicuña, B., Muñoz, R., Bhatt, S., & O'Keefe, V. (2012). "I'm not one of them": Barriers to help seeking among American Indians with alcohol dependence. *Cultural Diversity and Ethnic Minority Psychology, 18*(4), 352–362. doi: 10.1037/a0029757

rolled in an introductory sociology class were interviewed." When this is encountered, it may be safe to assume that a sample of convenience (not a purposive sample) was used. This should be regarded as a flaw in sampling.

EXERCISE ON TOPIC 68

1. Is purposive sampling widely used by "qualitative researchers" *or* by "quantitative researchers"?

2. Qualitative researchers make subjective judgments regarding the individuals to select on the basis of the likelihood of what?

3. What is the proper name for purposive sampling when there are a number of criteria to be applied in the selection of a sample?

4. Do all qualitative researchers seek diversity in their samples?

5. In a qualitative study, is the sole purpose for collecting demographic data to assist in the selection of participants?

Question for Discussion

6. Name a general topic on which a qualitative researcher might conduct research. Then, name at least four demographic variables for which it would be appropriate to collect data in light of the topic. At least two of them should be variables other than those mentioned in Example 3 from this topic.

For Students Planning Research

7. If you are planning to conduct qualitative research, do you plan to use "purposive sampling" *or* "purposive criterion sampling"? Explain your choice. If you plan to use purposive criterion sampling, name some of the criteria you plan to apply.

Sometimes qualitative researchers are interested in researching a problem that exists in a particular location or institution. For instance, a professor might want to understand why few women on his or her campus are majoring in engineering. For such a study, sampling women only from that campus would be appropriate.

When qualitative researchers are interested in results that may have broader applications, they should seek participants from a variety of sources. For instance, college women might be solicited from several different colleges for a study on why so few major in engineering. The use of participants from *diverse sources* is a methodological strength of a qualitative study when the researcher has a broader interest than just a single source (such as a single college campus). Example 1 illustrates how one group of researchers sought participants from diverse sources for a qualitative study.

EXAMPLE 1
Obtaining participants from diverse sources: A questionnaire assessing self-handicapping and defensive pessimism (see Martin, 1998) was administered to 584 first-year education students enrolled in three universities in metropolitan Sydney (Australia). Included in the questionnaire was an invitation for students to record their names and phone numbers if they were willing to be interviewed at a later time. In total, 134 students volunteered this information.[1]

One method to obtain data from diverse sources (including a national sample) is to rent a list of names and addresses of potential participants.[2] For instance, most major professional associations, such as the American Sociological Association, will rent lists for a reasonable fee to individuals who are conducting legitimate research. Its lists are segmented so that, for instance, a list of only those who belong to a particular interest group within the organization can be rented. Example 2 illustrates the use of a rented list to reach out to diverse sources for participants.

EXAMPLE 2
Obtaining participants from diverse sources using a rented list: Participants were selected based on purposive criterion sampling from a list, purchased[3] by the research team, that consisted of professionals who had managerial positions in business, governmental, or nongovernmental organizations in a western Canadian city. The criteria for participation included....[4]

Qualitative researchers usually use fewer participants than quantitative researchers. A brief survey of sample sizes was conducted by this writer. A random sample of quantitative and qualitative research articles in five journals published by the American Psychological Association showed the following:[5]

EXAMPLE 3
Sample sizes in five journals, each of which publishes both quantitative and qualitative research:
For qualitative research: Sample sizes ranged from 10 to 36, with a median (i.e., average) of 13.
For quantitative research: Sample sizes ranged from 25 to 766, with a median (i.e., average) of 82.

The major reason qualitative researchers use smaller samples than quantitative researchers is that qualitative data collection methods are often more expensive (including the expense of labor) and time-consuming than quantitative ones. For instance, a questionnaire for quantitative research can be distributed to hundreds of students in an auditorium relatively inexpensively. In contrast, individual interviews with students, each of which might last an hour or more, might make it possible to use only a dozen students, unless the researcher has major funding for the research.

---

[1] Martin, A. J., Marsh, H. W., Williamson, A., & Debus, R. L. (2003). Self-handicapping, defensive pessimism, and goal orientation: A qualitative study of university students. *Journal of Educational Psychology, 95,* 617–628.
[2] To locate specialized lists, use the term "list broker" (including the quotation marks) in a computer search using any major search engine. At the time of this writing, 80,800 websites for list brokers were identified in such a search.

[3] While some lists can be purchased for unlimited use, typically they are rented for a specific purpose and for a specific number of times that they may be used.
[4] Iwasaki, Y., MacKay, K. J., & Ristock, J. (2004). Gender-based analyses of stress among professional managers: An exploratory qualitative study. *International Journal of Stress Management, 11,* 56–79.
[5] The journals are *Journal of Counseling Psychology, Journal of Educational Psychology, Cultural Diversity and Ethnic Minority Psychology, American Journal of Orthopsychiatry,* and *Professional Psychology: Research and Practice.*

In addition, quantitative researchers often hope for statistically significant results using significance tests such as the *t* test. As indicated in Topic 58, the larger the sample, the more likely the results will be statistically significant. Qualitative researchers almost never test for statistical significance and, thus, do not need to use large samples for this purpose.

A criterion many qualitative researchers use for determining their sample size is called **saturation**. Briefly, this is how it is applied: As the data are collected (e.g., while the researcher is conducting interviews), the qualitative researcher conducts a preliminary, informal analysis, noting the major and minor themes that are emerging. At the point at which several additional participants fail to respond with new information that leads to the identification of additional themes, the researcher might conclude that the data collection process has become saturated. At that point, no additional participants are studied because new types of information are unlikely to be obtained by increasing the sample size. Thus, the point of saturation may determine the final sample size.

EXERCISE ON TOPIC 69

1. Are qualitative researchers always interested in problems that extend beyond one location or institution?

2. The use of participants from *diverse sources* is a methodological strength of a qualitative study when the researcher has what?

3. How might a qualitative researcher obtain names and addresses for a national sample?

4. On the basis of the brief survey reported in this topic, what was the average sample size for qualitative studies?

5. Do "qualitative researchers" *or* "quantitative researchers" tend to use more expensive data collection methods?

6. At what point might a qualitative researcher conclude that the data collection process has become saturated?

Question for Discussion

7. Are you surprised by the results reported in Example 3 from this topic? Explain.

For Students Planning Research

8. If you are planning to conduct qualitative research, do you plan to sample from diverse sources? Will you collect data until you reach saturation? Explain.

Semistructured interviews are by far the most widely used type of measure for collecting data for qualitative research. Typically, these are face-to-face interviews, which are often recorded. The obvious advantages of recording the interviews are that they can be examined carefully at a later date and can be examined by other researchers who are collaborating on the research project.

There should be an **interview protocol** consisting of written directions for conducting the interview as well as a standard set of predetermined questions to be asked of all participants. Ideally, the questions should be pilot-tested with at least a few individuals who will not be participants in the study. On the basis of the pilot test, the questions should be revised, if necessary. Also, when possible, the predetermined questions should be reviewed by experts in the area being investigated and revised as needed.

The initial questions should be designed to *establish rapport*. Example 1 shows three of the nine questions researchers asked in order to establish rapport with first-year university students at the beginning of an interview. Notice that the questions are quite general and do not deal with the direct topic of the research (i.e., self-handicapping, defensive pessimism, and goal orientation). These might also be thought of as warm-up questions.

EXAMPLE 1
Sample interview questions to establish rapport with first-year university students:

So now that you're at the university, what do you think?

Is the university what you expected?

Are you enjoying the university?[1]

Example 2 shows how a research team described their use of predetermined questions. Notice that they commenced with "broad, open-ended questions," followed by increasingly specific questions as the data collection progressed.

EXAMPLE 2
Use of predetermined questions in a semistructured interview: A set of predetermined questions guided

but did not limit the conversation. Interviews were about half an hour in length and commenced with broad, open-ended questions inviting participants to describe in their own words what assisted or impeded recovery during the six months immediately following discharge from treatment. As data collection progressed and emerging categories became apparent, participants were asked increasingly specific questions. In addition, summary statements and reflections were frequently made to validate responses and verify accurate understanding.[2]

"Semistructured" refers to the fact that the interviewer does not need to ask only the predetermined questions. First, if a participant does not seem to understand a question, it can be reworded by the interviewer. Second, if a response is too terse, the interviewer can ask additional questions, such as "Can you tell me more about it?" Third, the interviewer can probe with additional questions (in addition to the predetermined questions) in order to explore unexpected, unusual, or especially relevant material revealed by a participant.

It is especially important that qualitative interviewers be skilled because they are not simply following a predetermined script. This skill is acquired through practice. A novice who is planning qualitative research should conduct some practice interviews with individuals who will not be participants in the study. If possible, these practice interviews should be observed by an experienced qualitative researcher, who then provides feedback to the novice.

It is also important that an interviewer be unbiased. An interviewer can achieve an unbiased attitude through the process of **self-disclosure**. This refers to considering the research problem in relation to the interviewer's background and attitudes before conducting the interviews. For instance, if a team of qualitative researchers is planning to study child-rearing practices of recent emigrants from Asia, the researchers should consciously think about how they themselves were raised, their own experiences raising children, and any attitudes they have toward Asian Americans that might predispose them to skew the interview. The purpose of self-disclosure is to clear the air as well as to clear the

---

[1] Martin, A. J., Marsh, H. W., Williamson, A., & Debus, R. L. (2003). Self-handicapping, defensive pessimism, and goal orientation: A qualitative study of university students. *Journal of Educational Psychology, 95*, 617–628.

[2] Cockell, S. J., Zaitsoff, S. L., & Geller, J. (2004). Maintaining change following eating disorder treatment. *Professional Psychology: Research and Practice, 35*, 527–534.

mind before conducting the interviews. In some published reports of qualitative research, brief summaries of the researchers' self-disclosures are described.

Note that some of the predetermined questions should ask for **demographic information** (i.e., background information such as age and highest level of education), which will allow the researchers to describe the participants in a research report.

The next topic explores additional measurement issues in qualitative research.

EXERCISE ON TOPIC 70

1. Are semistructured interviews widely used for data collection in qualitative research?

2. What does an interview protocol consist of?

3. With whom should a pilot test of the interview questions be conducted?

4. The initial questions should be designed to do what?

5. In a semistructured interview, is it ever acceptable for an interviewer to ask questions not included in the list of predetermined questions?

6. What is the name of the process through which an interviewer can clear the air and clear the mind?

Question for Discussion

7. In your opinion, does the flexibility afforded by semistructured interviewing open the possibility that the interviewer might bias the interview so that the interviewer obtains results along the lines that he or she already expected? Do you think that fully structured interviews (with only predetermined questions) might provide more valid data?

For Students Planning Research

8. If you are planning to conduct qualitative research, do you consider yourself a novice? If yes, how do you plan to gain experience before conducting your research? Explain.

TOPIC 71 MEASUREMENT IN QUALITATIVE RESEARCH: II

Basic characteristics of semistructured interviews were described in the previous topic. This topic explores some additional issues regarding them and then describes other measurement methods used in qualitative research.

The use of interview data to explore complex issues raises the issue of reality. For instance, when participants describe how they were treated in some situation, the interview primarily exposes how participants perceive these matters. To many quantitative empiricists, *perception* is important but may not be as important as reality. To most qualitative researchers, however, objective factual reality[1] is not as interesting or informative as participants' perceptions. Examining perceptions is known as a **phenomenological approach** to acquiring knowledge. Almost all qualitative researchers are in some sense phenomenologists.[2,3]

In addition to one-on-one, semistructured interviews, qualitative researchers sometimes use **focus groups**. A focus group usually consists of 6 to 12 participants who are gathered to discuss a topic. The group is led by a **facilitator**,[4] as opposed to an interviewer. The facilitator describes the topic to be discussed and tries to create a nonthreatening environment in which all group members feel free to express their opinions, attitudes, and experiences— even if they differ from those of other participants. The facilitator should have a predetermined set of questions (also known as a *questioning route*) to ensure that all relevant aspects of the topic are discussed. In addition, the facilitator should probe for additional information when necessary.

Typically, a focus group lasts for about an hour. Also, it is typical to use two or more focus groups in a given research project.

A clear advantage of using focus groups is that the method reveals *the evolution of perceptions in a social context*. It is interesting to note that the focus group method began as a business marketing research tool when marketing researchers realized that the perceptions of an individual in isolation may be different from his or her perceptions as they develop in a social context. For instance, a new product that initially seems satisfactory to an individual may be seen as less desirable after he or she has discussed it with other individuals who may have different perspectives on it.

Example 1 shows a brief description of how data were collected with the focus group method in a study on stress.

EXAMPLE 1
Description of data collection using focus groups:
Each of the four groups of medical students who experienced the recovery teaching intervention participated in a 1-hour focus group at the beginning and at the end of their placement. A topic guide was used by the author to guide the discussion, and students were encouraged to talk to one another: asking questions, exchanging anecdotes, and commenting on each other's experiences and points of view. . . (p. 37).[5]

Appendix F at the end of this book shows the question route used by the authors of Example 1. Notice that the questions in the appendix move logically from broad to more specific, with the exception of the ending questions, which are broad.

Although it is widely discussed in research methodology textbooks, direct, physical observation is seldom used in published qualitative research reports in the social and behavioral sciences. Nevertheless, direct observation can provide valuable data. In qualitative observational studies, an important distinction is made between **nonparticipant observation** and **participant observation**. In *nonparticipant observation*, the qualitative researcher observes individuals as an outsider, for instance, sitting at the back of a classroom to observe student/teacher interactions. A particular concern with this type of observation is that the participants' behavior may change from its normal course because they know they are being observed.

In *participant observation*, the researcher be-

---

[1] Both qualitative and quantitative researchers realize that objective factual reality is elusive. The distinction here is in whether the researchers strive to obtain it.

[2] Both qualitative and quantitative researchers are interested in perceptions. The distinction here is in the degree to which the two types of researchers rely on perceptions for understanding a research topic.

[3] A full discussion of these issues is beyond the scope of this book. However, it is helpful to consider a trial in a court of law, in which a jury attempts to determine the reality of a situation, often relying heavily on witnesses' perceptions and recollections as well as any physical evidence.

[4] Facilitators can also be called **moderators**.

[5]Feeney, L., Jordan, I., & McCarron, P. (2013). Teaching recovery to medical students. *Psychiatric Rehabilitation Journal, 36*(1), 35–41. doi: 10.1037/h0094745

comes (or already is) a member of the group being researched and, thus, makes his or her observations as an insider. For instance, a teacher who is also a researcher who wants to study a high school that is widely known for academic achievement might arrange to teach at the school, providing an opportunity to observe while participating. Note that making participant observations without revealing to those who are being observed that research is being conducted may raise serious ethical problems.

Researchers who use observational methods often refer to their research as **field research**, which has historical roots in the field of anthropology. When the focus is on cultural issues, the research may be referred to as **ethnography**.

EXERCISE ON TOPIC 71

1. Examining perceptions is known as what type of approach to acquiring knowledge?

2. A focus group usually consists of about how many participants?

3. What are the two names for the individual who leads a focus group?

4. According to this topic, what is a clear advantage of using focus groups?

5. What is the name of the type of observation in which the researcher observes as an outsider?

6. When the emphasis in field research is on cultural issues, what may the research may be referred to as?

Question for Discussion

7. Do you think that it would be easier to analyze and interpret data from "individual interviews" *or* from "focus group discussions"? Explain.

For Students Planning Research

8. If you are planning to conduct qualitative research, do you anticipate using focus groups? Explain.

TOPIC 72 QUALITY CONTROL IN QUALITATIVE RESEARCH

This topic describes some of the specific techniques that qualitative researchers use to establish the dependability and trustworthiness of their data.[1]

One technique is to use multiple sources for obtaining data on the research topic. The technical name for this is **data triangulation**. For instance, for a qualitative study of age discrimination in an employment setting, a researcher might interview employees, their supervisors, and the responsible personnel officers. To the extent that the various sources provide similar information, the data can be said to be corroborated through data triangulation.

The methods used to collect data can also be triangulated. For instance, a researcher might conduct individual interviews with parents regarding their child-rearing practices and then have the same participants provide data on the same topic via focus groups. This would be an example of **methods triangulation** because two methods were employed to collect the data from one group of participants.

In review, note that in *data triangulation*, typically two or more types of participants (such as employees and supervisors) are used to collect data on a research topic. In contrast, in *methods triangulation*, only one type of participant (such as parents) is used to provide data, but two or more methods are used to collect the data.

An important technique to assure the quality of qualitative research is to form a *research team*, with each member of the team participating in the collection and analysis of data. This can be thought of as **researcher triangulation**, which reduces the possibility that the results of qualitative research represent only the idiosyncratic views of one individual researcher.

Sometimes, it is helpful to form a **team of researchers with diverse backgrounds**. For instance, for a study on the success of minority students in medical school, a team of researchers that consists of both medical school instructors and medical school students might strengthen the study by providing more than one perspective when one is collecting and analyzing the data.

The issue of having diversity in a research team is also addressed in Example 1. The researchers point out that age and gender diversity in their research team helps to provide a "comprehensive view" of the data obtained in interviews on age and gender discrimination in public employment.

EXAMPLE 1
Diversity in a research team: Age and gender issues were analyzed by all three researchers. A comprehensive view of the different meanings of age and gender issues was obtained by using a research team consisting of a 40-year-old man, a 55-year-old woman, and a 62-year-old man.

Oral interviews and focus groups are typically audiorecorded and then transcribed. Sometimes, transcription is challenging because of technical difficulties or participants not speaking distinctly. In addition, transcribers sometimes make clerical errors. Therefore, **checking the accuracy of a transcription** helps to ensure the quality of the data. This can be done by having an independent person compare the audiorecordings with the transcription. Often, it is sufficient to have this person check only a sample of the transcription. If the sample is satisfactory, it may be assumed that the entire transcription is accurate.

In the analysis of data, which is covered in the next two topics in more detail, the members of a research team should initially work independently (without consulting each other) and then compare the results of their analyses. To the extent that they agree, the results are dependable. This technique examines what is called **interobserver agreement**.[2] When there are disagreements, they can often be resolved by having the researchers discuss their differences until they reach a consensus. This process is described in more detail in Topic 74.

The use of an outside expert can also help to ensure the quality of the research. A researcher's peer (such as another experienced qualitative researcher) can examine the process used to collect data and the resulting data and the conclusions, and he or she can then provide feedback to the researcher. This process is called **peer review**. Under certain circumstances, the peer who provides the review is called an **auditor**, which is also discussed in Topic 74.

The dependability of the results can also be enhanced by a process called **member checking**. This

---

[1] The terms *dependability* and *trustworthiness* in qualitative research loosely correspond to the terms *reliability* and *validity* in quantitative research.

[2] In qualitative research, this is sometimes called *intercoder agreement*. In quantitative research, this concept is called *interobserver reliability*.

term is based on the idea that the participants are "members" of the research team. By having the participants/members review the results of the analysis, researchers can determine whether their results ring true to the participants. If not, adjustments can be made in the description of the results.

EXERCISE ON TOPIC 72

1. Suppose a researcher interviewed participants and then observed the behavior of the same participants. Is this an example of "data triangulation" *or* of "methods triangulation"?

2. In data triangulation, how many types of participants are used?

3. What is the name of the type of triangulation that reduces the possibility that the results of qualitative research represent only the idiosyncratic views of an individual researcher?

4. Is it ever desirable for a team of researchers to consist of individuals with diverse backgrounds?

5. In peer review, what is a peer?

6. Who are the members in member checking?

Question for Discussion

7. Name a research topic for qualitative research for which it might be helpful to have a team of researchers with diverse backgrounds. Explain why this might be helpful for the research topic you name.

For Students Planning Research

8. If you are planning to conduct qualitative research, which of the techniques described in this topic, if any, do you plan to use? Explain your choice(s).

To guide their data analysis, qualitative researchers usually select a general, overarching approach. Perhaps the most frequently used approach is **grounded theory**. At first, the term *theory* in *grounded theory* can be a bit misleading because it does not refer to an existing theory of human behavior. Instead, it refers to an *inductive method* of analysis that can lead to theories of behavior. In the inductive approach, which is characteristic of all qualitative research, the results (including resulting theories) emerge through consideration and analysis of the data. In other words, qualitative researchers start with the data and develop theories based on the data (i.e., grounded in the data). In contrast, many quantitative researchers start with an existing theory or deduce a new one from existing information and collect data to test the theory; they typically do not look to the data they have collected to develop new theories. Thus, quantitative researchers use a *deductive method*.

To put it more simply, quantitative researchers deduce theories from what is known and test the theories with research. In contrast, qualitative researchers collect data and analyze it in order to derive theories that explain the patterns noted in the responses of participants. In their seminal work on how to use the grounded theory approach, Strauss and Corbin (1998) said:

> It is through careful scrutiny of data, line by line, that researchers are able to uncover new concepts and novel relationships and to systematically develop categories in terms of their properties and dimensions.[1]

The grounded theory approach starts with **open coding**. In this stage, the transcripts of the interviews are examined for distinct, separate segments (such as the ideas or experiences of the participants), which are identified by type and "coded" with individual names. For instance, in a study of adolescent delinquents, each statement referring to overt aggression by the participant might be coded with a certain color of highlighter. Subcategories should also be developed, when possible. For instance, "overt aggression" might have two subcategories: "overt aggression toward peers" and "overt aggression toward adults, including parents and

teachers."[2] Preliminary notes on any overarching themes noticed in the data should also be made at this point.

The second step in the grounded theory approach to data analysis is called **axial coding**. At this stage, the transcripts of the interviews and any other data sources, such as memos written during data collection, are reexamined with the purpose of identifying relationships between the categories and themes identified during open coding. Some important types of relationships that might be noted are (1) temporal (X usually precedes Y in time), (2) causal (X caused participants to do Y),[3] (3) associational (X and Y usually or always occur at about the same time, but are not believed to be causally connected), (4) valence (participants have stronger emotional reactions to X than to Y), and (5) spatial (X and Y occur in the same place *or* X and Y occur in different places).

In the final stages of the grounded theory approach to analysis, qualitative researchers develop a **core category**, which is the main overarching category under which the other categories and subcategories belong. They also attempt to describe the *process* that leads to the relationships identified in the previous stage of the analysis. A process description should describe how the categories work together (or in opposition to each other) in order to arrive at the conditions or behaviors contained in the core category.

A key element throughout the analysis of data using the grounded theory approach is **constant comparison**, which is a technical term that refers to constantly comparing each new element of the data with all previous elements that have been coded in order to establish and refine categories. While this is being done, the analysis focuses on similarities and differences in the data that might be accounted for by a core idea.

---

[1] Strauss, A. L., & Corbin, J. (1998). *Basics of qualitative research: Techniques and procedures for developing Grounded Theory* (2nd ed.). Thousand Oaks, CA: Sage.

[2] In keeping with the inductive approach, categories and subcategories should be suggested by the data during data analysis, not developed prior to analyzing the data. Categories and subcategories developed at this stage should be regarded as preliminary and subject to change during the remainder of the analysis through the grounded theory approach.

[3] Participants' claims that "X caused me to do Y" should be viewed with caution because participants sometimes are not sufficiently insightful about the causes of their behavior.

EXERCISE ON TOPIC 73

1. In the term *grounded theory*, does the term *theory* refer to a theory that existed prior to conducting the research?

2. Does the grounded theory approach use the "inductive approach" *or* the "deductive approach"?

3. The grounded theory approach starts with what type of coding?

4. What is the name of the second step in the grounded theory approach?

5. In which type of coding is there an emphasis on identifying relationships?

6. What is the technical term that refers to constantly comparing each new element of the data with all previous elements that have been coded in order to establish and refine categories?

Question for Discussion

7. Do you think that the "inductive approach" (such as grounded theory) *or* the "deductive approach" (such as quantitative research) is more likely to yield important information? Are they equally likely to do so? Explain.

For Students Planning Research

8. If you are planning to conduct qualitative research, do you anticipate using the grounded theory approach? Explain. How prepared do you feel? If poorly prepared, how do you plan to learn more about it?

TOPIC 74 CONSENSUAL QUALITATIVE RESEARCH: ANALYSIS

As indicated in the previous topic, qualitative researchers usually select a general, overarching approach to the analysis of their data. In the previous topic, the grounded theory approach was described. In this topic, **consensual qualitative research (CQR)** is described.[1] Like all qualitative research, both approaches are *inductive* (see the previous topic for a discussion of the differences between the inductive and deductive approaches).

As its name implies, CQR strives to have a team of researchers arrive at a consensus on the meaning of the data collected (such as interview transcripts).

The first step in the CQR method is to **code into domains**. This refers to segmenting the data (such as interview transcripts) into groups according to the topics they cover. After the members of the research team have done this, they meet to discuss and refine the domains until they reach unanimous agreement on them.

The next step is to **develop core ideas within domains**. This is done by writing short summaries (i.e., abstracts) that reduce the original ideas of participants to fewer words. Notice that initially, the researchers work independently in developing core ideas.

The third step in CQR is called **cross-analysis**. In this step, the core ideas are grouped into categories based on similarities. This results in a higher level of generalization (i.e., the results are becoming less specific and more general).

Example 1 shows how one team of researchers described the above three steps.

EXAMPLE 1
Description of the use of CQR by a research team (bold added for emphasis): The CQR method (Hill et al., 2005, 1997) is characterized by the following three steps: **(1) developing domains and coding data into domains, (2) constructing core ideas (abstracts) from the data within each domain, and (3) conducting a cross-analysis by categorizing the consistencies across cases**. Hence, the analysis in this study was first done case by case, and later the data were examined across cases. At each step, the data were independently coded by each analysis team member, and then the team members met to engage in consensual discussion. Specifically, at the first

step, each analysis team member independently assigned each segment of data to various domains (e.g., stress, coping, relationships) and then met as a group to discuss the coding. After all of the data were coded into domains, at the second step, each team member again individually summarized the content of the raw data within each domain for each case, and then they met again as a team to engage in consensual discussion. The consensus versions of the summaries served as the core ideas (abstract) of the data. Subsequently, at the third step, the team members discussed possible categories that could be used to cluster similar core ideas across cases, independently coded the data, and then met again to discuss the coding.[2]

In CQR, there may be an external **stability check**, which can be done by examining data in addition to the interview transcripts (perhaps eyewitness accounts or physical evidence), if it is available.

Internal stability is examined in CQR by determining the extent to which each category was general, typical, or variant. Typically, domains that apply to all the participants are called **general**; those that apply to half or more of the participants are called **typical**; and those that apply to less than half but more than two of the participants are called **variant**. When writing up the results, researchers who use CQR usually use these labels throughout their results sections. Emphasis on enumerating the number of participants to which each domain applies is a distinctive feature of CQR. Example 2 shows a portion of the results section of a CQR study in which there is enumeration.

EXAMPLE 2
Enumeration in the results of a CQR study (bold added for emphasis): Results for European American therapists yielded one **typical** and two **variant categories** (neither of the variant categories emerged for the African American sample). As a **typical category**, these participants stated that, like their African American counterparts, they would address race when they deemed it relevant to the therapy process or relationship.... In the first **variant category**, these participants reported

---

[1] For more information on CQR, see Hill, C. E. (ed.). (2012). *Consensual qualitative research: A practical resource for investigating social science phenomena.* Washington, DC: American Psychological Association.

[2] Wang, Y.-W., & Heppner, P. P. (2011). A qualitative study of childhood sexual abuse survivors in Taiwan: Toward a transactional and ecological model of coping. *Journal of Counseling Psychology, 58,* 393–409.

that if a client raised the topic of race, the therapist would respond....[3]

The CQR method requires the use of an **auditor**, who is an outside expert. The auditor usually reviews the work of the research team after each major step in a study, not just at its conclusion. In a report on a CQR study, the following should be briefly described: the credentials of the auditor, the steps at which the auditor supplied feedback, and whether changes were made on the basis of the auditor's feedback. If changes were made, the types of changes made should be mentioned.

EXERCISE ON TOPIC 74

1. Unlike the grounded theory approach in Topic 73, CQR is *deductive*. Is this statement "true" *or* "false"?

2. What is the first step in analyzing data using the CQR approach?

3. Which step includes writing short summaries of participants' ideas?

4. What is done in the cross-analysis?

5. In CQR, what term is used for domains that apply to all the participants?

6. Does the auditor review the work of the research team only at the conclusion of the study?

Question for Discussion

7. Do you think that CQR (as you understand it from this topic) is likely to produce studies that yield important and valuable information? Explain.

For Students Planning Research

8. If you are planning to conduct qualitative research, do you anticipate using CQR? Explain. How prepared do you feel to use it? If poorly prepared, how do you plan to learn more about it?

---

[3] Knox, S., Burkard, A. W., Johnson, A. J., Suzuki, L. A., & Ponterotto, J. G. (2003). African American and European American therapists' experiences of addressing race in cross-racial psychotherapy dyads. *Journal of Counseling Psychology, 50*, 466–481.

PART J

PREPARING RESEARCH REPORTS

This part of the book provides an overview of how to structure a research report as well as how to describe the participants, measures, and results. Techniques for writing the Discussion section at the conclusion of a report are also presented. Finally, differences between typical research reports and theses and dissertations are covered.

NOTES

This topic describes the structure of a typical research report.

The first element is the **Title**. A typical title is concise, consisting of about 10 to 15 words, and should name the major variable(s). Populations of special interest may also be mentioned in a title. In Example 1, the variables are political activism and socioeconomic status, and the population consists of Asian American voters.

EXAMPLE 1
Title of a research report: The Relationship Between Political Activism and Socioeconomic Status Among Asian American Voters

Notice that the title in Example 1 does *not* describe the results of the research. In most cases, this is appropriate because the results of research are usually too complex to summarize within a short title.

The typical parts of a research report that follow the title are shown here:

Title
[Put author's name and affiliation here.]
Abstract
[Put introduction/literature review here.]
Method
Participants
Measures[1]
Procedure (optional)
Data Analysis (optional)
Results
Discussion
References

As indicated above, the title is usually followed by an **Abstract**, which is a summary of the research. The purpose of an abstract is to give readers an overview, which helps them determine whether the research is of interest to them. Writing abstracts is covered in more detail in the next topic in this book.

The abstract is followed by an **Introduction**. In short reports such as journal articles and term projects, the introduction contains a **Literature Review**. (See Part B of this book on reviewing litera-

ture.)[2] Preparing introductions and literature reviews for research reports is covered in Topic 77 in this book. Notice that there is no main heading for this part of the report. In other words, it begins immediately below the abstract.

Following the introduction/literature review is the Method section, which usually has its own major heading of **Method** (bold and centered). Immediately under this heading is the subheading *Participants* (in italics and flush left). Under this subheading, researchers state the number of participants, how they were selected, and demographics such as age and gender. Writing the description of the participants is described in more detail in Topic 78.

The next subsection under Method is *Measures* (with its own flush-left subheading), in which the measurement tools used in the research are described. Quantitative researchers usually use highly structured measures that can be objectively scored. Qualitative researchers use less-structured measures, often semi-structured interviews. Describing measures in quantitative and qualitative research reports is covered in Topic 79.

An optional subsection under the main heading of Method is *Procedure*. This subsection should follow *Measures* and be used to describe any physical steps taken by the researcher to conduct the research. For instance, if treatments were given in an experiment, the treatments could be described in detail in this subsection.

An additional subsection under the main heading of Method is *Data Analysis*, in which the method used to analyze the data is described. This subsection is optional in quantitative research when standard statistical techniques are used, but it is usually needed for describing the type of qualitative research used (e.g., describing how grounded theory or consensual qualitative research was implemented to analyze the data; see Topics 73 and 74).

The next major heading is **Results** (bold and centered). Considerations in presenting the results of research are described in Topic 80.

_____

[1] Some authors of research reports use the term *instrumentation* instead of *measures* to refer to measurement tools.

[2] In a traditional thesis or dissertation, Chapter 1 is an introduction to the research problem (with a limited number of citations to literature), while Chapter 2 is a literature review.

The next major heading is **Discussion** (bold and centered).[3] In this section, researchers present their interpretations of the outcomes of their research.

See Topic 81 for guidelines on writing the discussion.

The **References** conclude a research report. (See Part C for information on citing references.)

EXERCISE ON TOPIC 75

1. Should a title describe the results of the research?

2. The title is usually followed by what?

3. A typical title contains about how many words?

4. Is *Participants* a "major heading" *or* a "subheading"?

5. The measurement tools are described in which subsection?

6. Is *Procedure* an optional subheading?

7. Researchers present their interpretations of the outcomes of their research under which major subheading?

Question for Discussion

8. Consider this title for a research report: "Improving Mathematics Achievement." In your opinion, is the title adequate? Explain.

For Students Planning Research

9. Examine a research article related to the topic of your research. Does it follow the *exact* structure described in this topic? Explain. (Note: This topic describes common practices frequently followed by researchers; variations in structure are often permitted by journal editors as well as professors supervising research conducted as term projects.)

---

[3] In journal articles, some researchers use headings such as "**Discussion and Conclusions**" and "**Summary, Discussion, and Implications**."

An abstract is a summary of the research report. Journals often require relatively short abstracts, often limiting the number of words to no more than 250. The maximum word count for term papers, theses, and dissertations may vary.

In a very brief abstract, it is usually desirable to cover these three essential elements:

1. Research hypotheses, purposes, or questions. These may need to be abbreviated or summarized if they are extensive.

2. Highlights of the research methods, including mention of the participants and measures.

3. Highlights of the results.

Example 1 is an abstract with these three elements. The first sentence names the purpose. The second sentence mentions the participants and measures (e.g., interviews). The final sentences summarize the results.

EXAMPLE 1
An abstract with three essential elements: The purpose of this study was to determine the opinions of parents on the Community Drug Resistance Program (CDRP). A purposive sample of 36 parents of teenagers who participated in the program was selected to be interviewed individually. Three themes emerged from the interviews. First, all the parents strongly approved of the general purposes of the program. Second, most had little knowledge of the specific program activities. Third, all supported greater parental involvement in program implementation.

Note that specific statistical results are usually reported only sparingly, if at all, in abstracts. In Example 1, the term *most* refers to a statistical outcome in only general terms.

If space permits, consider starting the abstract with some brief background material. For instance, Example 1 could start with, "The Community Drug Resistance Program (CDRP) was first funded by the city council three years ago and has strong community support."

Space permitting, any important distinctive characteristics of the study could be mentioned in the abstract. Typically, these are characteristics that were not present in previous studies. For instance in Example 1, the author might say, "None of the previous evaluations included the views of parents." This might be included as part of the background information.

A longer abstract might end with a summary of the conclusions. For instance, Example 1 might end with, "Program directors should increase their efforts to involve parents and inform them of specific program activities."

Example 2 shows what Example 1 would look like with these additional elements.

EXAMPLE 2
An abstract with five elements: The Community Drug Resistance Program (CDRP) was first funded by the city council three years ago and has strong community support. However, none of the previous evaluations included the views of parents. The purpose of this study was to determine the opinions of parents on the CDRP. A purposive sample of 36 parents of teenagers who participated in the program was selected to be interviewed individually. Three themes emerged from the interviews. First, all the parents strongly approved of the general purposes of the program. Second, most had little knowledge of the specific program activities. Third, all supported greater parental involvement in program implementation. Program directors should increase their efforts to involve parents and inform them of specific program activities.

Consider including bold subheadings to identify the various elements in the abstract. This is done in Example 3.

EXAMPLE 3
An abstract with five elements identified with bold subheadings: **Background:** The Community Drug Resistance Program (CDRP) was first funded by the city council three years ago and has strong community support. However, none of the previous evaluations included the views of parents. **Purpose:** The purpose of this study was to determine the opinions of parents on the CDRP. **Method:** A purposive sample of 36 parents of teenagers who participated in the program was selected to be interviewed individually. **Results:** Three themes emerged from the interviews. First, all the parents strongly approved of the general purposes of the program. Second, most had little knowledge of the specific program activities. Third, all supported greater parental involvement in program implementation. **Conclusion:** Program directors should increase their efforts to involve parents and inform them of specific program activities.

Note that subheadings are required by some journals that publish research. In general, the longer the abstract, the more desirable it is to use subheadings.

Appendix G shows four effective abstracts. Note that they may differ somewhat from the recommendations made here, which is permissible.

Exercise on Topic 76

1. Journals often require relatively short abstracts, often limiting the number of words to no more than how many?

2. What is the first of the three essential elements in an abstract?

3. What is the last of the three essential elements in an abstract?

4. If background material is included, should it be the "first" *or* "last" element in an abstract?

5. Is it important to include specific statistical results in abstracts?

6. Are bold subheadings always required in abstracts?

Questions for Discussion

7. Examine the abstracts in Appendix G. Note that the first one does not have bold subheadings. In your opinion, would this abstract be greatly improved by the addition of bold subheadings? Explain.

8. Select one of the abstracts in Appendix G. Is it consistent with the suggestions made in this topic? What are its strengths and weaknesses, if any?

For Students Planning Research

9. Examine the abstract for a research article related to the topic of your research. Is it consistent with the suggestions made in this topic? What are its strengths and weaknesses, if any? Bring it to class for discussion.

The body of a typical research report begins immediately below the abstract, without a main heading. The introductory comments are usually integrated with the literature review. In fact, most researchers cite literature in their first paragraph.[1]

The first purpose of an integrated introduction and literature review is to identify the research problem area. The second purpose is to establish its importance. See Appendix C near the end of this book for sample first paragraphs of research reports. Each one introduces the problem and seeks to establish its importance.

The first paragraphs of an introduction, even if they are supported by citations to literature, should be reasonably specific to the research problem. For instance, if the research problem is childhood obesity in the United States, the first sentence in Example 1 is too global. An improved version is shown in Example 2.

EXAMPLE 1
Beginning of a research report (too broad for the topic): Obesity is a major public health concern in all industrial nations and is an important threat to the well-being of millions. Worldwide, rates of obesity range from....

EXAMPLE 2
Beginning of a research report (improved; more specific): Childhood obesity is a major public health concern in the United States, where rates of obesity for children 6 to 12 years of age have been estimated to range from....

One way to establish the importance of a problem is to cite statistics indicating its prevalence. For instance, for the topic of binge drinking among college students, statistics on how many college students engage in this behavior might be cited.

Another way to establish the importance of a problem is to describe the severity of its impact on individuals. For instance, a rare mental disease may affect relatively few individuals (low prevalence), yet have a devastating impact on those individuals. The severity of the impact can justify researching a problem, even if the problem is not widespread.

As indicated in Topic 16, a literature review should not consist of a series of summaries of pre-

viously published studies. Instead, generalizations about findings (i.e., the *trends* found in the research) should be stated, with references supporting them grouped together. Example 3 illustrates how this might be done.

EXAMPLE 3
Grouping references for a generalization: Several studies have indicated the weak effects of the Doe Drug Reduction Intervention Program when it is used with adolescents (Smith, 2012; Jones, 2010; Black, 2011).

To provide depth of information, it is acceptable to discuss selected studies in detail. For instance, Example 3 could continue with a statement such as, "Of these, Smith (2012) used the largest, most representative sample. She reported an average level of decrease in marijuana use from pretest to posttest of only 2.2% when averaged over...."

Note that specific statistics should be cited sparingly. Cite only those that are most relevant and can be easily understood out of the context of the original research reports. Readers can consult the original sources for additional statistical details.

Most research is designed to fill gaps in knowledge of a particular topic. When this is the case, it is important to explicitly point out those gaps in the literature review. This is illustrated in Example 4.

EXAMPLE 4
Pointing out a gap in the literature (after citing literature to establish that Latino adolescents are subject to stress due to discrimination, the authors state): "However, few studies have examined how Latino adolescents cope with discrimination, whether coping strategies might protect against the negative effects of perceived discrimination, and factors that promote the use of effective coping strategies."[2]

A combined introduction/literature review should end with a statement of the specific research hypotheses, purposes, and/or questions (see Topic 7). When there are several of them, they should be numbered or lettered, as in Example 5. Note that they should flow logically from the introductory material.

---

[1] In a typical thesis or dissertation, Chapter 1 is an introduction, with few literature citations, while Chapter 2 is a comprehensive literature review.

[2] Umaña-Taylor, A. J., Vargas-Chanes, D., Garcia, C. D., & Gonzales-Backen, M. (2008). A longitudinal examination of Latino adolescents' ethnic identity, coping with discrimination, and self-esteem. *Journal of Early Adolescence, 28*, 16–50.

Numbered hypotheses at the conclusion of the intro-duction/literature review: In light of the research findings described above, these hypotheses were for-mulated to be tested in the current research: (1) Col-lege students who are more involved in extracurricu-lar activities consume less alcohol, (2) have fewer friends who binge drink, (3) have....

EXERCISE ON TOPIC 77

1. Does a typical research report have the main heading **Introduction**?

2. What is the first function of an integrated introduction and literature review?

3. In this topic, two ways to establish the importance of a problem are mentioned. What is the second way?

4. Should a literature review consist of a series of summaries of previously published studies?

5. Should statistics in the literature be cited sparingly?

6. A combined introduction/literature review should end with what?

Question for Discussion

7. Examine a research article to determine whether the introduction/literature review is consistent with the recommendations in this topic. Describe any consistencies and inconsistencies.

For Students Planning Research

8. To what extent has the material in this topic helped to prepare you for writing an introduction/literature review? Explain.

TOPIC 78   DESCRIBING PARTICIPANTS

In research reports, the subheading *Participants* appears immediately under the main heading of **Method**. (See the outline in Topic 75.)

Obviously, the number of participants should be stated. This statement may contain information on selected demographics (i.e., background characteristics such as age and gender), as illustrated in Example 1.

EXAMPLE 1
Brief description of participants: A sample of 120 adolescents (12–16 years old, $m = 14.55$) participated in the study. There were 70 males and 50 females.

A wide variety of demographics may be reported. As indicated in Topic 28, some demographics are more relevant to a particular research project than others. For instance, in a study of mathematics instruction, students' grade level and GPA are more relevant than their religious affiliation.

It is usually desirable to indicate the method of recruitment (e.g., classified ads in a college newspaper or an offer of extra credit to students enrolled in a sociology course).

The response rate, if known, should be indicated. This is important because those who respond (known as *volunteers*) may be quite different from those who do not respond (see Topic 24).

When a *sample of convenience* (also called a *convenience sample*) is used, this should be mentioned (see Topic 24).

If *informed consent* was obtained, this should also be mentioned.

Example 2 shows an expanded version of Example 1 based on the above information.

EXAMPLE 2
Expanded description of participants (bold added for emphasis): All 250 students in a local middle school were **recruited** through letters mailed to their parents. Attached to the letters were **informed consent** forms for parents to sign if they agreed to allow their children to participate. Of the 250 parents, 120 returned the consent forms (a **48% response rate**), which resulted in a **convenience sample** of 120 adolescents (12–16 years old, $m = 14.55$), consisting of 70 males and 50 females.

When a large number of demographics are to be reported, researchers should consider reporting them in a statistical table. Such a table is especially important if two or more distinct groups were compared in a study. For instance, in a study comparing the academic achievement of girls attending a charter school with that of girls attending a traditional school, the demographics might be presented in a table such as the one in Example 3, where "free lunch" is an indicator of socioeconomic status because family income determines its availability. Such tables are efficient for the presentation of such information, and they help readers to spot important differences. For instance, the "free lunch" difference (20% vs. 42%) stands out in the tabular presentation in Example 3.[1]

EXAMPLE 3

Table of Demographics

	Charter	Traditional
Age	$m = 8.2$	$m = 8.8$
Age range	7–10	7–11
Free lunch (yes)	20%	42%
Intact family (yes)	78%	73%
Ethnicity		
Caucasian	75%	70%
African American	15%	20%
Asian	6%	5%
Other	4%	5%

Quantitative researchers emphasize *random selection* of participants from populations. (See Topics 25 and 26.) Thus, if random selection has been used in a quantitative study, it is important to mention it.

Qualitative researchers often employ *purposive samples*. As indicated in Topic 68, researchers who use this type of sample deliberately select individuals who they think might be rich sources of information on a particular research topic. Researchers who employ purposive sampling should explain their reasoning and the steps they took to implement it (see Topic 69). Without information of this type, readers are likely to assume that a *sample of convenience* (not a purposive sample) was used.

If *saturation* was used to determine sample size in a qualitative study, this should be indicated. (See Topic 69 for information on saturation.)

While limitations of a study due to poor sampling might be mentioned under *Participants*, researchers usually discuss this matter in the **Discussion** section of their research reports.

---

[1] Note that some researchers present detailed information on demographics in the Results section.

EXERCISE ON TOPIC 78

1. The subheading *Participants* appears immediately under what main heading?

2. Should the method of recruitment be described under *Participants*?

3. Is it appropriate to mention informed consent under *Participants*?

4. When is it especially important to use a table to report demographics?

5. Are "qualitative" *or* "quantitative" researchers more likely to use purposive sampling?

6. Is saturation more likely to be mentioned in a report on "qualitative research" *or* "quantitative research"?

Question for Discussion

7. Consider a researcher who has studied the school achievement of children who reside with their parents in a shelter for the homeless. Name two demographics that might be highly relevant and two that would be less relevant for inclusion in a research report on this topic.

For Students Planning Research

8. Examine a research article related to the topic of your research. Is the description of the participants completely consistent with the recommendations in this topic? Explain.

TOPIC 79 DESCRIBING MEASURES

Quantitative researchers usually use objective measures such as multiple-choice tests and attitude scales (e.g., "Strongly agree" to "Strongly disagree"). Note that *measures* are sometimes called *instruments*.

When a quantitative researcher uses a previously published measure, he or she should cite it and include a reference for it. For instance, a published achievement test would be cited and included in the reference list as a book, where the title of the book is equivalent to the title of the test. (See Part C on citing references.)

Many specialized measures are published only in the sense that they were included in journal articles. When one of these has been used, the original source should be cited, which is done in Example 1.

EXAMPLE 1
Brief description of a quantitative measure with citations: The Trait Forgivingness Scale (TFS; Berry, Worthington, O'Connor, Parrott, & Wade, 2005) assesses disposition to forgive. A sample item is, "There are some things for which I could never forgive even a loved one." Previous alphas range from .71 to .81, and construct validity has been established with constructs such as avoidance following a hurtful event.... [1]

Notice in Example 1, the authors (1) name the trait the measure is designed to measure (i.e., disposition to forgive), (2) provide a sample item, and (3) indicate that reliability (i.e., alphas) and validity have been established. All three elements are desirable in the description of a measure used in quantitative research. When space permits, more detailed descriptions of these three elements might be provided.

When a measure has been widely used, this should be noted (e.g., "the measure has been widely used by other researchers in a variety of settings"). This suggests that other researchers have found the measure useful.

Sometimes quantitative researchers construct new measures for a particular research project. Because information on them is not available elsewhere, it is especially important for researchers to provide detailed information on them in their research reports.

Qualitative researchers usually use less-structured measures than quantitative researchers. Despite the lack of high levels of structure, qualitative researchers should explicitly provide specific information on their measurement methods.

Perhaps the most widely used type of measure employed in qualitative research is the semistructured interview (see Topic 70). Example 2 shows how researchers briefly described the interview process they used.

EXAMPLE 2
Brief description of a semistructured interview: The in-depth, audio-recorded interviews were carried out at participants' homes and only the mother was invited. An open and accepting interview style based on phenomenology principles was used. The interview questions focused on how these mothers assisted their children's life adjustment at school, specifically with respect to T1DM [Type 1 diabetes mellitus]. Each interview began with the question: "What is your experience when assisting your child's life adjustment at school?" Facilitative techniques (e.g., "Hmm" and "Could you describe it more?") were used to obtain the most complete description possible. On average, interviews lasted approximately one hour. [2]

Notice in Example 2, the authors (1) state where the interviews were conducted and who was present, (2) name the focus of the questions, (3) provide a sample question as well as sample prompts (e.g., "Hmm"), and (4) indicate how long the interviews lasted. All of these are desirable elements.

When space permits, a description of a semistructured interview might also include background information on the interviewer, such as whether the interviewer in Example 2 above was, herself, a mother with a child with Type 1 diabetes.

Qualitative interviewers also frequently use focus groups to gather their data (see Topic 71). The description of focus group sessions should cover the same points as in Example 2 above. In addition, they should indicate how many focus groups were used and how many participants were included in each group.

---

[1] Hodgson, L. K., & Wertheim, E. H. (2007). Does good emotion management aid forgiving? Multiple dimensions of empathy, emotion management, and forgiveness of self and others. *Journal of Social and Personal Relationships, 24*, 931–949.

[2] Lin, H.-P., Mu, P.-F., & Lee, Y.-J. (2008). Mothers' experience supporting life adjustment in children with T1DM. *Western Journal of Nursing Research, 30*, 96–110.

EXERCISE ON TOPIC 79

1. Does Example 1 in this topic mention validity? If so, which type of validity is mentioned?

2. If a measure has been widely used, should this fact be mentioned?

3. When is it especially important for quantitative researchers to provide detailed information on the measures?

4. If semistructured interviews have been used, the researcher is relieved of the responsibility to describe them in detail. Is this statement "true" *or* "false"?

5. Is it appropriate to provide background information on the interviewer when semistructured interviews are used in the collection of data?

6. When focus groups are used, should the researcher indicate how many participants were in each group?

Question for Discussion

7. In your opinion, how important is it for researchers to provide the sample questions from their measures?

For Students Planning Research

8. Examine a research article related to the topic of your research. Is the description of the measures completely consistent with the recommendations in this topic? Explain.

As indicated in Topic 75, the Results section should have the main heading **Results** (bold and centered).

For research that has more than one hypothesis, purpose, or question, it is usually best to report the results for each separately in the order in which they were first presented in the research report. For instance, if there were two hypotheses, restate the first one and present the data for it. Then, restate the second hypothesis and present the data for that one.

In reports of quantitative research, researchers typically do not indicate how the statistical results were computed (e.g., they do not name the statistical computer program used), and they do not provide a reference for standard statistical formulas. For instance, a researcher would simply report the means and standard deviations relating to a hypothesis without discussing computational details. In these reports, descriptive statistics (e.g., mean, standard deviation, and percentage) should be reported first, followed by the results of tests of statistical significance (e.g., chi-square, *t* test, and ANOVA). This is illustrated in Example 1. Note that when there are hypotheses, the research should explicitly state whether the hypothesis was supported by the data.

EXAMPLE 1
Beginning of the Results section in a quantitative research report: The first hypothesis was that participants who attended the extended training sessions would report more satisfaction with the program than those who attended the abbreviated sessions. The mean satisfaction score for the extended group was higher ($m = 24.00$, $sd = 1.50$) than the mean for the abbreviated group ($m = 22.00$, $sd = 1.40$). The difference between the two means is statistically significant at the .05 level ($t = 3.30$, $df = 21$). Thus, the first hypothesis was supported.

The second hypothesis was that participants....

When there are a number of related statistics to report, it is usually best to present them in a table (instead of reporting them in sentences). Example 2 shows a table with a number of descriptive statistics. Highlights of the contents of statistical tables should be described in the Results section with statements such as, "The means in Table 2 show that the supervised practice group outperformed the unsupervised practice and control groups."

EXAMPLE 2

Table 2
Posttest Statistics for Three Groups

Group	n	m	sd
Supervised practice	21	55.78	8.27
Unsupervised practice	20	49.02	7.66
Control group	22	46.35	9.36

The Results sections for qualitative research differ in a number of respects. First, in reports on qualitative research, there is usually a discussion of the steps taken to analyze the data (such as the results of semistructured interviews), usually under the subheading *Data Analysis* (see the outline in the first column of Topic 75).[1] Here, the method of analysis (such as grounded theory or consensual qualitative research) should be named and the steps taken to implement the method described (e.g., how many coders were used and how a consensus was reached). See Appendix H for an example of how the data analysis method is described in a qualitative research report.

In the Results section of reports on qualitative research, there are usually few, if any, statistics reported. Instead, qualitative researchers discuss the primary themes that emerged from the data as well as any theories developed during the analysis. Example 3 shows the beginning of the Results section of a qualitative research report. Note that each of the themes mentioned in the example was used as a subheading within the Results section. Under each subheading, the researchers described the theme and illustrated it with verbatim quotations from participants to illustrate the meaning of the theme.

EXAMPLE 3
Beginning of the Results section in a qualitative research report: In this study we investigated the questions: What is collaborative health care? What occurs? How is it experienced? Qualitative data analysis produced six cultural themes: (a) characteristics of the environment, (b) characteristics of therapists, (c) the referral process, (d) characteristics of collaboration, (e) the psychotherapy process, and (f) social considerations. Taken together, they describe, at least in part, how collaborative health care is practiced at this site. The content and meaning of each cultural

---

[1] This subsection is placed under "Method," just above the Results section. It is seldom included in reports on quantitative research when standard statistical methods have been used.

theme will be described via a summarized version of patient, therapist, physician, and staff statements.[2]

Because statistics can be used to very concisely summarize quantitative data, the Results sections of reports of quantitative research tend to be much shorter than the Results sections of qualitative research reports.

EXERCISE ON TOPIC 80

1. For research that has more than one hypothesis, purpose, or question, is it usually best to report the results for each one separately? If so, in what order?

2. In reports on *quantitative research*, do researchers typically indicate how the statistical results were computed (e.g., do they name the statistical computer program used)?

3. Should "descriptive statistics" *or* "results of tests of statistical significance" be reported first?

4. When statistical tables are included in a Results section, which of the following is true?
   A. The tables should be presented without commentary.
   B. Highlights of the contents of statistical tables should be mentioned.

5. Is a subsection titled Data Analysis more likely to appear in reports of "quantitative research" *or* "qualitative research"?

6. Are verbatim quotations more likely to appear in reports of "quantitative research" *or* "qualitative research"?

7. Do reports of "quantitative research" *or* "qualitative research" tend to have shorter results sections?

Questions for Discussion

8. If you have access to a published report of quantitative research, examine it to answer these questions: Are statistics reported in tables? If yes, does the researcher describe the highlights of the results in the tables? Does the researcher discuss how he or she computed the statistics (e.g., by giving formulas and citations for them)?

9. If you have access to a published report of qualitative research, examine it to answer these questions: Is the Results section organized around themes? Does the Results section contain verbatim quotations from participants? If yes, are there many quotations?

For Students Planning Research

10. Examine a research article related to the topic of your research. Is the organization of the Results section in the article similar to the organization you plan to use? Explain.

---

[2] Todahl, J. L., Linville, D., Smith, T. E., Barnes, M. F., & Miller, J. K. (2006). A qualitative study of collaborative health care in a primary care setting. *Families, Systems, & Health, 24*, 45–64.

Topic 81   Writing the Discussion

As indicated in Topic 75, the last part of the body of a research report is the **Discussion**,[1] which has a main heading centered and in bold.

While there are many ways in which a Discussion section may be organized, the following information should usually be included.

Begin by referring to the *original purposes of the research*, which may have been stated as research questions, purposes, or hypotheses.

Second, indicate the extent to which the purposes were achieved as represented by the *research results*. Example 1 shows how the first two elements in a discussion might be presented. Note that specific statistics usually do not need to be presented here because a reader can refer to the Results section for them.

EXAMPLE 1
Beginning of a Discussion section: The purpose of this study was to test three hypotheses regarding the relationship between X and Z. The first hypothesis was that X would be directly related to Z in a sample of homeless children. This hypothesis was strongly supported by the data. The second hypothesis was....

Notice that the researcher who wrote Example 1 indicated that the hypothesis was "strongly supported." If a researcher knows of serious methodological weaknesses in the execution of the study *or* if the effect size is small (see Topics 62–64, more tentative language should be used such as, "The data offer limited support for the first hypothesis."

At this point, it is appropriate to briefly compare and contrast the results of the current research with the results reported in the literature review (e.g., "The support for this hypothesis is consistent with the results in a prior survey by Doe [2012]"). If any results of the current study are surprising in light of the information in the literature review, this should also be pointed out. For instance, a researcher might state, "The failure of the data to support the hypothesis for young children is surprising in light of the strong support for the hypothesis in the earlier experiment by Jones (2011), in which adolescents participated. A possible explanation for this inconsistency is...."

When the results have practical *implications*, these should be explicitly stated, and the researcher should indicate what actions a particular person, group, or organization should perform. In Example 2, the organization is "public health agencies," and the action is "providing bilingual diabetes outreach programs."

EXAMPLE 2
Practical implications in a Discussion section: The low rate of compliance by the Hispanic adults, most of whom were born in Mexico, may be due to language interference. Because many of these participants might not be fluent in English, public health agencies should consider providing bilingual diabetes outreach programs....

The Discussion section is an appropriate place to describe *limitations* (i.e., methodological weaknesses) and to indicate how the limitations might affect interpretations of the results. Although typical limitations are in sampling and measurement, a variety of other methodological problems may have affected the results, which should be considered in their interpretation. Example 3 indicates the nature of the limitation in sampling *and* its potential impact on the results.

EXAMPLE 3
Sampling limitation in a Discussion section: The volunteer sample for this survey consisted of disproportionately high middle- and high-socioeconomic-status individuals. Thus, the need for assistance in acquiring healthy food resources (e.g., fruits and vegetables) may have been underestimated in this study.

In the Discussion section, it is also appropriate to suggest directions for *future research*. Such suggestions should be specific because it is of little value to consumers of research to simply state that "more research is needed." Example 4 shows a discussion of future research. Notice that the suggestion is specific (i.e., use of a more limited vocabulary).

EXAMPLE 4
Directions for future research in a Discussion section: Because participant feedback indicates that some participants found the questionnaire difficult to comprehend, researchers should consider using a more limited vocabulary when constructing questionnaires during future research on this topic.

If a Discussion section is long, researchers sometimes include subheadings (in italics, flush left) to guide readers. On the basis of the above ma-

---

[1] In some research journals, this part is called "Conclusions." Other variations, such as "Discussion and Conclusions," may be found.

terial, here are subheadings that might be used in the Discussion section:

Research purposes and results
Implications
Limitations
Directions for future research

EXERCISE ON TOPIC 81

1. Should the heading "Discussion" be centered in bold?

2. The Discussion should begin with a reference to what?

3. Is it usually important to cite specific statistics when discussing research results in the Discussion section?

4. What should a statement of implication indicate?

5. When discussing limitations, it is appropriate to indicate how the limitations might affect what?

6. If a Discussion section is long, researchers sometimes include what?

Question for Discussion

7. Suppose a researcher only stated "More research is needed" in a discussion of future directions for research. Is this statement sufficient? Explain.

For Students Planning Research

8. In the Discussion section of your research report, do you plan to include all the elements discussed in this topic? Explain.

TOPIC 82 PREPARING THESES AND DISSERTATIONS

As indicated in Topics 75 and 76, in theses and dissertations Chapter 1 is the Introduction and is followed by Chapter 2, the literature review.[1] (See Topics 14–18 and 77 for information on writing literature reviews.)

Chapter 1 should start by introducing the problem area for the research and the reasons why it is important. When the researcher is establishing its importance, some literature may be cited, but only specific statistics (e.g., "up to 59% of adults are estimated to have…") and direct quotations. Note that direct quotations should be used exceedingly sparingly because they can interrupt the flow of the texts. The vast majority of the Introduction should be in the students' own words.

Although Chapter 1 should contain few references, mention of the literature in Chapter 2 may be made in Chapter 1. For instance, when establishing the importance of the problem area in Chapter 1, a writer might make statements such as "As the literature review in Chapter 2 indicates, this problem is pervasive throughout populations of homeless injection-drug users in urban areas." The researcher might also indicate gaps in the literature in Chapter 1 by stating that such gaps are described in detail in Chapter 2.

Any *theories* underlying the research should be briefly described in Chapter 1. The writer should indicate clearly how the current research is related to the theory or theories (see Topic 13). Note that a detailed discussion of the literature on relevant theories should be presented in Chapter 2.

After the researcher has introduced the problem area, establishing its importance and indicating its theoretical basis, an overview of the research approach *and* the rationale for using the approach should be presented. For instance, why was survey research selected as the approach (e.g., "…to establish the incidence of binge drinking at ABC College….")? Why was a qualitative research approach selected (e.g., "…to gather in-depth information from the participants' perspectives, which has hitherto not been obtained…")?

Chapter 1 should end with an explicit statement of the research purposes, hypotheses, or questions.

When there is more than one, they should be numbered (e.g., Hypothesis 1: Participants who….).

In addition to having a separate introductory chapter, theses and dissertations also differ from most other types of research reports in terms of the level of comprehensiveness and detail expected. This is because a thesis or dissertation is, in effect, a cumulative take-home examination in which students are expected to demonstrate a high level of ability to understand, organize, and present complex material. As a result, theses and dissertations tend to be much longer than other types of research reports.

To demonstrate an in-depth understanding of the material, students should be highly *reflective* and *critical*. For instance, when discussing the design selected for an experiment, a student could reflect on the merits and limitations of the particular design employed in the study. In another example, a student who conducted quantitative research might compare and contrast various measures (e.g., self-concept scales) and indicate the rationale for selecting one over the others for use in the thesis/dissertation research.

When students first become aware of the length expected in theses and dissertations, they are sometimes tempted to expand their dissertations by writing a long literature review consisting of detailed summaries of previous research, with the summaries strung together. As indicated in Topics 18 and 77, this is inappropriate because it fails to organize the literature and fails to create a synthesis.

Despite the restriction on stringing detailed summaries of previous research together, a long, detailed literature review can be created through the use of the following technique.

First, arrange studies into the smallest meaningful groups (e.g., the three studies using adolescents as participants could be in a different group from the two studies using adults). For each group, indicate the general nature of the findings, whether the findings are consistent from one study to the other, and any methodological flaws, especially ones that the studies in the group have in common (e.g., all studies using adults as participants used volunteer samples). Finally, select one study from each group to discuss in greater detail. Often, this will be a study judged especially strong in terms of its research methodology. In addition, it should be critiqued (i.e., its strengths and weaknesses should be described).

---

[1] In shorter research reports, such as research articles in journals and term projects, the introductory comments are usually integrated with the literature review.

The typical length of theses and dissertations intimidates many students. An effective technique for dealing with writer's block caused by the anticipation of composing a long document is to write small sections at a time (e.g., the description of a small group of related studies for the literature review). Writing small sections, which can later be pieced together and revised for flow, makes the task manageable.

EXERCISE ON TOPIC 82

1. Chapter 1 should start by introducing what?

2. Should direct quotations be used sparingly?

3. Is it permissible in Chapter 1 to refer to the literature review in Chapter 2?

4. Which chapter should contain a detailed discussion of the literature on related theories?

5. In Chapter 1, after the researcher has introduced the problem area, establishing its importance and indicating its theoretical basis, what should be presented?

6. Is it ever appropriate in a literature review to discuss one study in greater detail?

Question for Discussion

7. What is your opinion of the suggestion to concentrate on the composition of small sections as a way to overcome writer's block when preparing a thesis or dissertation? Have you ever used this technique when writing a long paper? Explain.

For Students Planning Research

8. Will you be writing a thesis or dissertation? If so, what problems do you anticipate?

APPENDIX A
ELECTRONIC DATABASES FOR LOCATING LITERATURE

Access Note

Access to all of the following electronic databases usually can be obtained free of charge through your college or university library, which probably maintains license agreements with the database publishers. Consult with your reference librarian for information on their availability at your library. Note that the *ERIC* and *PubMed/MEDLINE* databases are available free of charge to all individuals via the Internet.

Databases Discussed in Topic 15

Sociological Abstracts indexes and summarizes articles in more than 1,800 international journals and indexes and summarizes books and chapters in books. *Sociological Abstracts* indexes dissertations, book reviews, film reviews, and game reviews. An online thesaurus is available. Consult with the reference librarian at your college or university for information on accessing this database free of charge through your library's license agreement. Visit http://www.csa.com/factsheets/socioabs-set-c.php.

PsycINFO indexes and abstracts journal articles from more than 2,497 journals. Books, dissertations, and university and government reports are also included. Members of the public can access this database via the Internet for a daily service fee (charged to a credit card) at www.apa.org. Consult with the reference librarian at your college or university for information on accessing this database free of charge through your library's license agreement.

PsycARTICLES contains more than 154,000 full-text articles (not just abstracts) from 78 journals and selected chapters from books published by the American Psychological Association. Members of the public can access this database via the Internet for a daily service fee (charged to a credit card) at www.apa.org. Consult with the reference librarian at your college or university for information on accessing this database free of charge through your library's license agreement.

ERIC stands for Education Resources Information Center. The *ERIC* database contains more than 1.3 million abstracts of unpublished documents and published journal articles on educational research and practice. Hundreds of new records are added to the database daily. Visit www.eric.ed.gov for more information.

Other Electronic Databases

The *ABI/Inform* (*ProQuest*) database is a business and management database with abstracts and many full-text articles from U.S. and international publications. Topics include advertising, marketing, economics, human resources, finance, taxation, and computers.

The *Chicano Database* identifies all types of material about Chicanos. It incorporates the *Spanish Speaking Mental Health Database*, which covers psychological, sociological, and educational literature.

Child Development and Adolescent Studies includes abstracts from professional periodicals and book reviews related to the growth and development of children from 1927 to the present.

Contemporary Women's Issues provides full-text access to journals, hard-to-find newsletters, reports, pamphlets, fact sheets, and guides on a broad array of gender-related issues published since 1992.

ProQuest Criminal Justice contains full-text articles from criminology and criminal justice journal articles on law enforcement, corrections administration, social work, drug rehabilitation, criminal and family law, industrial security, and other related fields. There are also indexing and abstracts for 425 U.S. and international journals.

Dissertation Abstracts Online is a definitive subject, title, and author guide to virtually every American dissertation accepted at an accredited institution since 1861. Selected master's theses have been included since 1962. The electronic version indexes doctoral records from July 1980 (*Dissertation Abstracts International*, Volume 41, Number 1) to the present. Abstracts are included for master's theses from spring 1988 (*Master's Abstracts*, Volume 26, Number 1) to the present. This database has very wide subject matter coverage including, but not limited to, business and economics, education, fine arts and music, geography, health sciences, political science, language and literature, library and information science, psychology, and sociology.

Family Studies Database contains citations and abstracts for journal articles, books, popular literature, conference papers, and government reports in the fields of family science, human ecology, and human development since 1970.

International Index to Black Periodicals Full Text (*IIBP Full Text*) draws its current content from more than 150 international scholarly and popular periodicals. It covers a wide array of humanities-related disciplines including art, cultural criticism, economics, education, health, history, language and literature, law, philosophy, politics, religion, and sociology, among others. All records in the current file (1998 forward) contain abstracts.

PubMed/MEDLINE is the U.S. National Library of Medicine's (NLM) premier bibliographic database covering the fields of medicine, nursing, dentistry, veterinary medicine, the health care system, and the preclinical sciences. *PubMed/MEDLINE*, the primary subset of *PubMed*, is available on the Internet through the NLM home page at www.ncbi.nlm.nih.gov/pubmed and can be searched free of charge. No registration is required. Additional *PubMed/MEDLINE* services are also provided by organizations that lease the database from NLM. Access to various *PubMed/MEDLINE* services is often available from medical libraries and many public libraries.

Social Sciences Citation Index (*SSCI*®) and *Social SciSearch*® provide access to current and retrospective bibliographic information, author abstracts, and cited references found in more than 1,700 of the world's leading scholarly social science journals, covering more than 50 disciplines. They also cover individually selected, relevant items from approximately 3,300 of the world's leading science and technology journals. Note that the *Citation Index* lists cited authors and their works together with all authors who have discussed the cited works in their publications. This can be very helpful in conducting a literature search if a researcher starts with a classic older article that is highly relevant to the topic. By searching for all publications in which it was subsequently cited, the researcher can quickly build a collection of references that are likely to be very specific to the topic. Examining these sequentially permits the researcher to trace the history of thought on a topic or theory.

Appendix B
Electronic Sources of Statistical Information[1]

✎ Guideline 1
Web sources are often more up-to-date than professional journals.

When writing literature reviews, writers often need up-to-date information. Because of the ease of electronic publishing, the web is more likely to have such information than conventionally printed materials. Note that it is not uncommon for a printed journal article or book to be published a year or more after it was written. Despite this delay, professional journals are usually the primary sources of detailed information on how investigators conducted their research, so they remain premier sources of information for literature reviews.

✎ Guideline 2
Information on current issues can often be found using general search engines.

A general search engine such as Google can be used to locate information that might be included in a literature review. Consider the topic of smoking during pregnancy. A quick search using the search term "women smoking pregnancy" retrieved 62,000,000 sites with related information. The first site in the list, maintained by the March of Dimes, contains the information shown in Example 2.1.

Example 2.1
Sample topic delimited by "women smoking pregnancy":

Like drinking too much alcohol or doing drugs, smoking is also very harmful to your health. It can cause serious health conditions including cancer, heart disease, stroke and gum disease. It can also cause eye diseases that can lead to blindness. Smoking can make it harder for a woman to get pregnant.

Not only is smoking harmful to you, it's also harmful to your baby during pregnancy. When you smoke during pregnancy, your baby is exposed to dangerous chemicals like nicotine, carbon monoxide, and tar. These chemicals can lessen the amount of oxygen that your baby gets. Oxygen is very important for helping your baby grow healthy. Smoking can also damage your baby's lungs.[2]

✎ Guideline 3
FedStats.gov is an important source of statistical information.

Often, literature reviews begin with current statistics on how many individuals (and/or the percentage of individuals) are affected by the topic of the literature review, and up-to-date statistics are often available at www.FedStats.gov.

Statistics from more than 100 federal agencies can be accessed.[3] Prior to establishment of this website, individuals needed to search for statistics on an agency-by-agency basis. While the FedStats site still allows users to do this, they can also search by *topic* and the FedStats search engine will automatically search all agencies for relevant links to federal statistics. This is important for two reasons: (1) A user does not have to search each agency separately, and (2) an agency that a user is not aware of may have statistics relevant to his or her topic.

For instance, conducting a search by first clicking on "Topic links – A to Z" produces an alphabetical list of topics. Box 3A shows the topics under the letter C (at the time of this writing).

---

[1] This appendix was adapted from Chapter 4 of *Preparing Literature Reviews: Qualitative and Quantitative Approaches* (4th ed.) by M. Ling Pan (pp. 19–24). Copyright © 2013 by Pyrczak Publishing. All rights reserved.

[2] Retrieved from http://www.marchofdimes.com/pregnancy/alcohol_smoking.html on September 20, 2011.

[3] Be sure to go to www.FedStats.*gov* and *not* www.FedStats.*com*. The latter is *not* a government site.

Box 3A   *FedStats links for the letter C.*

Cancer:
-- *Atlas of Cancer Mortality in the United States*
-- Breast
-- Cervical
-- Lung
-- Mortality maps
-- Prostate
Charitable trusts
Children:
-- Administration for Children programs and services
-- Adoption
-- *America's Children* (ChildStats)
-- Behavior and social environment indicators
-- Child care
-- Child support enforcement
-- Cigarette smoking
-- Delinquency and victimization
    -- Delinquency case records (data and analysis software
       package)
    -- Juvenile arrests
    -- Juveniles as offenders
    -- Juveniles as victims
    -- Juveniles in court
    -- Juveniles in detention and corrections
-- Drug use
-- Economic security indicators
-- Education indicators
-- Foster care
-- HeadStart
-- Temporary Assistance for Needy Families
Health:
-- Child and infant
-- Indicators
-- Insurance
-- Population and family characteristics
-- Nutrition
-- WIC
Civil justice statistics
Coal
Commodity flow
Common cold
Communications:
-- Broadcast radio and television
-- Cable television providers by community served (size 9M)
-- Telephone industry and telephone usage
-- Wireless communications services
Computer and Internet use
Construction
Industry tax statistics:
-- Corporations

-- Exempt organizations' unrelated business
-- Partnerships
-- Sole proprietorship Consumer Credit
Consumer product safety
Consumer Price Indexes
Consumption, energy
Corporations
Country profiles
Crime (See also *Law enforcement*):
-- Characteristics of crime
-- Children
-- Crime in schools
-- Crimes reported to the police
-- Criminal offenders
-- Drugs
-- Firearms
-- Hate
-- Homicide
-- Prison inmates
-- Terrorism
-- Victims
-- Violent
Criminal justice:
-- Corrections
    -- Capital punishment
    -- Inmates
    -- Jails
    -- Prisons
    -- Probation and parole statistics
-- Courts and sentencing
    -- Court organization
    -- Criminal case processing
    -- Pretrial release and detention
    -- Sentencing
-- Criminal record systems
-- Employment and expenditure
-- Federal justice statistics
-- Indigent defense statistics
-- Law enforcement
    -- Campus law enforcement
    -- Federal law enforcement
    -- State and local law enforcement
-- Prosecution
Crops:
-- Crop progress and weather, weekly
-- Data by county
-- Data by state, historic
-- Field
-- Fruits and nuts
-- Vegetables

✎ Guideline 4
State government websites are a source of local statistics.

The main web pages for various states can be accessed by using the postal service's state names' abbreviations in URL addresses, such as www.ga.gov (for Georgia) and www.ca.gov (for California). While the organization of the home pages varies greatly from state to state, they contain links that can lead to a variety of statistical information, which can be useful when local statistics are needed for a literature review.

In addition, there are links to descriptions of a variety of government-funded programs. This information can be valuable for individuals who are reviewing literature on programs.

✤ Guideline 5
Use the raw statistics from governmental agencies, not statistics filtered by special interests.

Some individuals (such as politicians) and groups (such as advocacy groups) with special interests may understandably be selective in choosing which government statistics to report and interpret on their websites. Hence, it is usually best to obtain the original government reports either in print or via the web.

✤ Guideline 6
Consider consulting the Library of Congress's Virtual Reference Shelf on the web.

The Library of Congress maintains a website titled the Virtual Reference Shelf. It is an excellent site for general references such as dictionaries, general history, abbreviations, genealogy, and so on. This site's address is www.loc.gov/rr/askalib/virtualref.html.[4] Box 6B shows the main links on the home page of the site at the time of this writing.

Box 6B   *Links on the home page of the Library of Congress's Virtual Reference Shelf.*

Virtual Reference Shelf
Selected web resources compiled by the Library of Congress

• Abbreviations	• Education
• Almanacs and Fast Facts	• Encyclopedias
• Arts and Music	• Genealogy, Biography, and Archaeology
• Associations	• Grant Resource
• Awards/Prizes	• Health/Medical
• Books, Periodicals, and Publishing	• History (General)
• Business	• Language and Literature
• Calculators	• Law
• Calendars	• Libraries
• Clocks/Times	• Maps/Driving Directions
• Consumer Information	• Political Science and Government
• Current Events on the Web	• Quotations
• Dictionaries/Thesauri	• Science, Technology, and Engineering
• Directories	• Statistics

✤ Guideline 7
Consider accessing information posted on the web by professional associations.

A wide variety of associations post information (and statistics) on the web. While reviewers may already be familiar with the major organizations in their respective fields, there are many specialized organizations that deal with specialized issues.

To identify specialized associations, you may conduct a Google search for professional associations by using a search term specific to your major. For example, psychology majors may use the search term "professional associations psychology." Examples of some of the professional associations that come up during this search include the American Psychological Association, the American Board of Professional Psychology, and the National Alliance of Professional Psychology Providers.

In addition to posting information and statistics on the web, associations post position papers on a variety of contemporary issues relating to their fields. The positions taken by such associations might be cited in literature reviews.

---

[4] Rather than typing long URLs, you may find it faster to perform a quick search on a major search engine such as Google using a term like "Virtual Reference Shelf." Use the quotation marks around the terms to conduct an exact phrase match.

NOTES

Appendix C
Excerpts From Literature Reviews

The following excerpts show the beginning paragraph(s) of literature reviews. They should be referred to while you are answering Question 7 in the Exercise for Topic 16 (Organizing a Literature Review).

Excerpt 1: Relationships of HIV/AIDS Patients With Their Families

Individuals with HIV/AIDS and their caregivers in developing countries often suffer from various pressures, such as availability of adequate medical care, lack of formal support, declining resources, social isolation, stigma, and lack of community support (D'Cruz, 2003; Kelley & Eberstadt, 2005). Due to such pressures, HIV/AIDS patients and their caregivers are vulnerable to experience mental health symptoms including traumatic stress (McCausland & Pakenham, 2003; Owens, 2003) and depression (Land & Hudson, 2004; Wight, Beals, Miller-Martines, Murphy, & Aneshensel, 2007). The challenge of disclosing information to family members becomes another source of stress (Kalichman, Austiry Luke, & DiFonzo, 2003).

One of the major obstacles undermining the efforts to study the experience of HIV/AIDS in developing countries is the lack of access to information on the disease. Both Kelley and Eberstadt (2005) and Obermeyer (2006) question the accuracy of reported HIV/AIDS cases in Muslim and especially Middle Eastern countries. Most of the HIV/AIDS cases in developing countries are vulnerable to stigma and other forms of social isolation. Castle (2004) stated that negative attitudes toward people with HIV/AIDS in developing countries can be translated into harsh treatment and stigmatization by the community and, in some cases, by families of infected persons. Although stigma seems to be based on the values and attitudes of societies in developing countries, Ali (1996) noted changes in the views of people regarding HIV/AIDS. "A theology of compassion and approaches advocating harm reduction seem to be emerging in several Muslim countries, and greater acceptance of HIV positive people is justified with reference to religion" (cited by Obermeyer, 2006, p. 853).

The experience of HIV/AIDS can cause conflict within the family (Li, Jiang, Lord, & Rotheram-Borus, 2007), such as communication problems (Vangelisti, 1992) and problems in roles and family adaptation (Holmbeck, 1996). It is common to find the family is the only source of care and support for HIV/AIDS patients. That can become burdensome due to inadequate resources and assistance available for family caregivers and the unsupportive viewpoints existent in these societies (Kipp, Nkosi, Laing, & Jhangri, 2006). Therefore, it is important to explore the nature of interaction and relationship among HIV/AIDS patients and their families.

Source: Soliman, H. H., & Abd Almotgly, M. M. (2011). Psychosocial profile of people with AIDS and their caregivers in Egypt..*Psychological Reports*, *108*, 883–892. (Excerpt from pages 883–884.) Copyright © 2011 by Psychological Reports.

Notes:

_____

_____

_____

_____

Excerpt 2: Nurses' Medication Errors

Since the Institute of Medicine (IOM) report *To Err is Human* (Kohn, Corrigan, & Donaldson, 2000), the United States has made significant efforts to improve patient safety. With regard to medication errors, numerous studies have been published identifying the epidemiology and the etiology of medication errors, and hospitals, nursing homes, and other healthcare organizations continue to evaluate evidence-based interventions and to develop safety guidelines and protocols. Despite such progress, the IOM recently estimated that at least one medication error occurs every day for every hospitalized patient, suggesting that medication errors still remain a significant problem (IOM, 2006).

Safety culture has been emphasized as a necessary condition for patient safety, which includes reducing the number of medication errors (Kohn et al., 2000). A positive safety culture exists when group members share perceptions of the importance of safety, communicate with mutual trust, and have confidence in the efficacy of preventive measures (Health and Safety Commission, 1993). The Joint Commission included an annual assessment of safety culture in 2007 patient safety goals, and many healthcare organizations have embarked on efforts to assess safety culture or, on the surface, safety climate.

Although reducing medication errors is an important goal, there is consensus that eliminating them completely is unlikely, particularly when there are high volumes of activity. It has been estimated, for example, that a 600-bed teaching hospital with 99.9% error-free drug ordering, dispensing, and administration will still experience 4,000 drug errors a year (Leape, 1994). Therefore, organizations also must improve their strategies in dealing with errors when they occur. Unfortunately, there has been less emphasis on error management and the central feature, learning climate. The error management approach is focused on how to deal with errors when they occur. It emphasizes creating a positive learning climate, in which learning from errors is fostered in organizations. Although learning climate has been considered similar to, or incorporated into, safety climate, learning climate is focused on errors.

During the past decade, there has been increasing recognition in healthcare research of the significance of learning from errors (Berta & Baker, 2004; Edmondson, 2004; Rosen, & Carroll, 2006). Organizations with a positive learning climate have the competence to draw the appropriate conclusions from their safety information systems and the willingness to implement major reforms where needed (Department of Health, 2000). However, little is known about how learning climate contributes to error management and, ultimately, to error reduction. In fact, the current literature on medication errors tends to be focused primarily on work conditions that are conducive to error occurrence, complex work environment or inadequate staffing sources. Understanding the mechanism of learning in error management is therefore of importance for care organizations to achieve patient safety.

Source: Chang, Y. K., & Mark, B. (2011). Effects of learning climate and registered nurse staffing on medication errors. *Nursing Research*, *60*, 32–39. (Excerpt from pages 32–33.) Copyright © 2008 by Wolters Kluwer Health/Lippincott Williams & Wilkins.

Notes:

_____

_____

_____

_____

Excerpt 3: The Effects of Being Labeled a *Nerd*

In most schools, there seems to be a clear understanding of who is a nerd (B. B. Brown, Mory, & Kinney, 1994; Rentzsch & Schütz, 2011). According to B. B. Brown (1990), adolescents are assigned to a specific group by their peers because they have reputations and characteristics that fit with the stereotype of that crowd (see also B. B. Brown et al., 1994). The label *nerd* refers to one of the least liked crowds at school (B. B. Brown et al., 1994). It includes the following characteristics: being ambitious, intelligent, having good grades, studying a lot, displaying success publicly, being shy, having few friends, not wearing fashionable clothes, not being athletic, and not being physically attractive (Rentzsch & Schütz, 2011). The label *nerd* is feared by students who receive good grades (Pelkner & Boehnke, 2003; Pelkner, Günther, & Boehnke, 2002). Several labels are used for deprecating high-achieving students, such as *nerd* (e.g., B. B. Brown et al., 1994; Kinney, 1993), *brain* (e.g., Prinstein & LaGreca, 2002), *geek* (e.g., Tyson, Darity, & Castellino, 2005), or *teacher's pet* (e.g., Tal & Babad, 1990). The present study primarily refers to *brains* and *nerds* because of their similarity to the German label "Streber." (The German label is neither readily transferable to other derogatory terms used in school nor to the type of so-called nerds who are known for their enthusiasm about computers.) From an etymological perspective, "Streber" is a disparaging term that describes an overambitious, diligent person. Literally, it means a person who strives for success, achievement, etc.

Being labeled a nerd is not a trifle. If being labeled as such in class goes along with a lack of acceptance and being rejected, serious consequences can occur. Research shows that lack of acceptance is related to social isolation (Moulton, Moulton, Housewright, & Bailey, 1998), loneliness (Juvonen, Nishina, & Graham, 2000), reduced self-esteem (de Bruyn & van den Boom, 2005), and other forms of maladjustment (Parker & Asher, 1987). Furthermore, a 6-year longitudinal study by Prinstein and La Greca (2002) showed that students who were called *brains* by their peers exhibited increases in anxiety and loneliness as well as decreases in self-esteem over the course of time.

A potential consequence of being labeled a *nerd* is that the respective student might reduce future performance. If high-achieving students have to make a choice between doing well in school and being popular, they may try to achieve liking by decreasing success. Landsheer, Maassen, Bisschop, and Adema (1998) commented: "If high achievement in the sciences results in unpopularity, it could lead to lesser effort by better students" (p. 188). Similarly, Pelkner et al. (2002) found that the fear of being called a nerd predicted lower achievement in mathematics. Several discussion forums on the Internet, in which parents or students describe their concerns about being labeled a nerd, provide information about the social relevance of that topic (see http://bullying.org, http://www.schueler-gegen-mobbing.de), but up to now there are no systematic studies addressing the specific effects of various factors on the social evaluation of so-called nerds. In the next section, we discuss factors that may be relevant in social evaluation and then present two studies that tested the effects of these factors.

Source: Rentzsch, K., Schütz, A., & Schröder-Abé, M. (2011). Being labeled *nerd*: Factors that influence the social acceptance of high-achieving students. *The Journal of Experimental Education, 79*, 143–168. (Excerpt from pages 144–145.) Copyright © 2011 by Taylor & Francis Group, LLC.

Notes:

_____

_____

_____

_____

Excerpt 4: Nonstandard Work Schedule

In the last half century, the number of women participating in the labor force in the United States has increased dramatically, with particular increases among low-income women (Blank, 2002). At the same time, the nature of work in the United States has evolved. Service and sales sectors have expanded, and the economy increasingly operates around the clock, amplifying demand for workers outside the traditional 9-to-5 workday (Presser, 2003). It is now common for individuals to work nonstandard schedules—in the evening, nights, or on weekends—leading to concerns about the effects of work scheduling on families and children. Nonstandard work is more common among lower-income individuals (Presser), and so children in low-income families are more likely to be affected by their parents' nonstandard work schedules.

Research on the effects of nonstandard work schedules on both workers and their families has generally found that nonstandard work schedules have negative effects particularly in studies of mixed- and higher-income families (Han, 2005, 2006; Han & Waldfogel, 2007; Strazdins, Clements, Korda, Broom, & D'Souza, 2006; Strazdins, Korda, Lim, Broom, & D'Souza, 2004). Studies focused on low-wage workers, however, have

produced mixed results (Han, 2008; Hsueh & Yoshikawa, 2007; Joshi & Bogen, 2007; Phillips, 2002), and additional information is still needed about how mothers' nonstandard work schedules affect low-income families. Prior research has commonly compared parents categorized as working standard or nonstandard schedules, on the basis of a typical work week. That design has three limitations: unobserved selection into different schedules may bias results; "standard" and "nonstandard" categories may mask within-person variability in work schedules; and, in most studies, the "nonstandard" category includes both nights and weekends, although their consequences may differ.

Source: Gassman-Pines, A. (2011). Low-income mothers' nighttime and weekend work: Daily associations with child behavior, mother-child interactions, and mood. *Family Relations, 60*, 15–29. (Excerpt from page 15.) Copyright © 2011 by the National Council on Family Relations.

Notes:

_____

_____

_____

_____

Excerpt 5: Men's Health Behaviors

Approximately one third of all of the deaths in the United States might be prevented by the widespread adoption of health promotion behaviors and avoidance of health risk behaviors (Danaei et al, 2009). American men tend to engage in more than 30 controllable behaviors that increase their risk for disease, injury, and death (Courtenay, 2000a, 2000b), which may at least partly explain why American men live an average of 5.2 years less than American women (Minino, Heron, Murphy, & Kocharek, 2007). Men spend less time with their physicians; engage in fewer preventive health behaviors; consume more alcohol; use more tobacco products; have poorer diets, sleep hygiene, and weight management; and lower physical activity than women (Centers for Disease Control, 2004; Galuska, Serdula, Pamuk, Siegal, & Byers, 1996; Garfield, Isacco, & Rogers, 2008; Kandrack, Grant, & Segall, 1999; Shi, 1998).

These findings have brought men's physical and mental health to the forefront in current public health discourse (Addis et al., 2007; Baker, 2001; Bonhomme, 2007). Research on the variables that influence men's relative lack of engagement in health promotion activities and avoidance of health risk behaviors is thus of considerable importance. Masculine gender socialization is often cited as a major reason why men engage in poorer health behaviors than women (Courtenay, 2000a). Moreover, masculine gender socialization is also the major reason why men are significantly less likely than women to seek help for both mental health (Addis & Mahalik, 2003; Levant, Wimer, Williams, Smalley, & Noronha, 2009; Mahalik, Good, & Englar-Carlson, 2003) and physical health (Wyke, Hunt, & Ford, 1998). Masculine gender socialization thus appears to create a "double whammy" effect because it is associated with both poorer health behaviors *and* a reduced likelihood of using appropriate health resources when needed.

However, research on the relationships between masculine gender socialization and health behaviors is at a very early stage. Levant et al. (2009) reviewed a dozen published studies on the relationship between four measures of masculine gender socialization constructs and health behaviors and concluded that the endorsement of traditional masculinity ideology, conformity to masculine norms, masculine gender role stress, and gender role conflict are all associated with engagement in various risky health-related behaviors. Furthermore, only a handful of studies have directly compared the impact of various masculinity measures, and these studies have examined only a small subset of risky health behaviors (e.g., alcohol problems and aggression), while examining only one or two measures at a time.

Source: Levant, R. F., Wimer, D. J., & Williams, C. M. (2011). An evolution of the Health Behavior Inventory-20 (HBI-20) and its relationships to masculinity and attitudes towards seeking psychological help among college men. *Psychology of Men & Masculinity, 12*, 26–41. (Excerpt from pages 26–27.) Copyright © 2011 by the American Psychological Association.

Notes:

_____

_____

_____

_____

Excerpt 6: Delinquency and Substance Abuse

Over the past two and a half decades, a large body of research has been conducted on drug use among adolescent offenders. Across these studies, a rather robust and enduring relationship between delinquency and substance use has emerged. For example, the National Center on Addiction and Substance Abuse (2004) estimates that up to 78% of

arrested youths are alcohol or drug involved. Similarly, McClelland, Teplin, and Abram (2004) reported that 77% of the youths included in a sample of 1,829 Cook County, Illinois, juvenile detainees reported using drugs or alcohol in the past six months. Furthermore, based on the 1999 Arrestee Drug Abuse Monitoring (ADAM) results, the percentage of detained juveniles who tested positive for any drug ranged from 38% to 69% (National Institute of Justice, 2000). In addition, studies suggest that delinquency and drug use are two of the most resistant forms of problem behavior found in adolescence (Huizinga, Loeber, & Thornberry, 1994; Mann, 2003). These findings highlight a critical social problem in need of further study.

Despite consistent findings that substance use and delinquency are linked, the nature of this association varies by important sociodemographic factors including criminal history, age, gender, and race (Barnes, Welte, & Hoffman, 2002; Dembo, Wareham, & Schmeidler, 2007a; Huizinga & Jakob-Chien, 1998; Teplin et al., 2005), as well as type of substance used (Fagan, Weis, & Chang, 1990; Teplin, Mericle, McClelland, & Abram, 2003; Van Kammen, Loeber, & Stouthamer-Loeber, 1991; Wei, Makkai, & McGregor, 2003). For example, Dembo and colleagues examined a longitudinal sample of justice-involved youths and found significant sociodemographic differences in marijuana use. Males, older adolescents, and non-African American youths reported higher levels of marijuana use; however, no significant demographic differences were found in the use of cocaine (Dembo et al., 2007a,b). As such, it is important to consider the variation in drug use across these demographic subgroups, as well as across type of substance used.

Source: Childs, K., Dembo, R., Belenko, S., Wareham, J., & Schmeidler, J. (2011). A comparison of individual-level and community-level predictors of marijuana and cocaine use among a sample of newly arrested juvenile offenders. *Journal of Child & Adolescent Substance Abuse, 20*, 114–134. (Excerpt from page 115.) Copyright © 2011 by Taylor & Francis, LLC.

Notes:

_____

_____

_____

_____

APPENDIX D
A CLOSER LOOK AT THE STANDARD DEVIATION

In this appendix, some rules for interpreting the standard deviation in relation to the normal curve are described. In addition, the computation of the standard deviation is considered.

As indicated in Topic 55, going out one standard-deviation unit on both sides of the mean captures 68% of the cases in a normal distribution. It turns out that by going out two units on both sides of the mean captures approximately 95% of the cases.[1] For the distribution considered in Topic 55 with $M = 70$ and $S = 10$, it was noted that 68% lie between scores of 60 and 80. Going out $2 \times 10 = 20$ points (which is two standard-deviation units), scores of 50 and 90 (i.e., the mean of 70 *minus* 20 = 50, and the mean of 70 *plus* 20 = 90) are reached. This is illustrated in Figure 1.

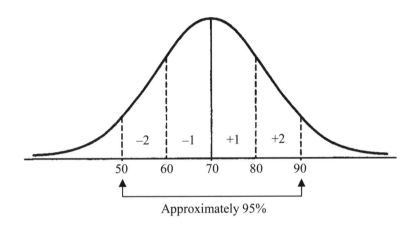

Figure 1. Normal curve illustrating approximate 95% rule.

Going out three standard-deviation units captures 99.7% of the cases, which is essentially all of the cases. Thus, there are about three standard-deviation units on each side of the mean in a normal distribution.

Considering how the standard deviation is calculated may help in understanding the standard deviation. As the formula below indicates, it is the *square root of the mean squared deviation from the mean*. Thus, the larger the deviations from the mean, the larger the standard deviation. Conversely, the smaller the deviations from the mean, the smaller the standard deviation.

The formula that defines the standard deviation is

$$S = \sqrt{\frac{\sum x^2}{N}}$$

The lowercase x stands for the deviation of a score from the mean of its distribution. To obtain it, first calculate the mean (in this case, 78/6 = 13.00) and subtract the mean from each score, as shown in Example 1. Then, square the deviations and sum the squares, as indicated by the symbol Σ. Then, enter this value in the formula along with the number of cases (N) and perform the calculations as indicated in Example 1.

---

[1] To capture precisely 95%, go out 1.96 (a little less than 2.00) standard deviations. Going out 2.58 standard deviations captures 99% of the cases.

EXAMPLE 1

Scores (X)	Deviations ($X - M$)	Deviations Squared (x^2)
10	$10 - 13.00 = -3$	9.00
11	$11 - 13.00 = -2$	4.00
11	$11 - 13.00 = -2$	4.00
13	$13 - 13.00 = 0$	0.00
14	$14 - 13.00 = 1$	1.00
19	$19 - 13.00 = 6$	36.00
		$\Sigma x^2 = 54.00$

Thus, for these data

$$S = \sqrt{\frac{54}{6}} = \sqrt{9.00} = 3.00$$

APPENDIX E
A CLOSER LOOK AT EFFECT SIZE

Reporting effect sizes in research reports has become common only in recent years, and they still are not universally reported. Hence, consumers of research (who typically do not need to compute statistics) may find it beneficial to be able to calculate some simple statistics that will allow them to more accurately interpret results in which effect sizes have been omitted in research reports.

In Topic 64, the calculation of Cohen's *d* was illustrated in the examples in which the two standard deviations were equal. When they are not equal, most researchers divide the difference between means by the "pooled standard deviation," which is a special type of average standard deviation that can be obtained by using the following formula. Its use is illustrated for an experiment in which the experimental group's standard deviation is 10.00 (with 15 participants, *n* = 15), and the control group's standard deviation is 14.00 (with 12 participants, *n* = 12). Note that for an experiment, the subscript "1" designates the experimental group, and the subscript "2" designates the control group.

$$sd_{pooled} = \sqrt{\frac{(n_1 - 1)sd_1^2 + (n_2 - 1)sd_2^2}{n_1 + n_2 - 2}} = \sqrt{\frac{(15-1)10.00^2 + (12-1)14.00^2}{15+12-2}} = 11.93$$

(Note that the pooled standard deviation of 11.93 is very close to the simple average of the standard deviations [10.00 + 14.00 = 24.00/2 = 12.00]. The larger the difference between the numbers of participants in the two groups and the larger the difference between the two standard deviations, the greater the difference between the pooled standard deviation and the simple average of the standard deviations.)

The usual formula for Cohen's *d* is the difference between the means divided by the pooled standard deviation, which is shown here in symbols:[1]

$$d = \frac{m_1 - m_2}{sd_{pooled}}$$

As a practical solution for consumers of research who do not want to engage in extensive calculations, a good *estimate* of *d* will usually be obtained by dividing the difference between the means by the *simple average* of the standard deviations. As indicated in the example above, the simple average of the standard deviations is 10.00 + 14.00 = 24.00/2 = 12.00. Divide the difference between the two means by 12.00 for an estimate. Another practical solution when one is conducting meta-analyses on experiments is to use only the standard deviation of the control group (and hence avoid averaging standard deviations altogether), as is discussed in the next paragraph.

When analyzing the difference between an experimental group and a control group, some researchers prefer to divide the difference between the means by the standard deviation of the control group only (as opposed to the pooled standard deviation for both groups). The resulting statistic is widely known as Glass's delta (Δ), although it is sometimes referred to as *d* in research literature. This is understandable because the value of *d* and the value of Δ are very similar when the two standard deviations are very similar. For instance, in a perfect case in which the two standard deviations are identical, the standard deviation of the control group will equal the pooled standard deviation of the two groups, so *d* and Δ will have exactly the same value.

In Topic 62, the examples are *experiments* (with experimental and control groups). Cohen's *d* is also appropriate for describing the difference between two means in *nonexperimental studies*. For instance, a re-

---

[1] Students who have taken statistics should note that the population value of the standard deviation (computed without the minus one [−1] in the denominator of the computational formula) should be used to obtain Cohen's *d*. If the sample standard deviation is used, the result is Hedge's *g*, which, for small samples, can differ noticeably from Cohen's *d*. Values of *g* can be converted to values of *d* with the following formula.

$$d = g\sqrt{N/df}$$

searcher could survey a random sample of girls and a random sample of boys (without any physical treatments), compute a mean and standard deviation for each group, and compare the two groups using d. In such a study, it is usually best to subtract the smaller mean from the larger mean (so that the difference is a positive number) and then divide by either the pooled standard deviation (for an exact value of d) or by the simple average of the two standard deviations (for an estimate of the value of d).

As indicated in Topic 64, when one is examining a body of literature, it is sometimes helpful to be able to directly compare the effect sizes represented by values of d with effect sizes represented by values of r. The following formula yields a good approximation of the value of d corresponding to a value of r.

$$d = \frac{2r}{\sqrt{1-r^2}}$$

The following formula is recommended for calculating the "effect size r" from a value of d. The subscript "es" for "effect size" is used in the formula to distinguish the result from a value of r that is computed directly from raw scores (as opposed to being computed from a value of d).

$$r_{es} = \frac{d}{\sqrt{d^2+4}}$$

APPENDIX F

OUTLINE OF QUESTION ROUTE FOR A FOCUS GROUP STUDY[1]

Opening comments:

Welcome and statements regarding the purpose of the study, focus group procedures, and ethical issues.

Opening comment:

"Please tell us a little bit about yourself."

Introductory question:

"Stress is prevalent in our everyday lives; many people feel stressed. In thinking about your daily life, what does stress mean to you?"

Transition questions:

"Is stress a negative factor in your life? If so, explain how it is negative."
"Is stress a positive factor in your life? If so, in what ways is it positive?"
    Subprobe: "What is it about stress that makes it good or bad?"

Key questions:

"What are the things that contribute to stress in your life?"
    Subprobe: (a) "How does this work? Does one thing contribute to stress more than others, or does the combination of many things contribute to stress?" (b) "Do you have any particular health concerns that contribute to your feelings of stress? Can you tell us more about them?" (c) "Besides possible health concerns, is there anything else that adds to your feelings of stress?" (d) "Does being a manager contribute to your feelings of stress? If so, describe how."

Ending questions:

"All things considered, what would you say is the major cause of stress in your life?"
"Is there anything about stress that we haven't talked about that you would like to discuss before we leave tonight?"

---

[1] Reprinted from page 62 of Iwasaki, Y., MacKay, K. J., & Ristock, J. (2004). Gender-based analyses of stress among professional managers: An exploratory qualitative study. *International Journal of Stress Management, 11,* 56–79.

NOTES

APPENDIX G

SAMPLE ABSTRACTS OF RESEARCH REPORTS

This appendix contains four sample abstracts, which appeared at the beginning of published research reports. Note that all indicate the nature of the findings, which is highly desirable. These abstracts should be referred to when you are answering Questions 7 and 8 for Topic 76.

Abstract 1: Abstract of a Survey

This study assessed work-related and driver-related factors in fatigue among Finnish heavy vehicle drivers. 683 professional drivers responded to a questionnaire, 27.8% of whom reported often feeling fatigue during their work shifts. Of the respondents, 27.5% reported having momentarily fallen asleep at the wheel while driving during the past year. Almost half (46.8%) of the fatigued drivers estimated the reasons for momentarily falling asleep were work-related. Long working shifts and short sleeps significantly increased the risk of momentarily falling asleep at the wheel. The risk of fatigue was the highest for the drivers who were unable to choose the time of their breaks.

Source

Perttula, P., Ojala, T., & Kuosma, E. (2011). Factors in the fatigue of heavy vehicle drivers. *Psychological Reports*, *108*, 507–514. Copyright © 2011 by Psychological Reports.

Notes:

_____

_____

_____

_____

Abstract 2: Abstract of an Experiment

Background: Adapting to living with chronic conditions is a lifelong psychosocial challenge.

Objective: The purpose of this study was to report the effect of a computer intervention on the psychosocial adaptation of rural women with chronic conditions.

Methods: A two-group study design was used with 309 middle-aged, rural women who had chronic conditions, randomized into either a computer-based intervention or a control group. Data were collected at baseline, at the end of the intervention, and 6 months later on the psychosocial indicators of social support, self-esteem, acceptance of illness, stress, depression, and loneliness.

Results: The impact of the computer-based intervention was statistically significant for five of six of the psychosocial outcomes measured, with a modest impact on social support. The largest benefits were seen in depression, stress, and acceptance.

Discussion: The women-to-women intervention resulted in positive psychosocial responses that have the potential to contribute to successful management of illness and adaptation. Other components of adaptation to be examined are the impact of the intervention on illness management and quality of life and the interrelationships among environmental stimuli, psychosocial response, and illness management.

Source

Weinert, C., Cudney, S., Comstock, B., & Bansal, A. (2011). Computer intervention impact on psychosocial adaptation of rural women with chronic conditions. *Nursing Research*, *60*, 82–91. Copyright © 2011 by Wolters Kluwer Health/Lippincott Williams & Wilkins.

Notes:

_____

_____

_____

_____

_____

Abstract 3: Abstract of a Program Evaluation

Objective: To reduce mental health symptoms and high-risk behaviors and increase social support and service utilization among street-living youth, the authors conducted a pilot study to assess the feasibility of the social enterprise intervention (SEI) at a homeless youth agency. *Method*: Convenience sampling was used to recruit 16 street-living youth from the agency. SEI participants received 7 months of vocational and small-business training and service referrals. A comparison sample of 12 agency youth was used. *Results*: Findings from independent sample *t* tests demonstrate that SEI participants displayed significant improvements at 9 months in life satisfaction, family contact, peer support, and depressive symptoms. ***Conclusions***: Preliminary findings suggest that the SEI was feasible within the agency setting and associated with higher mental health and social outcomes.

Source

Ferguson, K. M., & Xie, B. (2008). Feasibility study of the social enterprise intervention with homeless youth. *Research on Social Work Practice*, *18*, 5–19. Copyright © 2008 by Sage Publications.

Notes:

_____

_____

_____

_____

_____

Abstract 4: Abstract of a Qualitative Study

Abstract. **Objective**: The goal of this study was to identify factors that college students perceived as contributing to healthy and unhealthy eating patterns, physical activity (PA) levels, and weight change. **Participants**: Forty-nine 18- to 22-year-old students at a Midwestern university participated. **Methods**: Six focus groups (3 with each gender) were conducted, and data were analyzed using qualitative software to code and categorize themes and then reduce these to clusters according to commonly practiced methods of qualitative analysis. **Results**: Eating and PA behaviors appear to be determined by a complex interplay between motivations and self-regulatory skills as well as the unique social and physical environment comprising college life. Moreover, there appear to be gender differences in how these determinants impact behavior. **Conclusions**: Future research should examine these interactions in the college context in order to further our understanding of potential interventions or environmental modifications that support healthy eating and PA.

Source

LaCaille, L. J., Dauner, K. N., Krambeer, R. J., & Pedersen, J. (2011). Psychosocial and environmental determinants of eating behaviors, physical activity, and weight change among college students: A qualitative analysis. *Journal of American College Health*, *59*, 531–538. Copyright © 2011 by Taylor & Francis Group, LLC.

Notes:

_____

_____

_____

_____

_____

APPENDIX H

SAMPLE DESCRIPTION OF QUALITATIVE DATA ANALYSIS[1]

Qualitative Analysis of Relationship Dynamics

Thematic analysis was applied to the interview data (e.g., Aronson, 1994; Boyatzis, 1998; Lacey & Luff, 2001; Silverman, 2001). The goal of thematic analysis is to identify patterns in the data through an inductive process. It is a complex, iterative process that leads to an understanding of the participants' experiences. In this study, our goal was to understand the role of both partners' attachment patterns in their approaches to conflict, particularly violent conflict.

After listening to audiotapes of the interviews, the first author made extensive notes on each of the men's and women's interviews. Using index cards, she organized the preliminary data, including both partners' attachment profiles, levels, natures, and directionality of violence; the context of violent incidents; and relational dynamics leading up to and playing out in violent incidents. She used these cards to organize her extensive interview notes. She then wrote brief descriptions of the conflict dynamics of each couple, and the first, second, and third authors met to review and discuss the initial findings. Through this discussion, the researchers sought to identify relational dynamics that made sense of individuals' striking out abusively toward their partners. As a specific theme of relationship dynamics emerged, the group critically assessed its validity vis-à-vis descriptions of other abusive incidents described by the participants. When the researchers' interpretations did not converge or when one of the researchers questioned an interpretation, the first author revisited her notes and, if necessary, the audiotapes, and further discussion took place. This process was repeated until consensus was reached. When agreement was reached, the first author returned to the participant data to search for specific examples of the identified theme. Finally, we reviewed and critically assessed the themes of relational dynamics, concluding that

we had identified two overarching relational dynamics associated with incidences of partner violence.

As expected with thematic analysis, not all themes initially identified were maintained. A few themes did not hold up under further scrutiny. For example, in a few couples we initially identified a theme in which a man's violence appeared to be motivated by a desire to control his partner, even in the absence of perceived threats or emotional demands by the partner. However, when we examined this potential theme more thoroughly and studied the interviews of both partners in these relationships, we found that the men's violence could also be interpreted in terms of other identified themes (all of which included elements of control) and that this theme was not evident in most abusive incidents. Moreover, there was no consistent pattern in the couples in which this theme occurred. For example, it was not the case that this theme only emerged with dismissing men or in couples with male-only violence. Therefore, we did not feel comfortable in concluding that we had identified a consistent relational pattern associated with partner violence.

The two partners in a given couple often had somewhat different views on their relational dynamics. As well, they did not necessarily describe the same violent episodes. However, we found their stories to be remarkably consistent, in spite of the different points of view. For example, one member of the couple might see a partner's distancing behavior as indicating a lack of involvement in the relationship, whereas the distancing partner described the same behavior as stemming from being overwhelmed by a partner's demands. Thus, although their interpretations might differ, partners generally described similar relationship dynamics.

NOTES

Appendix I

A Closer Look at Abbreviated Page Numbers in ASA Style[1]

Example 1 illustrates the format for a typical journal article entry in a reference list. The entry ends with two page numbers: the page number on which the article begins (*beginning number*) and the page number on which the article ends (*ending number*). As called for in ASA Style, the *ending number* (462) has been abbreviated and is shown as 62.

Example 1

Doe, Jane. 2013. "A Survey of Ethnic Territoriality." Journal of Replicated Hypothetical Studies 23(3):456–62.

The *beginning number* is never abbreviated. The following are the rules regarding the abbreviation of *ending numbers*:

1. Do not abbreviate ending numbers that are less than 100.
2. Do not abbreviate ending numbers if the *beginning* number is a multiple of 100.
3. Do not delete numerals that are needed for unambiguous interpretation of an abbreviation.

The following are examples of correctly abbreviated numbers:

Unabbreviated Page Number	Abbreviated Page Number
110–112	110–12
828–833	828–33
1250–1256	1250–56
455784–455993	455784–993

---

[1] ASA Style is based on the recommendations made in *The Chicago Manual of Style*.

NOTES

Table 1
Table of Random Numbers

Row #						
1	2 1 0	4 9 8	0 8 8	8 0 6	9 2 4	8 2 6
2	0 7 3	0 2 9	4 8 2	7 8 9	8 9 2	9 7 1
3	4 4 9	0 0 2	8 6 2	6 7 7	7 3 1	2 5 1
4	7 3 2	1 1 2	0 7 7	6 0 3	8 3 4	7 8 1
5	3 3 2	5 8 3	1 7 0	1 4 0	7 8 9	3 7 7
6	6 1 2	0 5 7	2 4 4	0 0 6	3 0 2	8 0 7
7	7 0 9	3 3 3	7 4 0	4 8 8	9 3 5	8 0 5
8	7 5 1	9 0 9	1 5 2	6 5 0	9 0 3	5 8 8
9	3 5 6	9 6 5	0 1 9	4 6 6	7 5 6	8 3 1
10	8 5 0	3 9 4	3 4 0	6 5 1	7 4 4	6 2 7
11	0 5 9	6 8 7	4 8 1	5 5 0	5 1 7	1 5 8
12	7 6 2	2 6 9	6 1 9	7 1 1	4 7 1	6 2 0
13	3 8 4	7 8 9	8 2 2	1 6 3	8 7 0	4 6 1
14	1 9 1	8 4 5	6 1 8	1 2 4	4 4 2	7 3 4
15	1 5 3	6 7 6	1 8 4	3 1 8	8 7 7	6 0 4
16	0 5 5	3 6 0	7 1 3	8 1 4	6 7 0	4 3 5
17	2 2 3	8 6 0	9 1 9	0 4 4	7 6 8	1 5 1
18	2 3 3	2 5 5	7 6 9	4 9 7	1 3 7	9 3 8
19	8 5 5	0 5 3	7 8 5	4 5 1	6 0 4	8 9 1
20	0 6 1	1 3 4	8 6 4	3 2 9	4 3 8	7 4 1
21	9 1 1	8 2 9	0 6 9	6 9 4	2 9 9	0 6 0
22	3 7 8	0 6 3	7 1 2	6 5 2	7 6 5	6 5 1
23	5 3 0	5 1 2	1 0 9	1 3 7	5 6 1	2 5 0
24	7 2 4	8 6 7	9 3 8	7 6 0	9 1 6	5 7 8
25	0 9 1	6 7 0	3 8 0	9 1 5	4 2 3	2 4 5
26	3 8 1	4 3 7	9 2 4	5 1 2	8 7 7	4 1 3

NOTES

Table 2

Table of Recommended Sample Sizes (n) for Populations (N) With Finite Sizes[1]

N	n	N	n	N	n
10	10	220	140	1,200	291
15	14	230	144	1,300	297
20	19	240	148	1,400	302
25	24	250	152	1,500	306
30	28	260	155	1,600	310
35	32	270	159	1,700	313
40	36	280	162	1,800	317
45	40	290	165	1,900	320
50	44	300	169	2,000	322
55	48	320	175	2,200	327
60	52	340	181	2,400	331
65	56	360	186	2,600	335
70	59	380	191	2,800	338
75	63	400	196	3,000	341
80	66	420	201	3,500	346
85	70	440	205	4,000	351
90	73	460	210	4,500	354
95	76	480	214	5,000	357
100	80	500	217	6,000	361
110	86	550	226	7,000	364
120	92	600	234	8,000	367
130	97	650	242	9,000	368
140	103	700	248	10,000	370
150	108	750	254	15,000	375
160	113	800	260	20,000	377
170	118	850	265	30,000	379
180	123	900	269	40,000	380
190	127	950	274	50,000	381
200	132	1,000	278	75,000	382
210	136	1,100	285	100,000	384

---

[1] Adapted from Krejcie, R. V., & Morgan, D. W. (1970). Determining sample size for research activities. *Educational and Psychological Measurement, 30*, 607–610.

NOTES

INDEX

abstract 165

achievement test 93

alpha 89

analysis of variance 137–140

ANOVA 137–140

aptitude test 93

auditor 167, 172

averages 127–128

blind procedure 109

case study 9

causal-comparative 7, 9

census 9, 55

chi-square 121–124

citations 41–52

cluster sampling 61

coding
  axial 169
  open 169

coefficient of determination 133

conceptual definition 17

concurrent validity 76, 80

confidentiality 35

confound 109

consensual qualitative research (CQR) 171–172

constant comparison 169

construct validity 79–80

content validity 73, 80

control group 5

core category 169

correlational research 9

correlation coefficient 87, 133, 149–150

criterion-referenced tests (CRTs) 91–92

criterion-related validity 76, 79

Cronbach's alpha 89

cross-analysis 171–172

debriefing subjects 25

degrees of freedom 121

demographics 7, 63, 159, 164

dependent variable 11, 13

descriptive statistics 113–114

discussion, writing 187–188

dissertation 189–190

double-blind 109

effect size 145–150

empirical validity 75–76, 80

ERIC 33, 191

ethics in research 25–26

ethnography 166

experimental designs 99–108

experimental group 5

experiments 5, 7, 9, 99–100, 105–106

ex post facto study 7

external validity 103–104

face validity 73–74, 80

facilitator 165

field research 166

focus groups 165–167

formative evaluation 23–24

frequencies 113, 119

frequency distribution 113

frequency polygon 125

grounded theory 27, 169

Hawthorne effect 109

historical research 9–10

history in experiments 101

independent variable 11–13

inferential statistics 113–114

informed consent 25, 181

instrumentation 71

intelligence test 93–94

interaction 139

internal consistency 89–90

internal stability 171

internal validity 101–105

interobserver agreement 167

interobserver reliability 87

interquartile range 131–132

interval measurement 117–118

interview protocol 163

John Henry effect 109

judgmental-empirical validity 79–80

judgmental validity 73–74, 80

Kuder-Richardson 89

Likert scale 95–96

literature review 31, 35–40, 155–156, 175, 179–180

longitudinal research 9

main effect 139

margin of error 113

maturation 101–102

mean 127–129

measures of central tendency 128

median 127, 131–132

member checking 167

meta-analysis 151–156

mode 127–128

multiple comparisons 137

multiple-treatment interference 103

negative skew 125–126

nominal measurement 117, 119

nonexperimental study 5–12

normal curve 125, 129–130

norm-referenced tests (NRTs) 91

observation
  nonparticipant 165
  participant 165–166

operational definition 17

ordinal measurement 117

parallel-forms reliability 87, 89–90

parameters 113

participants, describing 19, 181

Pearson *r* 133–136

peer review 167

percentages 113, 119

phenomenological approach 165

pilot studies 67

placebo 109

poll 5, 9

population 55

positive skew 125–126

practical significance 141–142

precision in sampling 59

predictive validity 75–76, 80

preexperiments 105–106

program evaluation 23–24

projective techniques 95

proportions 119

PsycINFO 33, 191

purposive criterion sampling 159–160

purposive sampling 61, 159–160, 181

NOTES

NOTES